Should God Get Tenure?

Essays on Religion and Higher Education

Edited by

David W. Gill

William B. Eerdmans Publishing Company
Grand Rapids, Michigan / Cambridge, U.K.

© 1997 Wm. B. Eerdmans Publishing Co.

255 Jefferson Ave. S.E., Grand Rapids, Michigan 49503 /

P.O. Box 163, Cambridge CB3 9PU U.K.

Printed in the United States of America

02 01 00 99 98 97   7 6 5 4 3 2 1

Library of Congress Cataloging-in-Publication Data

Should God get tenure? : essays on religion and higher education /
edited by David W. Gill

p.   cm.

Includes bibliographical references.

ISBN 0-8028-4307-7 (pbk.: alk. paper)

1. Universities and colleges — United States — Religion.

2. Church and college — United States.

I. Gill, David W., 1946-   .

LC383.S46 1997

378'.01 — dc21   97-14229

CIP

For
Juniata College

in memory of
J. Omar Good
(1877-1969)

Contents

Acknowledgments

This collection of essays expresses a common debt by all of its authors to Juniata College and to the Trustees of the J. Omar Good Fund. Each of the authors represented in this collection has served at Juniata College as a "J. Omar Good Distinguished Visiting Professor of Evangelical Christianity." Each of us has been welcomed into the community of Juniata College for a year of teaching and research. Into the context of a very diverse liberal arts college we have been invited to bring some Christian perspective in our various fields of teaching. A reduced teaching load enabled us to carry out our various research and writing projects while at Juniata.

We are grateful for this welcome, support, and critical interaction that we enjoyed among the students, faculty, and administration during our years of service at Juniata College. Few other liberal arts colleges or universities can claim to have equaled Juniata College in sustaining such a successful and persistent conversation about God and religion within such a diverse, free-swinging, academic milieu.

These essays are an expression of our gratitude not only to the college but to the trustees of the J. Omar Good Fund for the honor of serving as "Good Professors." We are grateful to J. Omar Good for his generosity and vision, and to Lester and Pauline Rosenberger and their successor leaders of the Good Fund. We also wish to express our appreciation to William B. Eerdmans for undertaking publication of this volume.

In addition to the authors represented in this collection, four other distinguished colleagues, George Docherty, E. Earle Ellis, John Trever, and the late Chad Walsh, also served over the past twenty years as "J. Omar Good" professors at Juniata College.

Our purpose in writing these essays is not only to honor Juniata College and the memory of J. Omar Good — but also to contribute to the broader discussion of religion and higher education. While there is no single formula applicable to all institutions, we believe that religious thought and experience, that "God-talk," like all important aspects of human life and community, must occupy an important place in higher education. In this sense God should "get tenure" in our colleges and universities. To do otherwise is to ignore or repress a crucial dimension of life and learning.

North Park College graciously gave me a leave of absence during 1994-95 so I could serve as the J. Omar Good Distinguished Visiting Professor at Juniata College, during which time this project began. I am grateful for the support of both Juniata College and North Park College.

David W. Gill

Contributors

JILL PELÁEZ BAUMGAERTNER is Professor of English at Wheaton College, where she joined the faculty in 1980. She is a graduate of Emory University (B.A., Ph.D.) and Drake University (M.A.). In addition to many poems, articles, and reviews, she has published *Flannery O'Connor: A Proper Scaring* (Harold Shaw, 1988), *Poetry* (a college textbook) (Harcourt Brace Jovanovich, 1990), and *Leaving Eden* (White Eagle Coffee Store Press, 1995). Dr. Baumgaertner served as J. Omar Good Distinguished Visiting Professor at Juniata College during the 1995-96 academic year.

CARNEGIE SAMUEL CALIAN has been President and Professor of Theology at Pittsburgh Theological Seminary since 1981. From 1963 to 1981 he served on the faculty of the University of Dubuque Theological Seminary. He is a graduate of Occidental College (B.A.), Princeton Theological Seminary (B.D.), and the University of Basel (D.Theol.). He is the author of over two hundred articles and reviews and of nine books, including *Where's the Passion for Excellence in the Church?* (Morehouse, 1989), and *Theology without Boundaries: Encounters of Eastern Orthodoxy and Western Tradition* (Westminster/John Knox Press, 1992). During 1975-77, Dr. Calian served for two years as Juniata College's first J. Omar Good Distinguished Visiting Professor.

CORBIN SCOTT CARNELL is Professor of English at the University of Florida, where he has served on the faculty since 1958. He is a graduate of Wheaton College (B.A.), Columbia University (M.A.), and the University of Florida (Ph.D.). He is the author of many articles and reviews and of four books, including *Bright Shadow of Reality: C. S. Lewis and the Feeling Intellect* (Eerdmans, 1974). Dr. Carnell served as J. Omar Good Distinguished Visiting Professor at Juniata College during the 1984-85 and 1993-94 academic years.

ROBERT G. CLOUSE has been Professor of History at Indiana State University since 1963. He is a graduate of Bryan College (B.A.), Grace Theological Seminary (B.D.), and the University of Iowa (M.A., Ph.D.). In addition to many articles, chapters, and reviews he is the author or editor of several books, including *War: Four Christian Views* (InterVarsity, 1991), *The Cross and the Flag* (Creation House, 1972), *The Meaning of the Millennium: Four Views* (InterVarsity, 1977), *The Church in the Age of Orthodoxy and the Enlightenment* (Concordia, 1980), and *Two Kingdoms: The Church and Culture Through the Ages* (Moody, 1993). Dr. Clouse served as J. Omar Good Distinguished Visiting Professor at Juniata College during the 1983-84 academic year.

DONALD F. DURNBAUGH is Emeritus Professor of Church History, Bethany Theological Seminary. He has also served on the faculties of Juniata College and Elizabethtown College. He is a graduate of Manchester College (B.A.), the University of Michigan (M.A.), and the University of Pennsylvania (Ph.D.). In addition to many articles and reviews, he is author or editor of twelve books, including *European Origins of the Brethren* (Brethren Press, 1958), *The Brethren in Colonial America* (Brethren Press, 1967), and *The Believers' Church: The History and Character of Radical Protestantism* (Macmillan, 1968; 2nd ed., 1985). Dr. Durnbaugh served as J. Omar Good Distinguished Visiting Professor at Juniata College during the 1988-89 academic year.

W. WARD GASQUE is Dean and Professor of Biblical Studies at Ontario Theological Seminary in Toronto. He is a graduate of Wheaton College (B.A.), Fuller Theological Seminary (B.D., M.Th.), and Manchester University (Ph.D.). He has served on both faculty and administration of Regent College (Vancouver, British Columbia),

New College Berkeley (California), and Eastern College (Philadelphia). He is the author of *A History of the Interpretation of the Acts of the Apostles* (Hendrickson, 1989), editor of four collections of essays and twenty New Testament commentaries, and author of more than two hundred articles and essays. Dr. Gasque served as J. Omar Good Distinguished Visiting Professor at Juniata College during the 1987-88 academic year.

DAVID W. GILL is Professor of Applied Ethics at North Park College in Chicago. Before coming to North Park in 1992, he served on the faculty and administration of New College Berkeley for thirteen years. He is a graduate of the University of California, Berkeley (B.A.), San Francisco State University (M.A.), and the University of Southern California (Ph.D.). Among his publications are *The Word of God in the Ethics of Jacques Ellul* (Scarecrow Press, 1984) and *The Opening of the Christian Mind* (InterVarsity, 1989). He served as J. Omar Good Distinguished Visiting Professor at Juniata College during the 1994-95 academic year.

EARL C. KAYLOR, JR., is the Charles A. Dana Supported Professor of History, Emeritus, at Juniata College, where he taught for thirty-three years. He is a graduate of Juniata College (B.A.), the University of Notre Dame (M.A.), and Pennsylvania State University (Ph.D.). He is the author of many articles and reviews and of three books: *Truth Sets Free: A Centennial History of Juniata College, 1876-1976* (A. S. Barnes, 1977), *Out of the Wilderness: The Brethren and Two Centuries of Life in Central Pennsylvania, 1780-1980* (Cornwall Books, 1981), and *Martin Grove Brumbaugh: A Pennsylvanian's Odyssey from Sainted Schoolman to Bedeviled World War I Governor, 1862-1930* (Associated University Press, 1996). He has been closely identified with the J. Omar Good Fund since its inception, for many years as its administrator and now as one of its trustees.

H. NEWTON MALONY is a clinical psychologist and Senior Professor at the Graduate School of Psychology, Fuller Theological Seminary. He is a graduate of Birmingham Southern College (B.A.), Yale Divinity School (M.Div.), and Vanderbilt University (Ph.D.). He is the author or editor of more than thirty books, including *Psychology of Religion: Personalities, Problems, Possibilities* (Baker, 1991), *Religion in Psychodynamic Perspective* (Oxford, 1991), *When Getting Along Seems Impossible* (Revell, 1990), and (with Gary Collins) *Psychology and Theology: Prospects for Integration* (Abingdon, 1980). Dr. Malony served as J. Omar Good Distinguished Visiting Professor at Juniata College during the 1992-93 academic year.

PAUL A. MARSHALL is Senior Member in Political Theory at the Institute for Christian Studies in Toronto, Ontario. He is a graduate of the University of Manchester (B.Sc.), the University of Western Ontario (M.Sc.), the Institute for Christian Studies (M.Phil.), and York University (M.A., Ph.D.). Among his many publications are seven books, including *Human Rights Theories in Christian Perspective* (ICS, 1983), *Stained Glass: World Views and Social Science* (University Press of America, 1989), *Thine Is the Kingdom: A Biblical Perspective on Government and Politics Today* (Marshall, Morgan, and Scott, 1984), and *Labour of Love: Essays on Work* (Wedge, 1980). Dr. Marshall served as J. Omar Good Distinguished Visiting Professor at Juniata College during the 1991-92 academic year.

LAUREE HERSCH MEYER is Professor of Theology and Director of the Continuing Education and Doctor of Ministry programs at Colgate Rochester Divinity School/Bexley Hall/Crozer Theological Seminary. She has also served on the faculties of the University of Notre Dame, the University of North Carolina, and Bethany Theological Seminary. She is a graduate of Bridgewater College (B.A.) and the University of Chicago (M.A., Ph.D.). The author of many articles and reviews, Dr. Meyer served at Juniata College as J. Omar Good Distinguished Visiting Professor during the 1990-91 academic year.

RICHARD J. MOUW is President and Professor of Christian Philosophy and Ethics at Fuller Theological Seminary where he joined the faculty in 1985. He is a graduate of Houghton College (B.A.), the University of Alberta (M.A.), and the University of Chicago (Ph.D.). Prior to his coming to Fuller, he served for seventeen years as Professor of Philosophy at Calvin College. Among his many publications are *Politics and the Biblical Drama* (Eerdmans, 1976), *Called to Holy Worldliness* (Fortress, 1980), *The God Who Commands* (Notre

Dame, 1990), *Uncommon Decency* (InterVarsity, 1992), and (with Sander Griffioen) *Pluralisms and Horizons: An Essay in Christian Public Philosophy* (Eerdmans, 1992). Dr. Mouw served as J. Omar Good Distinguished Visiting Professor at Juniata College during the 1980-81 academic year.

MARK A. NOLL is McManis Professor of Christian Thought at Wheaton College, where he joined the faculty in 1979. He is a graduate of Wheaton College (B.A.), the University of Iowa (M.A.), Trinity Evangelical Divinity School (M.Div.), and Vanderbilt University (M.A., Ph.D.). He is the author or editor of several books on subjects in American religious and cultural history, including *Princeton and the Republic, 1768-1822* (Princeton University Press, 1989), *A History of Christianity in the United States and Canada* (Eerdmans, 1992), *The Scandal of the Evangelical Mind* (Eerdmans, 1994), and (as co-editor) *Evangelicalism: Comparative Studies . . . 1700-1990* (Oxford University Press, 1994). Dr. Noll served as J. Omar Good Distinguished Visiting Professor at Juniata College during the 1982-83 academic year.

BRUCE R. REICHENBACH is Professor of Philosophy at Augsburg College in Minneapolis, Minnesota, where he has been on the faculty since 1968. He is a graduate of Wheaton College (B.A.) and Northwestern University (M.A., Ph.D.). He is the author of many articles and reviews and of several books, including *On Behalf of God: A Christian Ethic for Biology* (Eerdmans, 1995), *The Law of Karma: A Philosophical Study* (Macmillan, 1990), *Evil and a Good God* (Fordham, 1982), and *Is Man the Phoenix? A Study of Immortality* (Eerdmans, 1978). Dr. Reichenbach served as J. Omar Good Distinguished Visiting Professor at Juniata College during the 1985-86 academic year.

ROBERT C. ROBERTS is Professor of Philosophy and Psychological Studies at Wheaton College. He is a graduate of Wichita State University (B.A.) and Yale University (B.D., Ph.D.). Dr. Roberts taught at Western Kentucky University from 1973-84 before joining the faculty at Wheaton. He is the author of many articles and reviews and six books, among which are *Spirituality and Human Emotion*

(Eerdmans, 1982), *The Virtues: Contemporary Essays on Moral Character* (Wadsworth, 1986), and *Taking the Word to Heart: Self and Other in an Age of Therapies* (Eerdmans, 1993). Dr. Roberts served at Juniata College as J. Omar Good Distinguished Visiting Professor during the 1989-90 academic year.

MEROLD WESTPHAL is Professor of Philosophy at Fordham University. He is a graduate of Wheaton College (B.A.) and Yale University (M.A., Ph.D.). Prior to his service at Fordham University he taught for eight years at Yale University and for eleven at Hope College. Among his publications are *God, Guilt, and Death: An Existential Phenomenology of Religion* (Indiana, 1984), *Kierkegaard's Critique of Reason and Society* (Penn State, 1991), *Suspicion and Faith: The Religious Uses of Modern Atheism* (Eerdmans, 1993), and *Becoming a Self: A Reading of Kierkegaard's Concluding Unscientific Postscript* (Purdue, 1996). Dr. Westphal served as J. Omar Good Distinguished Visiting Professor at Juniata College during the 1981-82 academic year.

Introduction:
Should God Get Tenure?

David W. Gill

Reactions to the title of this collection of essays have been mixed. Several of my friends mentioned a list of reasons "Why God Would Never Get Tenure" that they had seen posted anonymously on the Internet. Among the fourteen reasons: (1) He had only one major publication; (2) It wasn't published in a refereed journal; (3) The scientific community has had a hard time reproducing his results; (4) He expelled his first two students; (5) Although there were only ten requirements, most students failed his tests; and so on. Cute.

A publisher told me immediately on hearing it that he would like to buy my title — even if the essays were not of interest to his company. And a retired pastor worried that it sounded irreverent. But I do not mean to be either funny or irreverent by posing the question, "Should God Get Tenure?"

In higher education, "tenure" is granted because of one's performance (teaching, research and publication, service to college and community, etc.). While not exactly a guarantee of a lifelong position, tenure represents a certain level of job security. It intends to protect the freedom of the professional voice from ideological and political pressures. A tenured professor does not have to worry (at least, not as much as an untenured professor) if the administration

1

or the culture of the institution changes and one becomes politically incorrect or a minority voice.

During the twentieth century, theological and religious perspectives have been marginalized, if not utterly excluded, in much of our college and university education. In my otherwise outstanding experience as an undergraduate in history at the University of California at Berkeley in the sixties, it puzzled and troubled me that my courses in the late Roman Empire, in the Protestant Reformation, and in African-American history overlooked the importance of theological ideas and religious communities in interpreting those subjects. We were careful to study economic, political, demographic, and ethnic causes and correlations, but little or nothing was made of religious factors.

In the thirty years since my undergraduate experience, some positive steps, here and there, have been made in the opposite direction. Some of this is because African-American, Muslim, and other minorities have bravely insisted that we cannot study their culture or history without paying attention to the religion that stands at the heart of their experience. Nevertheless, God still does not have tenure in most institutions and academic disciplines. It is not unusual even at smaller, private, historically religious liberal arts colleges to hear faculties and administrations repeat, in one form or another, Tertullian's rhetorical question, "What has Athens to do with Jerusalem?" — and then deprecate Jerusalem.

The most innocuous, politically correct, ceremonial prayers addressed to "the spirit of love" or "the ground of all being" raise the hackles of many academics, who see this as an unwarranted intrusion of God into academia. Even in dealing with deep questions of moral values and the ends of life, students are often asked and expected to bracket out any religious perspectives or convictions — even though in reality such a neat separation is untrue and impossible for many. Students and faculty members of faith often find their interests ignored, ruled out of order, or treated with contempt.

Today's Conversation about God, Religion, and Higher Education

Should God Get Tenure? is not the beginning but the continuation of a discussion that has grown in quality and intensity over the past decade. Responding to the negative attitude toward religion in our broader culture and politics, Yale University law professor Stephen L. Carter wrote his recent, much-discussed book, *The Culture of Disbelief.* "In our sensible zeal to keep religion from dominating our politics, we have created a political and legal culture that presses the religiously faithful to be other than themselves, to act . . . as though their faith does not matter to them." Even though surveys indicate that more than nine of ten Americans today believe in God and four of five pray regularly, we have a trend toward "treating religious beliefs as arbitrary and unimportant" and a rhetoric that "implies that there is something wrong with religious devotion."[1]

Carter's first argument, then, is that people should not be required to deny who they are; their religious convictions are central to their personal and communal identities, and ought to be respected as such. But, second, political power and intellectual orthodoxy are healthiest not when unopposed but when in tension with opposing loyalties and perspectives. Religion is not just a personal philosophy or worldview; it is "at its heart, a way of denying the authority of the rest of the world" (p. 41). Religious commitments provide an important check on centralized power.

What Carter discusses in the broader political domain is equally important in higher education. His perspective is similar to what John Stuart Mill argued in his famous essay *On Liberty:* unpopular, minority opinions ought to be welcomed because (1) they might turn out to be correct, and (2) even if such opinions are incorrect, the truth is made stronger through encounter with opposing arguments.

Before Stephen Carter, historian Page Smith warned against "academic fundamentalism" in his *Killing the Spirit: Higher Education*

---

1. Stephen L. Carter, *The Culture of Disbelief: How American Law and Politics Trivialize Religious Devotion* (New York: Basic Books, 1993), pp. 3, 6.

in America.[2] "Academic fundamentalism" assumes that "only certain ideas are tolerated" in the "close-minded" academy; it is "the stubborn refusal of the academy to acknowledge any truth that does not conform to professorial dogmas." Smith illustrates this with a report on a college course on Gothic architecture that "made no mention of the religious passion out of which these grand structures rose," and a course on American Populism "that made no mention of the evangelical Protestantism . . . without some attention to which the movement remains uncomprehensible" (pp. 5-6). Of the many problems that the university faces, "the spiritual aridity of the American university is, for me, the most depressing aspect of all" (p. 20). "Although most Americans remain doggedly religious, academic fundamentalism banished from the academy any form of belief for which there was 'insufficient evidence' except the belief in the immutability and sufficiency of Science" (p. 107).

Page Smith calls for a renewed recognition and appreciation for *both* the "Classical Christian Consciousness" and the "Secular Democratic Consciousness" that have shaped our world and its universities. The latter has swallowed up the former over the twentieth century — but "declined into decadence . . . turned inward and became an end in itself" (p. 303).

Less polemical but equally powerful is George M. Marsden's painstaking history of *The Soul of the American University: From Protestant Establishment to Established Nonbelief.*[3] Marsden's history even-handedly tells the story of how religion has both nourished and challenged the development of American colleges and universities. Like Carter and Smith, Marsden concludes by calling for a renewed space for religion in the university.

For Marsden, the premises of secular naturalism that once justified the exclusion of religious and theological perspectives are

2. Page Smith, *Killing the Spirit: Higher Education in America* (New York: Penguin Books, 1990).

3. George M. Marsden, *The Soul of the American University: From Protestant Establishment to Established Nonbelief* (New York: Oxford University Press, 1994). See also George M. Marsden and Bradley J. Longfield, eds., *The Secularization of the American Academy* (New York: Oxford University Press, 1992), and Douglas Sloan, *Faith and Knowledge: Mainline Protestantism and American Higher Education* (Louisville: Westminster/John Knox, 1994).

no longer adequate. Thus, while "claims to private revelations or other religious attitudes that preempt intellectual inquiry are particularly problematic . . . there is no reason why it should be a rule of academia that *no* religious viewpoint shall receive serious consideration" (p. 431). Many religious perspectives have distinguished traditions and capable proponents. Pluralism and academic freedom, two widely held values in today's university, argue that not only Christian but other religious traditions should have a place in the forum. Given the overwhelmingly secular character of higher education, the diversity of religions, and the sharp divisions among Christians themselves, Marsden argues that any fears of reintroducing a virtual establishment of religion are misplaced.

Another important recent voice on this subject is Warren A. Nord, author of *Religion and American Education*.[4] Nord argues that "whether or not one is religious, one cannot deny that religion has been, and continues to be, tremendously important in shaping people's lives." Both for its beneficial and its negative effects, religion is important and worthy to be studied seriously. Because religion continues to play a vital role in our culture, "to be liberally educated students must hear the religious voices that are part of our cultural conversation; indeed, critical thinking requires the ability to be reasonable about contending points of view" (p. 377).

The Good Professorship

Some twenty years ago, well before this current conversation gathered momentum, the administrators of Juniata College and of the J. Omar Good Endowment saw the handwriting on the wall and decided to invite an annual "Distinguished Visiting Professor of Evangelical Christianity" to their college campus in central Pennsylvania. Those of us who have served in this capacity are under no illusions that we have been the "voice of God" on campus! But it has been our task to bring some theological perspective to the subjects and to the students we have taught during our year on campus.

4. Warren A. Nord, *Religion and American Education: Rethinking a National Dilemma* (Chapel Hill: University of North Carolina, 1995).

The essays which follow argue in many different ways for the critical, appreciative inclusion of theological and religious perspectives in higher education. All of the authors are of the Christian faith — but our arguments would also support the inclusion of Jewish, Muslim, Hindu, Buddhist, Native American, and other religious perspectives when and where appropriate. We are not arguing for permission to indoctrinate or proselytize, on the one hand; nor for an uncritical "feel good" affirmation of any and all things religious, on the other. "*Critical* appreciation" of the role of God and religion may be the best phrase.

What, then, might it mean for God to "get tenure"? Here are three basic possibilities: First, on a curricular level, courses in the Bible and in World Religions ought to become general education requirements (not just electives). Whether one is a "believer" or not, the great stories, personalities, themes, and ideas of the Bible have indelibly influenced our political, economic, health care, cultural, educational, and other institutions, movements, and debates. No one can be truly educated without some minimum level of biblical literacy, with attention to the ways Scripture has influenced art, music, literature, social reform, and popular culture. This is just a beginning, of course, and additional courses on "the Bible and . . ." or on other sacred religious texts are desirable if God has tenure.

In a world of global population movements, political-economic-technological networking, and multicultural diversity, a minimum of serious study of Christianity, Judaism, Islam, and other world religions is also essential for educated world citizens. The history, institutions, practices, and sacred literature of these religions ought to be required for study in all of our colleges and universities — not just for humanities and social science majors but for engineers, doctors, attorneys, mass communications majors, and others. Along with the study of such traditional religions, our students need to learn to use the tools of cultural, sociological, and psychological study to assess the roles of new religions, including "civil religion" and "secular religion" (such as Marxism, Darwinism, scientism, technologism, and other "isms" — which function in the role formerly occupied by traditional religions).

Second, in addition to such formal courses, "God-talk" and

religious perspectives ought to be given their due, whenever appropriate, in courses in history, literature, philosophy, and many other fields. In particular, when students wish to articulate or explore religious questions that are integral to their study of a given problem or field, we should encourage them to do so, critically and responsibly; we should not treat such interests as out of bounds or deserving of contempt.

Third, outside of the classroom, there is every reason to encourage student and faculty participation in religious practice and activism — just as we would encourage political, environmental, artistic, and community activism outside of class. Our goal in political science is not to kill off political activism; our goal in art history and criticism is not to repress artistic creativity. So too, our approach to critical religious study should not discourage religious practice.

Even in our secular, religiously disestablished era, religion (in one form or another) and God (or some substitute for God) continue to occupy an important and dynamic role in personal and social life. If our colleges and universities are to fulfill their higher aspirations of educating whole persons for the real world in all of its diversity and challenges, we need these days to go bravely against the flow and "give God tenure."

On Being a Professor:
The Case of Socrates

Bruce R. Reichenbach

I n the preface to his book on higher education, Mark Schwehn tells the personal story of being at a party where academics shared what they entered under the heading "Occupation" on the Internal Revenue form. The answers of one after another reflected the disciplines: historian, sociologist, psychologist. Schwehn then notes that "I admitted (it certainly felt like an admission) that I had written 'college teacher' under the relevant heading. This disclosure was greeted with what I can only describe (though it was doubtless a projection even then) as a combination of mild alarm and studied astonishment. I felt as though I had suddenly become, however briefly, an informant from another culture."[1]

Though in this age of fragmented university communities academic professionals tend to identify themselves and their colleagues by their narrow disciplines, society uses less discipline-oriented terms to denote those who professionally engage students in the classroom. They are variously called teachers, educators, instructors, lecturers, readers, tutors, professors, scholars, academicians, and more recently facilitators and co-learners. Though not carefully distinguished in common parlance, these terms are neither strictly equivalent nor pedagogically neutral. In particular,

---

1. Mark Schwehn, *Exiles from Eden* (New York: Oxford University Press, 1993), pp. vii-viii.

8

the terms can connote how professionals view their educational task and what instructional methods they typically employ.

The term most frequently used in postsecondary education is "professor." The term arose in the medieval universities to denote a person licensed to teach or dispute publicly. We capture this derivation when we define "profess" as to "openly declare or publicly claim a belief, faith, or opinion."[2] In professing, professors, in various contexts — writing, dialogue with colleagues, in the community at large, and, most importantly for education, in the classroom — not only entertain educated (informed and justified) beliefs about matters germane to the discussion but are willing to declare, recommend, and defend them publicly. Professors, in this sense, advance what they believe is significant, meaningful, true, justified, creative, and worthy of discussion and further exploration. Their expressions of belief constitute part of the public record to be understood, debated, evaluated, defended, altered, reconstructed, and applied.

But herein lies a difficulty: Is profession appropriate in the classroom? Does not a professor's profession of particular beliefs and general worldviews, whatever their stripe, conflict with the ideals of presuppositionless investigation, unbiased presentation of the materials, and open dialogue? The question is relevant, not only for all educators who function in this role, but most particularly for those whom we will term "Socratic professors," that is, those members of the academic community who trace their pedagogical heritage back to Socrates.

Our interest lies not merely with professors in general, but also with Christian professors, especially those who seek integration of their faith and learning. The beliefs of Christian professors will be situated in the larger Christian creational and redemptive worldview. In turn, this worldview, implicitly or explicitly, will underlie the professor's professing. So we might rephrase the question: Is it not the case that being a Christian professor is inimical to the educational process?

---

2. "Professor," *Oxford English Dictionary*, vol. VIII, p. 1429.

The Case of Socrates

If there is any philosophical hero, any model for the philosophical life, any ideal teacher of philosophy, it is Socrates. Indeed, he approaches pagan sainthood as a man martyred for his persistent questioning, for his endeavors to get others to think, even at the risk of offending the powerful who claimed to know. He believed that engaging his fellow Athenians in philosophical dialogue and debate made life worth living. His very life exemplified the philosophical truism that the unexamined life is not worth living.

Professors emulate Socrates not because he was successful in communicating content, for those whom he "taught" often left without a clear solution to the issue under discussion. Indeed, contemporary scholars identify the truly Socratic dialogues in part by Socrates' use of the *elenchus:* the adversarial refutation of other views. The opposing viewpoints refuted, discussion comes to an end but not a conclusion. The matter remains unresolved — postponed to a future meeting (*Protagoras* 361e; *Laches* 201e) or abandoned (*Lysis* 223a; *Euthyphro* 15e). It is as if for Socrates cutting a swath through the jungle of knowledge-claims was more important than arriving at King Solomon's rich mines.

Neither do teachers follow Socrates because he was loved by all of his students or debaters, for he was not. One might say that he received mixed student evaluations. Euthyphro, in frustration over his perception that Socrates stirred up arguments and set them in motion so that they always seemed to run in circles and never settled to a conclusion, pictured Socrates as the sculptor Daedalus, who created statues so real that they came to life (*Euthyphro* 11d). Thrasymachus became furious at Socrates, tossing out ad hominems and epithets when his arguments failed (*Republic* 336c-d, 338d, 340d, 343a).

Rather, we admire Socrates in part because he attempted to assist those who thought that they knew the answers to realize that they did not. He helped them painfully to scrub the scales of delusion from their eyes, to see more clearly their own ignorance. Socrates encouraged the young Theaetetus at the end of their apparently fruitless discussion, "Then supposing you should ever henceforth try to conceive afresh, Theaetetus, if you succeed, your embryo thought will be the better as a consequence of today's scrutiny, and if you remain barren, you will be gentler and more agreeable to your companions, having the good sense not to fancy you know what you do not know. For that, and no more, is all that my art can effect" (*Theaetetus* 210c).

What is striking about Socrates is the way he conducted his educational enterprise. Indeed, his pedagogical style has become so influential that we call it the Socratic method. Socrates operated as the persistent questioner, the intellectual midwife. "Heaven constrains me to serve as a midwife, but has debarred me from giving birth. So of myself I have no sort of wisdom. . . . The many admirable truths they bring to birth have been discovered by themselves from within. But the delivery is heaven's work and mine" (*Theaetetus* 150d). Epitomizing the admirable facilitator, he assisted, as with the case of the slave boy in the *Meno,* the student to recall knowledge from the mind's hidden recesses.

Socrates denied that he taught in the way that his listeners commonly understood the process. When brought to trial before his fellow-citizens, Socrates quickly rebutted the charge that he was a Sophist, the vocal purveyors of alleged knowledge who, at least in the eyes of both Socrates and his accusers, were hell-bent to make the weaker argument into the stronger so as to gain clients whom they could train to emulate their rhetorical methods (*Apology* 19d). Socrates also distanced himself from the report that he was a teacher who conveyed knowledge from his own vast storehouse (*Apology* 19e). Indeed, Socrates, with characteristic irony, contended that his very poverty evidenced the truth of his denial, for those who really knew should, by virtue of this valuable possession, be able to charge a handsome fee for their services. Rather, he taught by making others aware of their own ignorance while enabling them to discern or "discover for themselves the truth the teacher had held back."[3]

It was not that Socrates lacked wisdom; rather he professed a different wisdom, a limited wisdom that he took to be the beginning of all other wisdom. His wisdom concerned the nature of the knowing process. The first step of knowing, he argued, is being aware

---

3. Gregory Vlastos, *Socrates: Ironist and Moral Philosopher* (Ithaca, N.Y.: Cornell University Press, 1991), p. 32.

that one does not know.[4] Scholars debate the seriousness with which Socrates accepted the riddle of the enigmatic Delphic oracle, which claimed that Socrates was the wisest man. But he was serious about the task of arresting those in the Athenian community who claimed to be knowledgeable. As a result, his teaching style was adversative, critically examining the positions held by his interlocutors. Socrates used the *elenchus*, not to arrive at the coveted definitions of piety, friendship, or virtue, or to stake out his own position, but to refute the prominent views and those who advocated them. This refutation was not without merit, for the very act of investigating the meaning of the virtues and rooting out the errors of inadequate conceptions wherever they were found would improve a person's moral character.[5]

So where does this leave the Socratic professor, one who seeks to emulate Socrates as the model teacher? How can one who does not know (who is barren), who sees his or her role as a classroom midwife assisting students to bear ideas and then adversarially to test them for their "reality," profess anything? Is the term "Socratic professor" an oxymoron?

This is particularly difficult for the Christian Socratic professor who seeks to integrate faith and learning; this too smacks of being an oxymoron. To be a Christian is to espouse as true a particular worldview. All truth is grounded in or consonant with the wisdom of God. But if the professor only perpetually searches for the truth but never possesses or affirms it, if all discussion is elenchic, if in the academic context one is to be only an adversarial midwife who can no longer bear intellectual children, then the gulf between belief and profession is as wide as imaginable.

In fact, the Christian professor might be accused, as Socrates sometimes was (*Republic* 340d; 341a), of dishonesty in the class-

4. Vlastos notes that Socrates is not guilty of self-contradiction, for Socrates does not claim that he *knows* that he does not know; he *merely* affirms that he is not aware of such knowledge (p. 82, n. 4).

5. One might suggest that Socrates was less concerned with teaching others than with finding the truth for himself. In *Charmides* (166c-d) he notes that he "examines the argument chiefly for my own sake, though no doubt also for the sake of my friends." Since my concern is with the latter element, I will pass over this (not unimportant) feature of Socrates as educator.

room. If one professes to one's students that one does not know, that one is only a facilitator of recall, a co-learner and co-seeker, how can one at the same time put oneself forth to be a Christian, a person who entertains definite commitments about the world and its dependence on God, about what it is to be human as the *imago Dei*, and about the transcendent? One might seek an escape by saying that one's commitments are to the Supreme Person, but such a plea is not viable. To have Christian commitments involves having beliefs about that to which one is committed. Hence Christian professors (as indeed all professors, whatever their religious or non-religious stripe) cannot escape having beliefs — beliefs that, if they are honest, they espouse to be true and worthy of consideration and affirmation, not only by the professor, but by the students who hear the profession. Their educational task is more than adversarially elenchic: it is professorial.

So how, one might inquire, can one be a truly Socratic professor? Indeed, how can one be a Christian Socratic professor? How does the tension play out in the educational context?

The Myth of Neutrality

Socrates overtly proclaimed neutrality in his investigations. The career of midwifery began when one could no longer conceive; "they never attend other women in childbirth so long as they themselves can conceive and bear children, but only when they are too old for that" (*Theaetetus* 149b). By parallel reasoning, one might argue that only when professors eschew their own wisdom — or become too old — can they assist others to bear wisdom.

What are we to make of Socrates' claim of not knowing? Perhaps his profession of neutrality is best understood as irony. That is, his claim in the *Apology* not to know must not be taken simply at face value. While he claims that he lacks superhuman wisdom, he does possess limited human wisdom (*Apology* 20d). His "profession of ignorance [is] intelligible only if understood to disclaim one sort of knowledge, while claiming another in the same breath."[6]

6. Vlastos, *Socrates*, p. 13.

Even introductory philosophy students quickly see behind Socrates' questioning garb. For example, his discussion with Meno's slave boy rarely convinces them. Socrates is not neutral in pursuit of the origin of knowledge; he leads the boy to the correct answers. He knows the precise way he wishes to travel, even to the point of putting the correct answer in the boy's mouth, albeit in the form of a question. Socrates' dialectic at times is less an objective questioning than a subtle means to bring the other along in the journey already somewhat carefully conceived.[7]

Indeed, neither educators nor students come to the well without a jug of a particular shape and texture, molded by past experiences and the hands of parents, peers, teachers, ministers, and others. There is no complete professorial neutrality. Professors bring to their profession, both within and outside the classroom, their own noetic structure. They are not uniquely objective, if by "objective" we mean that they approach issues without presuppositions or biases. The biases run broad and deep. They include, at the basic level, the intentions and purposes behind their particular classroom communication. At the broadest level, they include a panorama of beliefs drawn from experiences and learning, beliefs that, insofar as they are integrated into theories or paradigms, form their worldview. Indeed, what is said and heard in the classroom, by professor and student alike, is viewed from the perspective of beliefs already entertained. Beliefs shape the way we understand questions and return answers. The hope is that what is unique about the perspectives of the professors is that they have conscientiously reflected on them and subjected them to scrutiny by themselves and their professional and academic community.

A common myth is that the burden of operating from presuppositions falls especially heavy on Christian or other faith-affirming professors. They are allegedly saddled with the uncommon burden

---

7. One might argue that the *Meno* is a work of Plato's middle period and thus reflects Plato's viewpoint rather than the tentative search of Socrates (e.g., Vlastos, *Socrates*, pp. 118-25). But even such undisputed early works as the *Apology, Crito*, and *Euthyphro* show the same evidence that Socrates is not aimlessly wandering in his questioning of his interlocutors.

of religious beliefs, from which non-Christian or nonreligious professors are free. One author writes, "The sort of 'truth' proclaimed by Christianity — like the fiats of theocratic and imperial authority — brooks no disagreement. It has thus crystallized as an orthodoxy, or a core of inalterable dogmas, that its followers are expected to steadfastly profess. . . . Dogmas, by their nature, are nondiscussable and nonnegotiable."[8] But though non-Christian and nonreligious professors are free from *Christian* presuppositions, they bring their own unique worldviews to the subject matter and to the classroom. They are no more free from presuppositions and biases than the Christian; it is only that they possess a partially differing set. They cannot be any more (or less) objective.

Where does this leave the Christian professor? Hopefully professing, but with the important caveat that the profession occurs in the context of the integration of faith and learning. This has several implications. First, faith must be subject to learning. Since faith-beliefs form part of the academic profession, they are subject to rational discourse, debate, and critical evaluation: to Socratic discussion. Protectionism is not a viable option for the professor. As the ideas of struggling students are placed on the table for discussion, so too are those of the professor, both within and outside the classroom. This is part of the price, if not the enjoyment, of participating in the academic community.

But at the same time, second, there is no reason to think that the beliefs must be subject to the latest intellectual fad. Alvin Plantinga has argued persuasively that there is a mistaken assumption in education that all must adhere to or be held accountable to the standards set by the secular community, as if these provide some sort of neutral ground on which to conduct discussion. Speaking about the philosopher, Plantinga writes,

> So the Christian philosopher has his own topics and projects to think about; and when he thinks about the topics of current concern in the broader philosophical world, he will think about them in his own way, which may be a *different* way. He may have

8. Aram Vartanian, "Democracy, Religion, and the Enlightenment," *The Humanist* 51, no. 6 (Nov./Dec. 1991): 12.

to reject certain currently fashionable assumptions about the philosophic enterprise — he may have to reject widely accepted assumptions as to what are the proper starting points and procedures for philosophical endeavor. And — and this is crucially important — the Christian philosopher has a perfect right to the point of view and pre-philosophical assumptions he brings to philosophic work; the fact that these are not widely shared outside the Christian or theistic community is interesting but fundamentally irrelevant.[9]

He terms this "integrality."

In sum, professing is perspectival, worldviewish. The professor who is the barren midwife will never be able to profess; empty jugs can pour no water. In recognizing this, professors are freed from the unnecessary burden of trying to prove that they possess the illusory property of objectivity. They are also freed from the delusion that students are incapable of evaluating for themselves what is professed, without being overwhelmed by the power or position of the instructor. This view makes students to be less than they are, thinking them liable to undue persuasion by the teacher, incapable of taking their own stand. Some students are especially vulnerable, but protecting them hardly merits the risk of disvaluing, by the deceit of alleged objectivity, the abilities of most to be independent thinkers.

At the outset of this section I suggested that Socrates' profession of neutrality at times might be ironic. What matters is not his profession of neutrality, but his persistent search for the truth. In doing so he modeled this professorial dimension for his students. Students "need a teacher as a catalyst and guide, one who has struggled and is struggling with similar questions and knows some of the pertinent materials and procedures."[10]

9. Alvin Plantinga, "Advice to Christian Philosophers," *Faith and Philosophy* 1, no. 2 (July 1984): 256.

10. Arthur Holmes, *The Idea of a Christian College* (Grand Rapids: Eerdmans, 1975), p. 48.

The Myth of Expressionism

The Socratic method appeals to the doctrine that learners unknowingly already possess knowledge and truth within themselves. Thus education should provide the opportunity for these to be expressed and, if possible, integrated with the expressions of others. But if everyone already comes loaded with knowledge, then it seems that there is little room for professing "experts," only for those skilled in the art of midwifery to elicit the hidden.

In the 1970s' days of "groupiness" — group love, group think, group discussion, sensitivity groups, and the like — it was acceptable to let group ignorance pass for knowledge. After all, what was of primary importance was to share one's beliefs. There was no truth to be sought after, only feelings and opinions to be expressed. The very expression provided the needed cathartic experience, best exemplified in "I'm okay; you're okay."

But as we discovered, this is not education. Indeed, pooling ignorance can be diseducation. To reiterate one's ideas without any challenge, to solicit acceptance on the grounds that you believe it sincerely, is to reinforce the wrong elements. Socrates is positively shocked at Euthyphro's suggestion that he can legitimately prosecute his father for impiety, especially considering Euthyphro's shaky, unreflective understanding of piety.

For Socrates, no one comes to the discussion possessing a *tabula rasa*, a mind devoid of truths. The Socratic dialectic would prove fruitless from the start, after all, if there were nothing by which one could sort out true from false beliefs. The interlocutors could not recognize when a claim was to be rejected.[11]

But contrary to the myth of expressionism, Socrates' belief is consistent with the professorial role of experts. First, as Vlastos notes, Socrates seeks not merely to root out conceit of knowledge but also to advance the quest for truth by worming it out of those in whom it is hidden. Thus, he must assume that "his interlocutors always carry truth somewhere or other in their belief system," truth that eventually they might recognize under his guidance.[12] But Socrates did not

11. Vlastos, *Socrates*, p. 15.
12. Vlastos, *Socrates*, p. 114.

allow just any expression to pass for knowledge. He strongly believed that there was truth that transcended individual possession, for which one was to seek. He argued, "I do not insist that my argument is right in all other respects, but I would contend at all costs both in word and deed as far as I could that we will be better men, braver and less idle, if we believe that one must search for the things one does not know, rather than if we believe that it is not possible to find out what we do not know and that we must not look for it" (*Meno* 86b-c).

The professor must agree with Socrates that it is essential that we search for the things we do not know *with the expectation that there is something to know.* This last part is what many in our era of postmodern thought miss, but which the professor must profess. Unless there is something to know, unless there is truth, it hardly matters being a *professional,* let alone a Christian, professor. Any kind of professor or facilitator will do. Education reduces to sensitivity, which paradoxically cannot have among its core beliefs that it is true that sensitivity matters.

Second, Socrates himself is not above professing, though he does it in his own dialectical way. The questions he asks often are rhetorical. Is quality of life better than quantity? Must one never willingly do wrong? Is it right to do an injury in retaliation? Ought one fulfill all one's moral agreements? From these Socrates concludes that one ought not to injure the state by breaking its laws (*Crito* 48b-50a). Is virtue something good? Is the good beneficial? Is not the benefit to be found in right use and harm in wrong use? And once these points are readily conceded, Socrates quickly draws the conclusion that virtue is knowledge (*Meno* 87d-88d).

One might respond that the conclusion Socrates draws in the *Meno* remains tentative, for he goes on to wonder why there are not teachers of virtue if virtue is knowledge. But this, too, must be properly understood. On the one hand, Socrates often is not tentative. For example, when affirming that evildoers are unhappy, Socrates asks Polus whether he wants to refute such a claim. Polus notes that this "would be more difficult to refute than [Socrates'] first point," to which Socrates replies that it is "not difficult, but impossible, for the truth is never refuted" (*Gorgias* 473b).[13]

13. "These facts . . . are buckled fast and clamped together — to put it

On the other hand, Socrates' tentativeness — his rejection of dogmatic certainty — provides an important model for the professor. It is the paradox of profession: what one professes must be a live profession, one that the professor profoundly believes, yet one that also lies open to question and investigation. It must be grounded in and testable by experience and reason. Socrates' method never yields certainty, for every belief advanced is subject to scrutiny, the outcome of which remains tentative even should it survive Socratic questioning.[14] The tentativeness comes from the recognition that knowledge is not indubitable certainty. At the same time, however, neither are we left with agnosticism, which places all claims on equal footing.

By being testable I mean that the claims are open to examination, analysis, and discussion. One must do more than merely assert that this is the way things are because that is what I believe them to be or how I feel about the matter. Reasoned investigation is required, investigation that brings all of the resources of the humanist, the natural scientist, and the social scientist to bear on the issue. The proclamation, though believed, is advanced in the community of learning as a thesis worthy of being both believed (since thought to be true) and investigated (since its truth must be confirmed, especially by those to whom it is recommended for belief).

Educators, among others, have wrung their hands over the apparent tension between affirmation and openness. Might it not be the case that where convictions are so strong, as often they are with religious and moral beliefs, one cannot countenance the other side? How can one be open to what one believes to be false, and perhaps at times even demonic? Can one really be open to racist or sexist positions? Should professors tolerate, even allow, the advocacy of politically incorrect positions in the classroom?

---

somewhat crudely — by arguments of steel and adamant — at least so it would appear as matters stand. And unless you or one still more enterprising than yourself can undo them, it is impossible to speak aright except as I am now speaking. For what I say is always the same — that I know not the truth in these affairs. . . . And so once more I hold these things to be so" (*Gorgias* 509a).

14. Vlastos, *Socrates*, p. 114.

The conflict, I submit, arises from two things. First, it originates from a confusion between the academy and the "pulpit" (or faculty lounge or locker room). In the former, open, civil debate must in principle rule, no matter how false or despicable one thinks the opposing viewpoint. Indeed, if one believes, as Socrates does, that truth will win out, only by exposing false dogmas to the *elenchus* can one show the advocate (or at least the bystanders) that the position is indeed false and not worthy of belief. In the nonacademic setting, however, one need not be open to the other perspective (though civility might remain a virtue). Here the goal often is mere persuasion, not education.

Second, the conflict arises from the way the matter is asserted. I affirm what I believe to be true. To affirm it dogmatically creates conflict, for I have not left any options for the academic community, which seeks the truth, except to believe it on evidence of my mere assertion. If, however, I affirm the belief nondogmatically, the conflict disappears. For though I have affirmed the truth of the belief, I leave it open for the members of the academic community to search out for themselves its truth and supporting evidence.[15] Thus, though in my profession I believe that I am correct and indeed am willing to make the relevant commitments based on that belief — and in the case of religious beliefs, the risk of faith — yet I am willing to have others explore the truth-claim for themselves. Profession and tentativeness are not incompatible in the classroom, except for the dogmatist. On this Socrates would agree.

Education, then, involves more than elicitation of expression. Unreflective experience provides a beginning source for acquiring knowledge. One must begin with the assertions of what one believes as true, as well as connecting what one hears with what one already believes. But a task remains for the professor, a task that goes beyond mere adversarial *elenchus* that elicits opinions

15. It is important to note that the openness is not that of relativism, where all opinions are equal, and appreciation rather than careful, critical evaluation is the order of the day. Rather, it is the "openness that invites us to the quest for knowledge," that submits ideas to the bar of reason and experience. Allan Bloom, *The Closing of the American Mind* (New York: Simon & Schuster, 1987), p. 41.

from students. A philosopher once told me that the business of philosophy was garbage disposal. He was only partly correct. Professors engage in more than the trash-sorting and disposal business; they must be committed to helping restock the food shelves. They are obliged to supply elements whereby others can make new or replacement truth-claims. Allan Bloom recalls, "When I was a young teacher at Cornell, I once had a debate about education with a professor of psychology. He said that it was his function to get rid of prejudices in his students. He knocked them down like tenpins. I began to wonder what he replaced those prejudices with. . . . Did he believe that there are truths that could guide their lives as did their prejudices?"[16] Professors present claims, not to be asserted dogmatically or taken uncritically, but truth-claims nonetheless, subject to investigation and recommendations to be accepted and acted upon.

The Myth of Denigration

The final myth I want to address is that profession demeans the listener. Professing is held to demean in that it allegedly attempts to coerce or compel listeners to a certain position, rather than allowing them to think for themselves. Students and listeners should be respected, the argument goes. They should be given the tools to construct their own worldview and belief system, not persuaded or cajoled into that advocated by the professor.

The premises advanced in this argument are true. Education is not equivalent to mere persuasion. If it were, use of any of the multitude of rhetorically persuasive devices would be sanctioned in the academic community, so long as they were successful. Rather, education should assist students to discern the truth and should do this by reasoned presentations of the perceived facts and their justification. The end is that students come to hold justified beliefs. Thus, education is incompatible with compulsion, or even with advocacy of belief on the basis of *mere* authority. Students, if they are to become lifelong learners, must be provided

16. Bloom, *Closing*, p. 42.

the intellectual tools to be able to distinguish true from false claims, good from bad reasoning, fact from wishful thinking, evidence from pseudoevidence or emotional appeal.

But though the reasons advocated by the myth of denigration are true, the conclusion that profession demeans fails to follow. It is not profession itself that is problematic; it is the use (or better, misuse) of profession. If, on the one hand, profession is used to badger students into agreeing with the professor, then profession is being wrongly used. It becomes a tool of proselytizing rather than of education.

So how might profession be properly employed? First, professors should put the issues squarely on the table. They should state clearly what is in question and why it is important or significant. Education, while noting ambiguity, should never allow obfuscation.

Second, professors should stake out a thesis regarding the issue. They might do this boldly and assertively; they might do it tentatively and hesitantly. The degree of certitude professed should depend on the perceived strength of the evidence and the willingness of the believer to commit to that position.

Third, profession, when properly grounded, should provide students with reasons for thinking that what is professed is true or probably true. This will assist students (whether hearers or readers) to distinguish profession from propaganda. Within the educational context, discussion should be carried on in a reasoned, civilized fashion. Ad hominems, red herrings, and sundry other illegitimate appeals must be avoided, for they move the discourse from an honest dealing with the issue to valuing only listener agreement. Education must stand for integrity.

Fourth, professors should engage those who think differently, but neither to construct straw persons to be easily vanquished nor to demean or belittle opposing views or the persons holding them. Rather, others' views should be taken seriously: stated with the same clarity as those one professes, developed with the appropriate nuances, provided with their soundest and strongest reasons, and evaluated fairly. Socrates in the *Theaetetus* provides a model, for time and again he brings back Protagoras (in a rhetorical fashion, Protagoras not being present at the debate) to defend his claims, lest Theaetetus think that Socrates won the debate unfairly.

Fifth, professing must be done from humility brought on by the recognition of our extreme finitude. It is an old saw that the more one knows, the more one realizes how much there is to know and what little one knows. Further, as Paul wrote in 1 Corinthians, we now see through a glass darkly. Our vision is flawed, imperfect, limited, imprecise, skewed. Accordingly, we need the help of others to see the path of knowledge. No, it is not the blind leading the blind, but those with partial and perhaps better sight, those who have developed skills of the other "senses," that we call on to guide us in our pronouncements. Socrates was correct: to recognize one's limits is the beginning of wisdom. What Euthyphro lacked most of all was humility.

Sixth, professors, if truly Socratic, should challenge the students with the profession. Nicias says of Socrates, "Any one who is close to Socrates and enters into conversation with him is liable to be drawn into an argument and whatever subject he may start, he finds that he has to give account both of his present and past life, and when he is once entangled, Socrates will not let him go until he has completely and thoroughly sifted him" (*Laches* 187e). There should be a certain tension in the classroom, occasioned by profession that at times will make others uncomfortable but that also will provoke creative responses.

Socrates likens his professing task to the stinging fly that goads the lazy horse into action. In this he is not always the model professor.

> It is plain that Socrates, besides being an original and powerful mind, was also something of an intellectual clown, a reveler in circus debate, a diabolical needler of his contemporaries. . . . He chooses his antagonists, fixes on the subject, . . . elicits from him an opinion, a speech, a dogma, and then proceeds to counterpunch the poor man and his opinion to death, mixing in his blows not only philosophical points and arguments but also sarcasm, irony that borders on insincerity, and personal insults; and he does not rest until he has extracted from his victim a public confession of utter helplessness. At the end, when it is painfully

obvious that his opponent will never recover, he proposes that they all go home and start all over again another time. It is no wonder that he never has a second dialogue with the same man.[17]

At the same time, there is little doubt that some of his interlocutors needed to be stung out of their lethargy.

This raises the question concerning to what extent students are fragile. It depends on the student. Socrates himself sometimes adapted to his interlocutors, as one can readily see by contrasting the way he handled Thrasymachus and youthful Theaetetus. The overriding concern is "exhorting you and elucidating the truth for everyone that I meet" (*Apology* 29d); how best this is done will vary with the context and one's students.

Finally, professors should leave it open to the students to develop and make their own professions. This will allow for openness, for breathing room, for a space where the students can, for themselves and in their own time and way, carefully think through the issues before them. Success in profession of beliefs should never be equated with agreement of listeners. Should we do so, truth becomes a matter of who and how many believe it. But truth is never discerned merely through democratic voting. Professors should encourage critical thinkers, not disciples.

If professors are truly convinced of the truth of their position, and if they truly believe that in the end truth will prevail — perhaps not entirely and decisively, but gradually with the preponderance of its weight — then they need not pressure, cajole, or close down the options. Rather, they will state their case and enable the students to come to their own decisions. Put another way, the obligation to profess is not equivalent to the obligation to convert. That task belongs to the Spirit.

Perhaps the operative word here is "enable." Profession without enabling can often look like coercion, especially when it is coupled with persuasive techniques or with the power of authority at times wielded by or accompanying the position of the professor. Profession, if it is to succeed, must be made from the position of

---

17. Gerasimos Xenophon Santas, *Socrates* (Boston: Routledge & Kegan Paul, 1979), p. 6.

weakness not strength (here I refer to the presentation, not the quality of the reasoning), from humility and not pride, from openness and not dogmatically. Only as the one in the position of knowledge, power, and authority can withdraw can others be freed to look at what is professed in its own light, to assess it clearly and believe it for its merit.

Profession properly employed does not demean learners. Rather, they are enabled to come to an open-minded, fair, reasoned, judicious, and carefully qualified position of their own. In this they are respected, indeed, most highly respected, for in professing, professors are sharing what is of great importance for their own worldview. Professors put their beliefs out into that marketplace of ideas. They do not cast pearls before swine, but pearls before the jewel merchants, who must themselves decide what the wares are worth.

Professing and Piping

Successful profession involves more than presentation. As W. K. C. Guthrie notes regarding Socrates, "Dialectical skill was for him only the means to moral reform, which will always fail unless there is an initial current of sympathy between teacher and disciple."[18] Socrates possessed a certain magnetism that in spite of, or perhaps even in part because of, his appearance, drew persons to him. Alcibiades likens Socrates to the piper Marsyas, who merely by playing could bewitch his listeners. "Now the only difference, Socrates, between you and Marsyas is that you can get just the same effect without any instrument at all — with nothing but a few simple words. . . . When we listen to you, . . . we're absolutely staggered and bewitched" (*Symposium* 215c-d).

The Socratic professor pipes. Successful profession requires a connection between the professor and the pupil, an empathy. Socrates at times terms it a divine voice that warns him when the pupil is incapable of conceiving ideas (*Theaetetus* 151a). But however one describes it, profession occurs most effectively when there is a

18. W. K. C. Guthrie, *Socrates* (Cambridge: Cambridge University Press, 1971), p. 81.

personal connection between professor and listener that attracts, motivates, and stimulates the search for truth.

But it must not be the piping of proselytizing, which turns students into disciples. (In this respect, Guthrie has it wrong.) Whereas proselytizing makes for followers who primarily emulate the leader, education creates students who reflectively go beyond the professor. The piper of education plays the passionate song that frees listeners from the bondage of ignorance, to pursue determination of the truth of the tune. The piper models profession, touting the tune that enables others to play their own.

The Socratic professor pipes no oxymoronic tune. Once the faulty myths of neutrality, expressionism, and denigration are debunked, the allegedly Socratic objections to profession are less weighty. Indeed, Socrates can still function as a model once it is seen that the Socratic method involves more than the *elenchus*, when it is seen to advance the truth no matter how tentatively. One need not have an excuse to profess Socratically nor see it as an unwelcome side of the educational task. Rather, proper professing stands at the heart of the educational enterprise.

Academic Excellence:
Cliché or Humanizing Vision?

Merold Westphal

Colleges and universities that are academically serious are in the habit of talking a lot about academic excellence.[1] Even at the level of just talking, that is the easy part. The hard part is saying what we mean.

Sometimes we move almost immediately to talking about how successful we have been in getting our students into the most prestigious graduate and professional schools or corporations. This is unfortunate for at least two reasons, even — and perhaps especially — where that record is impressive. In the first place, such a record may or may not be a *measure* of academic excellence, but it is surely not a *cogent account* of what we mean by academic excellence, at least if what we mean stands in any positive relation to the liberal arts tradition. Whether and to what degree placement success is a measure of more than itself will depend on what academic excellence is. And to move immediately from the mention of academic excellence to our placement record may be to distract attention from that fact that we have not said, perhaps because we do not really know, what we mean by academic excellence.

More serious, perhaps, is a second problem. When we speak of academic excellence in the way just described, we may very well

1. This essay appeared in an earlier form in *Thought* 63, no. 251 (Dec. 1988): 348-57. It is reprinted with minor changes and with permission of Fordham University Press.

create in the minds of our students, their parents, and even ourselves the impression that we have defined academic excellence. Placement success, which may not even be a very reliable *measure* of academic excellence in the tradition we profess to embody, can easily be taken to be the very meaning of that excellence. In other words, that education is excellent which produces placement success, because that is the very purpose of education. Thus, while verbally honoring the liberal arts tradition, we reinforce our own society's reduction of education to the acquiring of marketable skills. And when we bemoan the fact that we do not find in our students that love of learning which we would like to see, something we do as regularly as they complain about the food in the cafeteria, we have not only them but also ourselves to blame.

What follows is an attempt to say what we mean (have meant in the past, are trying to mean at present) when we talk about academic excellence in liberal education. Its point of departure is a piece of diction that is probably as familiar to all of us as it is, I believe, unfortunate. With increasing frequency we hear reports that liberal arts graduates are in growing demand in the business world. Corporations seem to be noticing that liberal arts graduates tend to go higher in their companies on average than their colleagues and that a surprisingly high percentage of CEOs majored in a liberal arts discipline. While this is doubtless good news in some sense to those who take liberal education seriously, I find this way of speaking troublesome. What bothers me is the way that this familiar usage links the concept of the liberal arts, and with it the concept of liberal education, to specific disciplines, especially those that belong to the humanities and fine arts. Thus a friend of mine who is deeply committed to the ideal of liberal education recently spoke to me about students taking courses in math, physics, and the liberal arts.

A mutual friend of this friend and mine once referred to these as the "ancillary disciplines." Why he chooses to teach at a liberal arts college while holding a view so diametrically opposed to its ideals I do not know. What concerns me here, however, is not the view of this second friend, an enemy of the liberal arts, but the view of the first friend, a friend of that tradition. For I believe that the concept of the liberal arts and of liberal education which can help us to understand what we mean when we speak of academic excellence must free itself from the view that the burden of liberal education belongs with certain disciplines. Just as I resist the suggestion that my own discipline, philosophy, is an "ancillary" one, so I resist the suggestion that mine is one of those few that, by virtue of their subject matter, render education liberal.

Humanistic Education

In place of both of these views I want to suggest a holistic vision of the entire educational enterprise in terms of which we can view it as truly liberating. I turn to the ancient Greeks for help. Our concept of excellence comes from their concept of virtue *(arete)*, especially as developed by Plato and Aristotle. In everyday Greek everything that had a specific function or task *(ergon)* had its corresponding virtue. Both artifacts and artisans were "virtuous" if they performed their special task well. A virtuous ballpoint pen would be one that could write through butter, and a virtuous computer programmer one who could write programs quickly and without bugs.

Plato and Aristotle brought the term closer to the more familiar usage, which links virtue to matters of morality, when they asked the question, What is the task we have simply as human beings, regardless of vocational and other differences, and what would it be to perform this task well?

The concept of human rationality, which underlies this question, is the foundation of classical humanism, just as the concept of creation in the image of God is the foundation of biblical humanism. A distinctively Christian approach to liberal education would have at its foundation a conception of our common human task, which begins with the concept of *imago Dei* and works its way through such concepts as covenant and kingdom to the crucial concept of *imitatio Christi*.[2]

---

2. Here it will be important to remember that the *imitatio Christi* is above all the way of the cross and that this involves an outward journey (cleansing the temple, confronting the Sanhedrin, Pilate, and Herod) as well as an inward journey (the battle for submission to the Father's will in Gethsemane). There

A philosophy of education that seeks to root itself in an understanding of Christian humanism faces two problems, one traditional, one distinctively contemporary. The traditional issue is the relation between Christian humanism and classical humanism (together with all the other humanisms of the Renaissance, Enlightenment, and so forth, which do not make biblical faith their point of departure). Tertullian's question, What has Athens to do with Jerusalem? and Karl Lowith's question, Can there be a Christian gentleman? call attention to the important differences between the two.[3] What biblical faith means by the *imago Dei* is not the same as what the Greeks meant by the divinity of the soul. Nor is an understanding of the *imitatio Christi* derived from the New Testament very close to the *imitatio* of the forms one finds in Plato.

Still, there are important continuities as well as discontinuities. That is why Augustine can give thanks for what he found in the "books of Platonists" as well as call attention to what he did not find there.[4] Whether we choose to emphasize the distance between Athens and Jerusalem or the closeness, for present purposes the point is simply this: Our concept of excellence has its foundation in a concept of a generic, shared human identity (singular) and task (singular) that goes beyond our many differential identities and tasks, in particular our vocational identities (plural) and tasks (plural). What is at issue is not simply better doctors or better managers or even better philosophers, but better human beings.[5]

It is precisely this fundamental concept of humanism in all its versions which raises the distinctively contemporary problem. In-

---

is thus not only the inwardness of the spiritual disciplines, as portrayed classically, for example, by Thomas à Kempis. There is also the political side of bearing the cross, confronting the principalities and powers. For a powerful presentation of the outward, political dimension of *imitatio Christi,* see John Howard Yoder, *The Politics of Jesus* (Grand Rapids: Eerdmans, 1972), esp. chaps. 6-8.

3. Karl Lowith, *Nature, History, and Existentialism* (Evanston, Ill.: Northwestern University Press, 1966), pp. 204-13.

4. St. Augustine, *Confessions* VII.9, 20-21.

5. Anyone who has seen the looks of blank disbelief on student faces when they are told that the primary goal of their philosophy course is "to become more nearly human" will have a sense of the strangeness of the humanistic ideal in our culture.

tellectual currents often summed up with the term "postmodern-ism" have challenged the validity of any kind of humanism. Truth is to be replaced by interpretation, and the human subject is to be denied, not merely decentered.[6] The death of foundationalism leaves the idea of a normative human task unfounded. The death of God turns out to entail the death of "man."[7]

Postmodernism must be taken seriously by any who wish to speak of academic excellence in anything like the traditional sense, for it tends to assimilate the traditional concepts to geocentric astronomy and phlogiston theory. Foundationalism may be dead and with it the confident, even arrogant, humanism of the Enlightenment.[8] But Christian humanism has powerful resources for drawing less destructive conclusions from the genuine insights of postmodernism than does postmodernism itself. Its understanding of human finitude and fallenness provides an alternative interpretation of the limits of human access to truth, while its theology of creation and redemption makes it possible to keep human thought related to a divine truth which it never possesses finally, fully, or without distortion. A Christian humanism that wishes to draw from the well of Greek humanism will have to be a humble humanism. But then humility is a Christian virtue.

But colleges and universities with a Christian identity should not confuse bashfulness with humility. The bold articulation of a Christian humanism as the context for a clear alternative to con-

6. Jean-François Lyotard, *The Post-Modern Condition* (Minneapolis: University of Minnesota Press, 1984); Richard Rorty, *Philosophy and the Mirror of Nature* (Princeton, N.J.: Princeton University Press, 1979); Seyla Benhabib, "Epistemologies of Postmodernism: A Reply to Jean-François Lyotard," *New German Critique* 33 (1985): 103-26; Albrecht Wellmar, "On the Dialectic of Modernism and Postmodernism," *Praxis International* 4 (1985): 337-62.

7. Mark Taylor, *Erring: A Postmodern A-Theology* (Chicago: University of Chicago Press, 1984).

8. In *The Arrogance of Humanism* (New York: Oxford University Press, 1975), David Ehrenfeld has explored the arrogance of Enlightenment humanism in the context of the environmental crisis, but the issues are obviously much broader. Albert Camus, *The Rebel: An Essay on Man in Revolt*, trans. Anthony Bower (New York: Random House, 1956), speaks of rebellion instead of arrogance, but his account of the arrogance of Enlightenment and Romantic humanism is even more devastating.

temporary vocationalism has perhaps never before been more needed. And, thanks in large part to postmodernism, it has become (with apologies to my English teachers) more possible just as it has become more necessary. For postmodern critiques have shown the secular humanism of the Enlightenment to be a particular faith and not the universal voice of a reason too pure to be shaped by special interests and contingencies. Christian faith need not be intimidated by appeals to such a "Reason," once this Wizard of Oz has been found out.

Holistic Education

Turning then again to the Greeks, we move a step closer to the concept of academic excellence that we are seeking with Aristotle's distinction between moral virtue (excellence in action and feeling) and intellectual virtue (excellence in thinking). As we shall shortly see, this is anything but the modern distinction between subjective values and value-free scientific thought. Precisely because Aristotle's holistic account of intellectual virtue is not synonymous with the modern concept of research rationality, I find in it a helpful framework for thinking about the nature of liberal arts education.

At its core Aristotle's is a theory of three intellectual virtues, three ways in which thinking is excellent. One is purely theoretical; the other two involve, as we would say, practical or applied knowledge. Although these are not their usual names, our discussion will be helped if we call them *contemplation, moral know-how,* and *technical know-how.*[9]

For our purposes the particulars of Aristotle's view of pure theory are less important than the fact that he includes pure theory in his account of human excellence. (I include here his discussion of *nous, episteme,* and *sophia.*) We fulfill our common human task and are thus more fully human when we exercise our minds in the understanding of God, the world, and ourselves just for the sake of understanding. This is knowledge which is its own end, which does not need to justify itself in terms of some result other than itself,

9. Aristotle, *Nichomachean Ethics* VI.1-7.

which it helps to produce. It is valued not because of its applications but for the awe and wonder that are essential components of it, and because it is the actualization of the potential that defines, in part, what it is to be human. Why do we use our rational capacity in this way? Because it is there. A human being who will not think in this way is like a pen that will not write. Or, to be more precise, when our need to understand is limited by the need to make and to do, we are like a car that will not start. We just are not what we advertise ourselves to be.

If careful attention is given to the definition just given to contemplation, it will be clear that it includes a wide variety of mental activities. It will also be clear that the distinction between pure and applied research is more relevant for understanding the concept than the distinction between speculation and empirical observation. Of course, religious meditation and philosophical speculation would be examples of contemplation as defined above (unless, for example, one engaged in TM in order to cure one's acne). But it is just as true that empirical research in the natural or social sciences would count as contemplation when its underlying motive is the sheer joy of discovery or delight in understanding. And when I define contemplation as seeking to understand God, the (natural and social) world, and ourselves for the intrinsic and not instrumental value of that understanding, I think of understanding broadly enough to include the "production" and "consumption" of art. The understanding we gain from art and science, religion and philosophy can be valued as a means to some end other than itself. But when it is valued for its own sake, it is contemplation.[10]

10. John Henry Newman, *The Uses of Knowledge: Selections from The Idea of the University* (New York: Appleton-Century-Crofts, 1948), p. 17, speaks of the usefulness of liberal learning in a chapter entitled, "Knowledge Its Own End." He there applies to knowledge what Aristotle says regarding property. "Of possessions those rather are useful which bear fruit; those *liberal, which tend to enjoyment*. By fruitful, I mean, which yield revenue; by enjoyable, where *nothing accrues of consequence beyond the using*." Incidentally, where Newman's translation says "liberal," the Oxford translation says "gentlemanly" (Aristotle, *Rhetoric* I.5). For a parallel discussion of the "usefulness" of the religious life, see Merold Westphal, *God, Guilt, and Death: An Existential Phenomenology of Religion* (Bloomington: Indiana University Press, 1984), pp. 122-59.

The two other divisions of intellectual virtue for Aristotle are moral know-how *(phronesis)* and technical know-how *(techne)*. In both cases, as the term "know-how" suggests, we are dealing with knowledge that leads directly to action. Its value is in its application, in the behavior that it informs. But the distinction between the two forms of know-how is as sharp for Aristotle and as important for us as the distinction between both of these forms of know-how and contemplative reason.

Aristotle distinguishes between two kinds of (nonintellectual) behavior. One involves activity that is its own end, that is valued for its own sake. The other is a means to an end. It is valued for its result, something it produces but that could, at least in principle, be produced otherwise. The former Aristotle calls doing or acting *(praxis)*, the latter making *(poiesis)*. The child who jumps up and down for sheer joy is acting. The jogger who dutifully runs in order to lose weight or reduce the risk of heart attack is making. If there were a harmless pill that produced the same results, the jogger, at least the one I have in mind, would quickly trade in the running for the pill. The activity of running is valued only for results quite different from itself.

Since Aristotle thinks that the distinction between these two kinds of behavior is very important, it is not surprising that he distinguishes the know-how that shapes the one from the know-how by which the other is guided. Moral know-how *(phronesis)* is the knowledge that shapes acting or doing *(praxis)*. Technical know-how *(techne)* is the knowledge that guides making *(poiesis)*.

It is, of course, important not to identify moral know-how with moral virtue. It is an intellectual virtue. My ability to make sound moral judgments always exceeds my practice of the virtues. (That is Calvin, Luther, Augustine, or Paul dressed up as Aristotle. What he calls weakness of will, they call bondage to sin.) But while moral know-how is not a sufficient condition of moral virtue, it is a necessary condition. Moral virtue depends on this intellectual virtue. Moreover, Aristotle is convinced that learning to make sound moral judgments is an essential part of training the mind, of cultivating intellectual virtue or excellence.

Finally, there is technical know-how, instrumental reason or the ability to find the most effective means for achieving our ends.

This definition makes it clear that the selection of our ends is not the task of technical know-how. And since that task cannot belong to contemplative reason, which is not the guide of either making or doing, the choice of ends will either be subjective and sub-rational or it will belong to moral know-how. The latter is obviously Aristotle's position. This crucial division of labor results. It is the task of moral know-how to decide what ends we should seek and what means are *legitimate* in their pursuit. It is the task of technical know-how to discover what means are most *effective* in the pursuit of our ends. Subject to the dual moral constraints on the choice of our ends and of the means by which we may rightly pursue them, the job of technical know-how is to increase our skill at getting what we want, so far as what we want can be made or produced in Aristotle's sense. The production of goods and services is guided by moral values rather than simply by the market. Marketable skills are subordinated to moral commitments.

In our own language, technical know-how is the vocational component in Aristotle's theory of education. (The term "vocation" oscillates between the quite different concepts of calling and career. I would like to rescue its linkage with the former, but am here capitulating to the current tendency to make vocation and career synonymous.) In today's marketplace there is relatively little demand for contemplative wisdom or for moral know-how. The acquiring of marketable skills falls all but entirely within the domain of technical know-how.

This brings us to a crucial point, for liberal education is so often contrasted with vocational education. Such a contrast often leads us to speak of students taking courses in physics, math, and the liberal arts, since the vocational marketplace is more interested in people with training in physics and math than in those who have studied literature or art history.

We must be careful at this point. Some people have been able to market their skills in literature or art history. Or consider my college friend, Dlorem. We took philosophy and geology together. For him, we might say, philosophy was the liberal arts part of that semester, while geology was his vocational training, for upon graduation he went off to the Sunbelt to find oil. But for me, philosophy was my vocational training and geology was my liberal arts component that semester. We might, I say, speak this way. It has the advantage of drawing the distinction between liberal and vocational education not in terms of disciplines but in terms of usage, in terms of what knowledge is taken to be "for."

But Aristotle suggests to me a different, and I think better, way of speaking. It will still involve the difference between vocational and liberal education. But it will not conceive of these as two mutually exclusive pieces of the educational pie. Rather, vocational education will be, as expected, that education which focuses on the teaching and learning of the technical know-how needed for healing sick people, marketing products, teaching students, and so forth. It will consist fundamentally in the attaining of marketable skills.

Liberal education, by contrast, will be the holistic project that includes all three of Aristotle's intellectual virtues. Liberal education will include vocational education, as it did for me and my friend Dlorem, but the vocational component will be different by virtue of its place in a larger whole. It will be an integral part of the process, but just as integral will be the development of theoretical and moral reason. Learning how to make a living will be only part of the larger project of learning how to live.[11] The acquisition of marketable skills will be integrated with serious reflection about what goals we ought to seek, including their relative priority, and about what means are legitimate in their pursuit. This will serve as a reminder that education is not only designed to make us marketable but also to contribute to our moral sensitivity. And in addition to all of this, there will be a sense of the development of our intellectual powers simply for the sake of better understanding the general scheme of things and our place in it.

---

11. It is interesting to notice how the phrase "the good life" changes its meaning depending on which of these concepts controls it. Where it is controlled by the concept of making a living, it has its modern, materialistic sense. Where it is controlled by the concept of learning how to live well, it has its classical, moral meaning.

Academic Excellence

It is now possible to answer two questions at once. The first is the question, What do we mean by academic excellence? The second is the question, How do vocationally oriented programs such as Business Administration, Education, and Nursing relate to a liberal arts program?

When we speak of academic excellence we mean an educational enterprise that (1) aspires to cultivate all three intellectual virtues, understanding for its own sake, moral know-how, and technical know-how, (2) does a good job of developing each of these, and (3) integrates them into a balanced and harmonious whole. Academic excellence involves comprehensive vision, multifaceted achievement including but not limited to the acquiring of technical know-how (marketable skills), and the ability to make a coherent whole out of the various facets. Vocationally oriented programs can become the tail that wags the educational dog for those involved in them. But they need not. The vocational component in each student's program can be presented and understood as an essential but not primary element in a larger whole whose goal is to make the student not just employable but as fully human as possible.

It becomes immediately clear that our placement of students in the more prestigious companies or graduate and professional schools is not a measure of academic excellence. It is a significant, if not infallible, measure of how well we do at producing technical know-how. But it says little or nothing at all about the vision that aspires to cultivate all of the intellectual virtues, about the degree to which contemplation and moral know-how are achieved, or about the degree to which these various components are cogently integrated. Whenever we succumb to the temptation to define our academic excellence in terms of placement, we announce to the world that in spite of our professed commitment to the liberal arts we really do not know how to be more than a vocational school. We tell the public that we are giving them what they want, even when we suspect that our announced mission is to provide something better than that.

Of course, excellence defined as I have suggested is all but impossible to quantify, by contrast with placement. In a society that tends to worship quantification and the empirical testability it makes possible, the classical concept of excellence is something of a fish out of water.

But this is only one indication of the tension between the ideal of liberal education and contemporary American culture. Because of our national preoccupation with matters economic (our materialism, to speak frankly), we are a society inclined toward a philosophy of education that tilts heavily, at times even exclusively, toward the production of technical know-how.[12] Our highest priority tends to be the gross national product and, educationally speaking, the knowledge that enables people to provide those goods and services for which the market has a demand. That is what underlies the previous reference to giving the public what they want. Our students, and perhaps even more their parents, are sufficiently part of the American scene that they approach college with expectations that are largely job-oriented. In other words, the idea of a liberal education that I have tried to spell out in this essay is less the product of the culture in which we live than the subversive relic of another culture. Since it is hard to market subversion, that creates a certain cognitive dissonance for colleges that retain the liberal arts ideal as more than a *shibboleth*. Perhaps that is why it is so hard to do so.

At any rate, it may be worth turning once again briefly to Aristotle, this time for a sketch of that society in which liberal education is truly at home. His discussion of intellectual virtue is part of his ethics, and his ethics is part of his politics. Like Dewey's, his is a vision of education for citizenship. But his *polis* is not grounded in a materialistic philosophy. It does not worship its economic sector nor define the good life in terms of the goods and services it produces.

This does not mean for a moment that Aristotle's *polis* is a monastic community, grounded in an ascetical philosophy of life.

---

12. The critique of instrumental reason in the political context by the Frankfurt school is relevant here. The political and educational contexts are inseparable, both in theory and in practice. See Max Horkheimer, *Critique of Instrumental Reason*, trans. Matthew J. O'Connell et al. (New York: Seabury, 1974), and Jurgen Habermas, *Toward a Rational Society: Student Protest, Science, and Politics* (Boston: Beacon, 1970).

It just means that for the society he has in mind happiness and success are defined in terms of virtue rather than in terms of pleasure, wealth, or status. For this reason, while technical know-how is indispensable, it is not central. Because the purpose of human life does not consist in making a living, or, as Jesus puts it, our life does not consist in the abundance of our possessions (Luke 12:15), technical know-how plays a subordinate role to moral know-how and to contemplation (in the broad sense here defined). The highest destiny of reason is the contemplative and moral life, and the *polis* is the place where individual lives and social intercourse are grounded in these values.

No doubt Aristotle shortchanges the genuinely human significance of labor, production, and the knowledge that guides them. And no doubt this is largely due to the role of slaves in his society.[13] But if his emphasis on contemplation and moral virtue yields an excessively idealistic humanism, it serves as a useful point of reference for recognizing the materialism of our own society, where the theories that guide our quest for ever-higher levels of productivity and profitability show little sign of the constraints of morality or the context of contemplation. Perhaps the postmodernism that would eliminate all forms of humanism is more the effect than the cause of this social climate. Perhaps it has simply drawn the philosophical conclusions of dominant aspects of the world we live in.

This question about the kind of society in which liberal education is truly at home provides another good opportunity for reflection about the distinctives of such education in a Christian context. Even if we apply a corrective to Aristotle's disdain for labor and production, it is clear that the ideal of liberal education presented here is at odds with the primacy of instrumental reason in our society. One possibility is that the rhetoric of liberal education will be retained while the substance of education quietly adapts itself to the demands of the economy. The only alternative to this,

---

13. Had he had the chance to read Hegel, Aristotle would never have praised him as Marx did for adopting "the standpoint of modern political economy" and recognizing labor as the "self-confirming essence of man." Karl Marx, *Karl Marx: Early Writings*, trans. T. B. Bottomore (New York: McGraw Hill, 1964), p. 203.

other than giving up all pretense of liberal education and becoming purely vocational, is for colleges and universities to bite the hand that feeds them by challenging the materialistic, instrumental assumptions so close to the heart of corporate and consumer America. If the Christian faith cannot provide the moral and intellectual resources for making such a challenge creatively and compassionately, I am not sure where else to look. It may be that the religious context is the only one in which the tradition of liberal arts education can survive in today's world. But this requires Christian institutions that are willing and able to articulate and to implement a philosophy of education in keeping with their Christian identities.

Perhaps the political turn of the discussion has seemed sudden or jarring. But there is no tension between saying that the harmonious development of the three intellectual virtues is essential to being fully human and saying that such development is essential to good citizenship. In fact, the former probably implies the latter. For on the view here presented, where education is lopsidedly directed toward the cultivation of technical know-how and the associated marketable skills, individuals are less than fully human and the society that they constitute is dehumanizing as well. Perhaps we serve best when we do not automatically identify what the age demands with what the age needs.

Religion, Science, and the Humanities in the Liberal Arts Curriculum

H. Newton Malony

A humorous story attributed to Newt Gingrich, Speaker of the United States House of Representatives, depicts a young man waiting in the check-out line of a grocery store in the Boston area. The sign over the line in which he was waiting said, "6 items or less; cash only." He had 8 items and wanted to pay by check. The clerk counted his items, looked at his check, and pointed to the sign, and exclaimed, "You are either a student at MIT who can't read or a student at Harvard who can't count!" Gingrich suggested that this humorous incident reflected the observation made by C. P. Snow that there are two intellectual traditions in America: that of the sciences and technology — and that of the humanities and the arts.[1]

Gingrich and Snow were correct as far as they went. However, I am convinced that there is a third culture that must be considered — that of religion. I have no ready answer as to how a clerk might have identified a student from Boston University's School of Theology at this check-out counter, but I am convinced that religion represents a dimension of life that is distinct from the sciences and the humanities. Further, I believe that if an institution of higher learning claims to provide education in the liberal arts tradition, it should require that as much attention be given to religion as to science and to the

---

1. C. P. Snow, *The Two Cultures: A Second Look* (Cambridge: Cambridge University Press, 1959, 1979).

humanities in its curriculum. An adequate overview of culture demands it. Why and how this can be done is the thesis of this essay.

After further distinguishing the cultures of science, humanities, and religion, I will probe the psychodynamics of late adolescence, which tend to make confrontation with religious issues easy to avoid. Then I will elucidate a historical understanding of the goals of education in the "liberal arts," using Juniata College in Huntingdon, Pennsylvania, as an example. Finally, I will offer some suggestions as to how liberal arts education could be reconstrued to better include religion in the interaction among America's *three*, not just *two*, cultures.

America's Three Cultures

There are three distinct intellectual cultures operative in the Western world, of which American life is representative. They are the cultures of science, of the humanities, and of religion. While persons never exist totally in one of these cultures to the exclusion of the others, as the grocery store clerk's judgment might imply, there is evidence that the worldviews operative in each of these three cultures *do* result in a degree of selective perception. More important, these distinctive worldviews tend to dominate and color general attitudes and actions to a significant degree.

How might we define the differences among science, the humanities, and religion? While no one will be fully satisfied with my definitions, for purposes of this discussion let us say that (1) the *sciences* attempt to understand the general conditions that regulate the physical and social world through replicable experiments, sensate experience, and logical reasoning;[2] (2) the *humanities* attempt to comprehend the cultural attainments of human beings through historical, philosophical, anthropological, literary, and aesthetic description and analysis;[3] and (3) *religion* attempts to deal with the

2. A. N. Whitehead, *Religion in the Making* (Cleveland: World, 1960), p. 233; Arthur Peacocke, *Theology for a Scientific Age: Being and Becoming — Natural and Divine* (Oxford: Blackwell, 1990), p. 9.

3. National Endowment for the Humanities, 1965.

ultimate struggles of humans in facing the enigmatic, the tragic, and the mysterious experiences of life.[4]

In a drastically oversimplified sense, one could say that the sciences deal with "practical" realities, the humanities deal with "social" realities, and religion deals with "personal" realities. Although postmodern philosophic analysis makes these distinctions more artificial than ontologically real, my contention is that they do, indeed, have a significant *functional* reality in the experience of the typical college student.[5]

I can vividly remember my own college experience in a church-related liberal arts college. There were buildings for both the natural and biological sciences. There were other buildings for history, literature, and the arts. Except for required introductory courses, majors in either of these several buildings never entered each other's domains or had any dialogue with one another. I resonated completely with Snow's anecdote about the president who, after noting that diners at a Cambridge College high table were not conversing with a visitor, said "Oh, those are mathematicians! We never talk to *them.*"[6] This lack of conversation among the sciences, the humanities, and religion was definitely true where I went to college even though it claimed to be a liberal arts institution where interdisciplinary conversation was the norm.

On my campus, there was the definite feeling that the "hard" disciplines were in one place and the "soft" disciplines were in another, and "never the twain should meet." Religion, of course, was associated with "soft" studies and with preministerial students who worked in churches on the weekends. The three cultures operated separately and independently. More important, it was implicitly assumed that the hard disciplines, the sciences, dealt in *facts* while the soft disciplines, the humanities, dealt in *ideas* and *opinions*.

This arrangement led to two types of options. One option was for some of my professors to take the positivistic position that only

4. J. M. Yinger, *The Scientific Study of Religion* (New York: Macmillan, 1970), p. 7.

5. See Thomas S. Kuhn, *The Structure of Scientific Revolutions,* 2nd ed. (Chicago: University of Chicago Press, 1970), and Nancey Murphy, *Theology in the Age of Scientific Reasoning* (Ithaca, N.Y.: Cornell University Press, 1990).

6. Snow, *Two Cultures.*

those statements which could be verified by reference to sensate, shared events had meaning. Of course, this option implied that only their scientific statements made sense. Most statements in the humanities and *all* statements in religion were nonsense; they had no meaning. The other option was to conclude that there were different types of meaning. Science, from this point of view, had empirical meaning for understanding the physical world, while religion had moral meaning for personal motivation and existence. Statements in the humanities had only descriptive meaning; they predicted nothing and were post-hoc narratives of what existed or occurred.[7]

These two options can still be found in colleges and universities. Postmodern philosophy of science and culture has concluded, however, that neither option is fully satisfying.[8] On the one hand, it is now generally acknowledged that all scholarly work begins with a priori assumptions. No academic enterprise collects theory-free facts. Science, like religion and the humanities, begins with assumptions. And this is true of the natural as well as of the social sciences.[9]

Further, it is generally recognized today that the very act of study changes the object of study. Kant was right. We never know "the thing as such." The wave-particle distinction in the study of light convinced Niels Bohr that there was no objective reality — a conclusion that deeply disturbed Einstein even though such relativistic conclusions were at the very core of the quantum physics that he had initiated![10] What has become a truism in modern science has been known in theology for some time. Feuerbach in the nineteenth century concluded that humans made their gods in

---

7. Ian G. Barbour, *Myths, Models and Paradigms: A Comparative Study in Science and Religion* (New York: Harper & Row, 1974).

8. Thomas A. Oden, *Requiem: A Lament in Three Movements* (Nashville: Abingdon, 1995).

9. See Kuhn, *Structure;* Barbour, *Myths, Models, Paradigms;* Gary Collins, *The Rebuilding of Psychology: An Integration of Psychology and Christianity* (Wheaton, Ill.: Tyndale, 1977); D. Browning, *Religious Thought and the Modern Psychologies* (Philadelphia: Fortress, 1987); L. Laudan, *Progress and Its Problems: Towards a Theory of Scientific Growth* (Berkeley: University of California Press, 1977).

10. E. Regis, *Who Got Einstein's Office? Eccentricity and Genius at the Institute for Advanced Study* (New York: Addison-Wesley, 1987).

their own image and Tillich in the twentieth century asserted that there would always be a God *above* the God of the theologians' best thinking and conceiving.[11] The sharp division between facts and opinions that I experienced in my undergraduate career may not, in truth, exist.

However, there is yet another characteristic of my alma mater that seems to be the same today as it was when I was a student there. Although touted as education in the liberal arts tradition, my college's publications, from that day to this, have delineated the number of students who have gone on for postgraduate studies in religion, the sciences, or the humanities. I take this as an indication that my college has always been more interested in perpetuating the polarization of intellectual cultures than it has been concerned to graduate persons who took away a liberal arts education replete with broad interdisciplinary learning. Not unlike institutions that make no claims to be "liberal arts colleges," my college was, and is, primarily "preprofessional." Unfortunately, such emphasis on preprofessional training, as I hope to establish, violates the intent of the liberal arts tradition.

Liberal arts colleges should be most pleased that their students are broadly, not narrowly, educated. They should take pride that they train persons who are prepared to face a world in which the boundaries of the three cultures have become blurred. They should boast that they are preparing those who will function not as specialists, but as extensively informed generalists; citizens who, while continuing to seek new knowledge, need never take another course for credit to be educated persons.

The Psychodynamics of Late Adolescence

Among the three cultures, religion has played an increasingly minor role in liberal arts education. This has become true for three reasons. The first pertains to academicians themselves. As a group, professors

11. Ludwig Feuerbach, *The Essence of Christianity* (1857; New York: Harper, 1957); Paul Tillich, *Systematic Theology*, vol. 1 (Chicago: University of Chicago Press, 1951).

in institutions of higher learning continue to be significantly less traditionally religious than the general public, and they tend to espouse agnostic or anti-religious convictions in their teaching and in their personal lives.[12] The religious skepticism of the eighteenth century continues to dominate the academy. Second, as a result of this and other cultural trends, religion has been increasingly relegated to subcultural privatism during the twentieth century. This has led to a bias against required or public discussion of these issues and a general depreciation of religion's value.[13] The third reason for religion's deemphasis, and the one I would like to examine here, has been the psychodynamics of late adolescence. The majority of the questions that religion addresses, while fairly universal, are not central to the developmental stage of life in which most college students find themselves.

Although an increasing number of students return to college in mid-adulthood, the dominant age group in most undergraduate student bodies is still late adolescence, 17-23 years. Quite apart from whether these students are primarily motivated by hopes of money or job or self-fulfillment, their role in culture remains that which Erik Erikson correctly identified as one of "moratorium."[14] Moratorium is a term that implies a legal or authorized *delay* in the performance of some activity. Erikson observed that youth, at this age, are culturally permitted to delay their entrance into the adult world for several years while they explore, test, and critique their culture. While in college, they are allowed to have no full-time job, to spend their time in study, to think about the meaning of life, to decide on a vocation, and to explore every aspect of the society of which they will later become a part. They are encouraged to lower their dependence on home and family and to launch out into an independent existence.

Often, in the moratorium of late adolescence, religion is the first thing that students critique. In the lives of many youth, reli-

12. C. P. Ragan, H. N. Malony, and B. Beit-Hallahmi, "Psychologists and Religion: Professional Factors and Personal Beliefs," *Review of Religious Research* 21 (1980): 208-17.

13. Stephen L. Carter, *The Culture of Disbelief: How American Law and Politics Trivialize Religious Devotion* (New York: Basic Books, 1993).

14. Erik Erikson, *Identity and the Life Cycle: Selected Papers* (New York: International Universities Press, 1959).

gious participation has been a familial mandate that had little meaning beyond accommodation to the home environment. If the essence of religion is, as Yinger defined it, the way that people make meaning of the enigmas, the tragedies, and the mysteries of life, the average young person has faced few of these issues that evoke genuine religious involvement.[15] Life presents them with an open future. Only in the unusual case do late adolescents face major life crises while in college.

Enigmas are injustices, coincidences, preferences, and biases of fate, environment, and life predicaments that tear at the fabric of self-esteem and hopes for the future. *Tragedies* are the unexpected, undeserved, and unexplainable misfortunes that disrupt life and require radical readjustment of plans and expectations. *Mysteries* are the imponderables of ultimate meaning and purpose that transcend empirical survival and/or momentary happiness.

Although no generalizations are without exception, few youth have experienced such stresses as these at the time they enter college. Life, of course, is replete with these difficulties, but persons face most of them in the years that follow late adolescence. When youth enter college, therefore, religion has met few, if any, real needs other than that of cultural conformity and peer group affiliation. The culture of "religion" assumes little importance, therefore. Religion becomes an option rather than an obligation. Choosing to become religiously uninvolved is a benign way to show defiance and independence.

The cultures of the sciences and the humanities do not suffer the same fate. Continued interest in science and the humanities is sustained and, in fact, mandated in the form of required courses. The typical college curriculum does not allow students to lay aside involvement in science and the humanities. Cultural awareness and appreciation are the goals of the humanities. Rationality and explanation are the goals of the sciences. These have been the core of modern liberal arts education.

There is one exception, however, to the observation that the life crises to which religion provides answers have not been faced by late adolescent individuals. This is the issue of *personal identity*. While

15. Yinger, *Scientific Study of Religion.*

achieving "personal" identity is typically associated with finding "vocational" identity, the process is more complex than this.[16] Late adolescence is a time in which persons come to an understanding of their place in history, not just their role in the world of work. Late adolescent individuals are able to appreciate the contribution their culture has made to the failures, as well as to the successes, of their society. They can recognize injustice and reflect on their own culpability. They can identify with ideals and commit themselves to causes of social reconstruction. Often, they are haunted by their own materialistic preoccupations. In a somewhat tongue-in-cheek self-description, Joshua Janoff depicted the typical college student with these words: "I'm a 22 year-old freshman at a small New England liberal-arts college. I take classes in subjects like writing and sociology. The school newspaper I write for is filled with aspiring muckrakers, and most people here followed Teddy Kennedy's re-election bid with enthusiasm. A casual outside observer might say that I fit the mold of the left-wing, out-of-touch, spotted-owl-saving, liberal-loving student. A stereotypical Generation Xer suffering from a short bout of college-induced idealism, right?"[17]

From a psychodynamic point of view, late adolescence can become a time of intentionally shaping one's life in terms of "ego ideals." And ego ideals are not only ethical values but exemplary persons with whom youth can identify and whose example they feel called to follow.[18] While this identification process can be aided and abetted by studies within the humanities, optimally this process is a religious one, as the late Harvard psychologist Gordon Allport noted.[19] Within the dominant Christian tradition of the West, Jesus often serves as an "ego ideal" figure with whom college youth can identify.

Two aspects of Jesus' life are focal for this dynamic: his lofty, postconventional, moral teachings and his sacrificial death. These can inspire youth to a way that is life transforming, as one of

16. Erikson, *Identity and Life Cycle.*
17. J. B. Janoff, "A Gen-X Rip Van Winkle: Looking the Part Doesn't Mean that I'm a Stereotypical Twenty-something," *Newsweek,* 24 April 1995, p. 10.
18. Abraham Maslow, *Religion, Values, and Peak Experiences* (Columbus: Ohio State University Press, 1964).
19. Gordon Allport, *The Individual and His Religion* (New York: Macmillan, 1950).

America's early psychologists, G. Stanley Hall, stated in his insightful theory of adolescent conversion.[20] Hall suggested that all persons are born with an impulse toward, and a capacity for, altruistic, unselfish existence. As persons develop and grow up, Hall concluded, they become encrusted with selfish, egoistic motives that suppress this innate concern for others' welfare. Hall used the image of a geode rock to depict this process. The inner crystal of the geode is hidden by the ugly crust of rock that surrounds it. The geode must be broken open by a powerful force to reveal its inner beauty.

According to Hall, as they confront their own identity crises, late adolescents experience a haunting nostalgia for the deep, inner, unselfish, altruistic part of themselves that has been neglected in the course of their development. They become inspired by the accounts of Jesus' high moral teachings and by his martyrdom for what he believed. In Hall's opinion, however, although Jesus' teaching and his martyrdom have a magnetic influence on youth, they do not have sufficient power to effect a radical change in their life goals or behavior. Only the *story* of a God who loved humans enough to die for them can penetrate youth's personalities and enable them to commit themselves to lives of service and unselfishness. This is the *work* of Jesus that the Christian church has proclaimed as central to the meaning of his life. This story carries a truth that supplements his *person* and *teachings*.

While the traumatic life events to which religion speaks may have occurred among only a few college students, most college students do have to face this kind of identity crisis in which religion can be extremely influential. While many courses in religion do not intentionally address this developmental concern, many campus ministries build their programs around opportunities for students to reflect upon such "ego ideals" as Jesus. They also lift up the faith of the Christian church and call youth to commit themselves to lives of service, morality, and social justice. These kinds of events offer youth the *in-vivo* opportunities to process their identity crisis in a religious framework.

20. H. Newton Malony, "G. Stanley Hall's Theory of Conversion," *Newsletter of Division 36 (APA): Psychologists Interested in the Psychology of Religion* (Fall 1983): 3-5.

While this discussion has centered on the role that the Christian faith might play in the developmental ego identity crisis of adolescence, it does not mean that Christianity is the only option for including religion within the liberal arts curriculum. Western, and particularly American, culture is dominated by the Judeo/Christian tradition and the centrality of that tradition should be acknowledged. Most college students will come from that tradition, although there is an increasing religious diversity in student bodies. This plurality of traditions should eventuate in campus ministries staffed by representatives of non-Christian traditions so that students can have viable options. Nevertheless, Christian campus ministries should not be discounted.

The Liberal Arts Ideal

Most colleges that espouse the educational ideals of the liberal arts tradition state that they intend to awaken and cultivate independent thinking.[21] The Mission Statement of Juniata College illustrates this common goal. Juniata's aim is to

> awaken students to the empowering richness of the mind and to enable them to live fulfilling and useful lives. . . .
>
> Individual growth first requires the development of basic intellectual skills: the ability to read with insight, to use language clearly and effectively, and to think analytically. . . . Juniata students are stimulated to exercise creativity and to develop those fundamental values — spiritual, moral, and aesthetic — which give meaning and structure to life. . . .
>
> The qualities of mind and character nurtured within the Juniata community permit our students to realize their full potential as contributors to society, informed citizens, and caring and responsible adults.[22]

21. F. Eby and C. F. Arrowwood, *The History and Philosophy of Education: Ancient and Medieval* (New York: Prentice-Hall, 1942).
22. Juniata Mission Statement (1992-93), p. 6.

This statement grounds Juniata's educational goals solidly within the tradition of the liberal arts as it was conceived by the Greeks and transformed by the Renaissance and the Enlightenment. From the ancients to the present, liberal education has been guided by the principle that "the good life is the life guided by rational thought."[23] Education in the liberal arts is preeminently education of the *mind*. It is education in a way of thinking, as the Juniata statement forcefully states.

Liberal arts education today, however, no longer advocates *thinking* to the exclusion of *doing*. Aristotle called practical training "vulgar," as opposed to "liberal." He, with his teacher Plato, believed it right that the philosophical class should think — leaving work for the artisans and slaves. Liberal education was reserved for philosopher-citizens who spent their time thinking and reflecting on the "good." To them was given the business of ruling the state because they were the ones who had the leisure to think before they acted and who could comprehend what was best for society.

Today's liberal arts education no longer depreciates practical vocations — nor does it presume that there are innate subservient classes in society who are to be governed by philosopher elites. The Juniata Mission Statement specifically asserts that it hopes to enable students to "live fulfilling and *useful* lives." Nevertheless, it still promotes the idea that action should by guided by thought, and that the mind has to be trained to think well. Controlling one's impulses and directing one's existence do not come naturally or easily.

Juniata's Mission Statement also includes a reference to "fundamental values — spiritual, moral, and aesthetic — which give meaning to life." Many, though not all, programs in the liberal arts argue that educating students to live lives grounded in *ideals* is a worthy goal. This moral objective has been an essential component of the liberal arts tradition for over two thousand years. Aristotle said that any education "which makes the body or soul or mind of the freeman less fit for the practice or exercise of *virtue* is vulgar."[24] Plato proposed that students should be trained to get in touch with

23. Eby and Arrowwood, *History and Philosophy*, p. 729.
24. Eby and Arrowwood, *History and Philosophy*, p. 430.

the life of the soul before it becomes imprisoned in the body. Students should be trained to seek and know the will of the transcendent One — "the good" — that which could then guide them to live above the level of passions and desire. Whether we call it virtue, the good, altruism, or fundamental values, this is a critical component to be addressed in a liberal arts education.

In my opinion, religion can and should play a central role in meeting this goal of inculcating "moral and spiritual values" in students' lives. Such values exceed the "functional ideals" of adjustment and achievement within a society. They transcend the materialistic egotism that tends to dominate the motivation of the average late adolescent. I am convinced that "Senior Values Seminars," such as have been required of students at Juniata and other colleges, fall short of their goal if they do not include a significant religious component. Kant's "moral proof for God" is still highly compelling.[25] Kant, like G. Stanley Hall, presumes that human beings possess an innate component that is moral, altruistic, and unselfish. "Values Seminars" will remain tame, inconclusive, and ineffective unless the discussion is grounded in the kind of transcendent reality about which religion speaks.

Explicit attention to religion, Christian or otherwise, should be included alongside of the informed, independent, reflective thought that curriculum planners assume students bring to dialogues as a result of their training in science and the humanities. Until and unless students acknowledge that the moral call is at the essential core of their personhood, they will tend to relativize their own obligations and leave justice concerns to others who seem to prefer such involvements.

The inclusion of religion in liberal arts education has a long history. During the Middle Ages, theology was the umbrella discipline for the seven liberal arts. In a university education one was taught "the elements of the seven liberal arts — grammar, rhetoric, logic, arithmetic, geometry, astronomy, music — and *theology*."[26]

---

25. Colin Brown, *Philosophy and the Christian Faith: A Historical Sketch from the Middle Ages to the Present Day* (Downers Grove, Ill.: InterVarsity Press, 1968, 1979), pp. 99ff.

26. Eby and Arrowwood, *History and Philosophy*, p. 665; emphasis added.

The loss of theology, or religion, in the liberal arts tradition has been grievous. The relegation of religion to a mere elective within the humanities has been a significant departure from the tradition and a loss of one of the prime motivators for ethical living. Religion's demise has probably been as much due to the ascendance of the culture of disbelief within the academy as to the assignment of religious belief to private opinion in the general public.[27]

A Proposal for Incorporating Religion

Having said that there are three, not two, cultures in the Western world, and having asserted that religion addresses a developmental need, I should now like to propose a curriculum model for liberal arts education in which religion is given a more prominent place. This would signal a partial return to a tradition that has characterized the liberal arts since the Middle Ages. I say *partial* return, because there is no doubt that the Reformation, Renaissance, and Enlightenment revolutions in education emphasized the "personalistic" rather than the "dogmatic" basis of learning that had characterized the earlier Scholasticism. However, as Trotter observes, in the educational dialogue there has been an "unfortunate separation of this enormous revolution in human learning and thought from its religious origins. . . . That separation has brought us, several centuries later, to the point where the moral uses of knowledge are once again the overwhelming question of our time. . . . Whereas Erasmus and Luther and Calvin and Valla and Pico and Colet sought to liberate the individual from the moral capacities of traditional religious thought, now our task is to wonder just how to insinuate moral discourse into the scientific world view."[28]

It is my conviction that limiting religious input merely to elective courses within the humanities is insufficient to address this problem. The first step, as I envision it, would be to establish a separate Religion Division in the liberal arts curriculum. This Reli-

27. Carter, *Culture of Disbelief.*
28. E. T. Trotter, *Loving God with One's Mind* (Nashville: United Methodist Church, 1987), p. 46.

gion Division would have equal status with the Science and Humanities divisions. This would be an explicit structural acknowledgment that *three*, not *two*, cultures should be addressed in liberal arts education.

Curricula within such a division would, like its counterparts in science and humanities, include both an informative and an applied component. Just as the sciences include lectures and laboratories and the humanities include aesthetic involvement as well as course content, so offerings in religion would include both scholarly courses and participation in campus ministry activities. It would be the purpose of these courses and activities to stimulate personal commitment alongside intellectual reflection. John Wesley, the founder of Methodism, called this a combination of "knowledge and vital piety."[29]

This combination of informational and practical components within the Religion Division would rest on the universal need of persons to address life's enigmas, tragedies, and mysteries through a philosophy of life that is transempirical and transcultural. It further acknowledges the critical development phase of identity formation in which college students are involved and the responsibility of liberally educated persons to commit themselves to virtuous existence as well as to scholarly reflection.

It also recognizes the need to address two intellectual concerns raised by the sciences and the humanities. These are (1) the need to reconcile the explanations of science with the affirmations of religion and (2) the need to discover a way to transcend the cultural relativism of the humanities in daily life. As Kant so intuitively observed, there is a difference between theoretical and practical reasoning. There are unavoidable religious dimensions in both.

The offerings of such a Religion Division might include courses in the Judeo-Christian Heritage, Comparative Religions, Modern Culture and Religion, Religious Pluralism in America, and the Philosophy, Psychology, and Sociology of Religion. Further, required religious practica might include worship, field work, retreats, conferences, and visits to religions other than one's own. The inclusion of this praxis dimension in the Religion Division would be parallel

---

29. Trotter, *Loving God.*

to the labs and aesthetic participation required in the science and humanities cultures. Such requirements would not be religiously coercive because they would be varied enough to provide for all religious, as well as philosophical, traditions.

Capstone seminars such as the Juniata "Senior Values Seminar" would be mandated for graduating students. These experiences would allow for clarification and analysis of the basic assumptions on which graduates would be building their identities. Open discussion of religion would be acknowledged as a legitimate basis for self-determination. No automatic exclusion of overt religious talk would be allowed on the presumption that religion is a totally private affair. The explicit inclusion of religion in these dialogues can be directed in a manner that avoids proselytism and respects personal decision-making.

"Dialogue Seminars" with the sciences and the humanities also would be required. These seminars would focus on two general issues: "Questions in Religion and Science" and "Questions in Religion and the Humanities." The science/religion seminars would consider the implications of recent discoveries in cosmology and physics such as the Big Bang Theory, Quantum Mechanics, and the Anthropic Principle.[30] The humanities/religion seminars would focus on the problems of cultural relativism, universal justice, environmental ecology, historical teleology, and community ethics.[31]

My proposal for including this third culture, religion, in a more explicit manner within liberal arts education is a radical one that might meet with strong opposition among curriculum planners. But the issues underlying this proposal must be discussed and de-

30. Possible resources for such science/religion dialogues might include Ian G. Barbour, *Issues in Science and Religion* (New York: Harper Torchbooks, 1966, 1971), and *Religion in an Age of Science* (San Francisco: Harper, 1990); Langdon Gilkey, *Religion and the Scientific Future* (New York: Harper & Row, 1970); R. Peters, ed., *Cosmos as Creation: Theology and Science in Consonance* (Nashville: Abingdon, 1989); J. M. Templeton and R. L. Herrman, *The God Who Would Be Known: Revelations of the Divine in Contemporary Science* (San Francisco: Harper & Row, 1989).

31. Possible resources for the religion/humanities seminars could include Carter, *Culture of Disbelief*; Martin E. Marty and F. E. Greenspahn, eds., *Pushing the Faith: Proselytism and Civility in a Pluralistic World* (New York: Crossroad, 1988).

bated. As the title of Mark Noll's book *The Scandal of the Evangelical Mind* attests, there has been a rightly deserved impression among scholars that religious persons are more interested in experience than in thought.[32] Although I contend that it is perfectly legitimate to advocate an experiential or applied dimension to religion (similar to those required in science and the humanities), my interest is also to make religion a serious part of the scholarly dialogue. Rational reflection is no more a stranger to religion than it is to science and the humanities. There are critical interdisciplinary issues that should include religion for any liberally educated person.

It is no accident that I propose a model of the liberal arts that combines religion, science, and the humanities. The Methodist tradition of which I am a part has always sought to actualize John Wesley's hope to unite the "warm heart and the sound mind." Methodism was born in Oxford University. It was a product of the eighteenth-century Enlightenment, not of the sixteenth-century Reformation. John Wesley always referred to himself as a "Fellow of Lincoln College," rather than as a "pastor." Methodism has spawned over twelve hundred colleges and universities in America since its first official church conference in 1784 — at which one of the first decisions was to establish a college. Methodists have always attempted to love God with their *mind,* fearing neither science nor the humanities. Our faith has been that each of these cultures has provided a way that contributes to "putting it all together" in the best religious sense.

32. Mark Noll, *The Scandal of the Evangelical Mind* (Grand Rapids: Eerdmans, 1994).

Tolstoy and Freud on Our Need for God

Robert C. Roberts

Central to a Christian account of personality is the premise that the human heart needs God.[1] Søren Kierkegaard put it this way: "The simple and humble thing is to love God because one needs him. . . . This in the deepest sense is the inquiry about one's welfare: Do I love God?"[2] In individual cases the need may not be conscious, and that is why we speak of need rather than of desire. When Augustine prays that "man desires to praise Thee,"[3] or Kierkegaard says that the self is in despair unless it "rests transparently in the power that established it,"[4] — they are not saying that each of us can, upon consulting the contents of our minds, find in ourselves

1. I write from a broadly Christian perspective, and in the conviction that personality psychology is always heavily perspectival, that is, dependent on contestable philosophical or theological commitments about the nature of persons and the nature of the universe in which we live. This will be true no matter how "scientific" the account purports to be. But the commitments that imply the construal of our need for God that is commended in this essay are not confined to Christianity. Such outlooks as Judaism and Islam will interpret our need for God in much the same way. Thus, "Jewish psychologist" or "Muslim psychologist" can often be substituted for "Christian psychologist" when the latter phrase appears in the essay.

2. *Christian Discourses*, trans. Walter Lowrie (New York: Oxford University Press, 1940), p. 197.

3. *Confessions*, trans. E. B. Pusey (New York: Dutton, 1962), I.1.

4. *Sickness Unto Death*, trans. Howard V. Hong and Edna H. Hong (Princeton: Princeton University Press, 1980), p. 49.

a desire to praise God, or an emotion of despair that is obviously a frustrated state of our God-libido. Even if we are aware of wanting *something* that is not among the objects of our finite life, we may not know that we want God. We may be like the pubescent boy, underinstructed about sex, on whom it dawns that he wants *something*, and that *something* is in the general vicinity of girls, but he does not know more definitely what he wants. In any case, the Christian understanding of the psyche is that it is "restless until it rests in God"; it needs a positive and happy relationship with God as a condition of its being mature and healthy. In this, Christian psychology differs from virtually all theories of personality offered today.

When a Christian psychologist like Saint Augustine, Søren Kierkegaard, Fyodor Dostoyevski, or Simone Weil alleges that the human heart desires God, the claim is generic: It is in the basic structure of the psyche to need connection with God, in much the same way as it is in the structure of the human body to need food, drink, a certain environmental temperature range, and sexual contact. Of course, some individuals have a poor appetite for some of these things; but that is usually taken as a sign that something is wrong with them. Or perhaps better, it is like the need for human contact and nurturing: people who do not get enough of this at a crucial stage of development do not mature properly; and if one has too little, or not the right kind, of it in adult life, one does not flourish (the failure to feel a need for human fellowship that we see in some people is itself a symptom of dysfunctional formation).

To liken the need for God with these other needs is to say that it is not a product of human culture, such that people from one culture could be expected to have it but not people from another culture. (An anthropologist studying the Ilongot headhunters of the Philippine island of Nueva Viscaya will not be surprised to find that they have no desire for computers; but she will be surprised if she finds that they never get hungry or have no sexual interests or no interests in friendly associations with other human beings.)

Compatible with this claim of genericness, however, is the fact that some cultures do a better job than others of expressing and eliciting the desire. For example, the Puritan culture in early America did a better job of it than did the culture of Harvard's philosophy department in the 1960s. In this respect the need for God differs from the need to defecate. It can be far less obvious and urgent, is much easier to repress or ignore, and is more susceptible to cultural discouragement.

Like the sex drive, the natural need for God may be contingent upon maturation, and the consciousness of it may be contingent upon an appropriate stimulus-situation. Augustine took quite a long and detoured path to find out that it was really God he wanted. The lapse of time may not so much clarify an already full-grown desire as develop that desire to the point where God can clearly be its satisfaction. Often, people do not realize how much they need God until some situation of crisis or loss gives them perceptual clarity about the nature of their life. The experience of Tolstoy that we will look at in a moment illustrates this possibility.

The psychological need for God that the Christian tradition ascribes to humans has several dimensions that correspond to generic features of our human life as they interact with features of God as he is conceived in the Christian tradition. First, part of our need for God is a need for something completely trustworthy to depend on, something that will provide absolute security; and God is trustworthy in a way that transcends anything that can be trusted in our finite, mortal life. Second, God loves us, and we need to be loved (that is, appreciated, accepted, valued, rejoiced in, solicited, admired) by One who knows us perfectly and whose love is absolutely worthy and completely trustworthy. Third, we are beings who live on "meaning" in the sense of life-purposes, some kind of directing orientation for our activities; and beyond all of the finite orientations and purposes of our actions, we need One that is absolute.

Clearly, all three of these interlocking and overlapping needs have finite counterparts the satisfaction of which is quite important in itself — we need sources of security like present health and employment, a bank account and so forth; family and friends who accept and appreciate us; and goals like earning a degree, writing a book, raising healthy children, and making a success of our business. But Christian psychology says that in addition to the need for these finite forms of security, love, and meaning, we need a form of them that can come only from God.

Three tasks of the Christian psychologist are (1) to clarify what is meant by the claim that humans have a psychological need for God, (2) to consider the evidence for it, and (3) if possible, to explain this need (bringing it into explanatory connection with other features of the psyche as observed and as construed in Christian terms). These tasks intertwine: As we consider the evidence, we become clearer what claim is being made, and possible explanations of this feature of the psyche suggest themselves; as we clarify the claim, we come to see better what would count as evidence for it and likewise are presented with some possible explanations. In the present section I have done a bit to clarify the claim, identifying features of the need for God by comparing it with other appetites and needs and dividing it into three aspects. In the next section I shall focus on a certain kind of evidence — broadly speaking, "clinical" — and my example will be a famous crisis and its resolution in the life of Leo Tolstoy. I shall then consider a standard way of dismissing this evidence, whose classic statement is found in Sigmund Freud's *The Future of an Illusion*. In the last section I shall comment about the nature of any resolution of the "debate" between Freud and Tolstoy.

Tolstoy's Crisis[5]

As a child and youth Tolstoy strove for moral perfection, but early in his youth he realized that he did not believe the doctrines of the Orthodox church. Through association with his upper-class peers he was drawn into a vain, sensuous, and egoistical view and lifestyle. He succeeded at all he did, particularly in his writing but also in achieving physical strength, influence among his peers, and success with his estate. He accepted a nineteenth-century version of what we would call scientific positivism, namely that the physical sciences are the court of last appeal on questions of what is real. He adopted a typical nineteenth-century intellectual philosophy of the

---

5. Quotations in this section are from Tolstoy's confession in "*A Confession*" *and* "*What I Believe*," trans. Aylmer Maude (London: Oxford University Press, 1940).

progressive perfectibility of humankind, and believed that he and his literary associates were the teachers of humankind. But as he says, he had no idea *what* he was teaching, for really he had nothing to teach. And human progress, whether his own or humanity's, fell far short of satisfying his spiritual needs. He wrote, "I devoted myself to [my writing] as a means of improving my material position and of stifling in my soul all questions as to the meaning of my own life or life in general" (p. 15). But at about age 50, "something very strange began to happen to me. At first I experienced moments of perplexity and arrest of life, as though I did not know what to do or how to live; and I felt lost and became dejected. But this passed, and I went on living as before. Then these moments of perplexity began to recur oftener and oftener, and always in the same form. They were always expressed by the questions: What is it for? What does it lead to?" (p. 15).

Tolstoy says that these questions seemed childish, but when he "touched them and tried to solve them" he realized that they were the most momentous of life's questions and that he had no answer to them.

> Before occupying myself with my Samára estate, the education of my son, or the writing of a book, I had to know *why* I was doing it. As long as I did not know why, I could do nothing and could not live. Amid the thoughts of estate management which greatly occupied me at that time, the question would suddenly occur: "Well, you will have 6,000 *desyatínas* of land in Samára Government and 300 horses, and what then?" . . . And I was quite disconcerted and did not know what to think. Or when considering plans for the education of my children, I would say to myself: "What for?" Or when considering how the peasants might become prosperous, I would suddenly say to myself: "But what does it matter to me?" Or when thinking of the fame my works would bring me, I would say to myself, "Very well; you will be more famous than Gógol or Púshkin or Shakespeare or Molière, or than all the writers in the world — and what of it?" And I could find no reply at all. The questions would not wait, they had to be answered at once, and if I did not answer them it was impossible to live. But there was no answer. (Pp. 16-17)

Of course Tolstoy could have given the conventional, finite reasons for improving his estate, educating his son, and so forth. But his spiritual crisis consisted precisely in the fact that *such* reasons no longer struck him as adequate to give meaning to the activities in question, to supply the motivation needed to "keep going." These finite reasons would make sense, it seemed to him, only if tethered to something larger, something eternal.

The evacuation of meaning from reasons not tied to something eternal was a consequence of having a vividly clear larger view of what his life consisted in and whither it tended. "Today or to-morrow sickness and death will come (they had come already) to those I love or to me; nothing will remain but stench and worms. Sooner or later my affairs, whatever they may be, will be forgotten, and I shall not exist. Then why go on making any effort? . . . How can man fail to see this? And how go on living?" (pp. 19-20). To live requires being "intoxicated with life," that is, confined to a short view of it. And yet even this short, intoxicated view is not merely finite, after the manner of brute-consciousness; rather, the everyday human consciousness supplies a pseudo-infinite deceptive overlay that gives activities meaning. (The adolescent sense of "immortality" differs from the time-consciousness of animals in that all activities are invested with a sense of infinite future.) Drunkenness was some relief, for it allowed Tolstoy to feel motivation by a sort of inertia of habit from a past in which his goals had made sense to him. But as soon as he was sober again, he would realize that such habit-motivation was a delusion, that there was in fact "nothing to wish for. I could not even wish to know the truth, for I guessed of what it consisted. The truth was that life is meaningless" (p. 17).

Tolstoy stresses that his life was, by normal human standards, in no way pathological, deficient, or problematic. He was in vigorous middle-age, still able to work both mind and body for long hours. He loved and was loved by the wife who had borne him vigorous well-adjusted children. His estate was improving steadily; he was respected by acquaintances and relations; he was famous as an author. "And in this situation I came to this — that I could not live, and, fearing death, had to employ cunning with myself to avoid taking my own life" (p. 19). Many atheists and agnostics find much meaning in their families, but without something eternal to tie them to, Tolstoy found his family, whom he loved, a source of intensified pain: " 'Family' . . . said I to myself. But my family — wife and children — are also human. They are placed just as I am: they must either live in a lie or see the terrible truth. Why should they live? Why should I love them, guard them, bring them up, or watch them? That they may come to the despair that I feel, or else be stupid? Loving them, I cannot hide the truth from them: each step in knowledge leads them to the truth. And the truth is death" (p. 21).

The life of the creation of works of art and the contemplation of other people's works afford many people meaning, even in the absence of any eternal meaning.[6] But, Tolstoy suggests, this is because people accept a concocted sense of the meaning of life that is created by a consensus that life makes sense and that art mirrors that sense. "But when I began to seek the meaning of life and felt the necessity of living my own life, that mirror became for me unnecessary, superfluous, ridiculous, or painful. I could no longer soothe myself with what I now saw in the mirror, namely, that my position was stupid and desperate" (p. 22).

Some who have felt the emptiness of life in the contemplation of the worms and of the collapse and oblivion in which all of their interest and striving end have coped by resignation. The despair derives from aspiring to what the universe cannot supply; so let us reduce our aspirations, measuring them to reality. This Stoic solution is the one to which Freud also urges us, and which he predicts will be naturally adopted as the human race comes to psychological maturity. Tolstoy rejects it as impossible to him. "Had I simply understood that life had no meaning I could have borne it quietly, knowing that that was my lot. But I could not satisfy myself with that. Had I been like a man living in a wood from which he knows there is no exit, I could have lived; but I was like one lost in a wood who, horrified at having lost his way, rushes about wishing to find the road" (p. 22).

---

6. See Bertrand Russell, "A Free Man's Worship" in *Mysticism and Logic* (Harmondsworth, Middlesex: Penguin Books, 1953). Although art is the solution that Russell offers to Tolstoy's problem, the solution is not really adequate, even by Russell's lights, as indicated by the rather shrill and melancholy attitude expressed in the essay.

In other words, Tolstoy could not shake the aspiration toward a transcendent positive meaning of his life. He found in himself what Kierkegaard calls "the passion of the infinite," which is characteristic of people who, unlike those whose spiritual sensibilities have been dulled, know "what it means to exist."[7] To resign himself in the Stoic way would be to shut out an insistent part of his being and thus to be dishonest. It would be to adopt, under ostensible honesty and resignation, the kind of self-deception that Solomon more forthrightly commends: Indulge in pleasant activities, and "[you] will not much remember the days of [your] life because God keeps [you] occupied with joy in [your] heart" (Eccles. 5:20). Furthermore, thinks Tolstoy, this part of his passional nature is something noble, which to deny would be degrading.

Eventually, Tolstoy comes to see that his despair depends on his accepting a certain conception of reason, whose principle (as we might put it) is that reasoning is valid only insofar as it is limited to the finite. One example of such reasoning is that of the natural sciences.

> . . . in this sphere of knowledge the only answer to my question, "what is the meaning of my life?" was: . . . "you are a transitory, casual cohesion of particles. The mutual interactions and changes of these particles produce in you what you call your 'life.' That cohesion will last sometime; afterwards the interaction of these particles will cease and what you call 'life' will cease, and so will all your questions. You are an accidentally united little lump of something. That little lump ferments. The little lump calls that fermenting its 'life.' The lump will disintegrate and there will be an end of the fermenting and of all the questions." So answers the clear side of science and cannot answer otherwise if it strictly follows its principles. (P. 31)

Another kind of example of "reason" is that of the philosophers. Schopenhauer, Solomon, and the Buddha ask "What is the meaning of a human life?" and each, in his own way, says that

---

7. Søren Kierkegaard, *Concluding Unscientific Postscript*, trans. Howard V. Hong and Edna H. Hong (Princeton: Princeton University Press, 1992), p. 249.

there is no meaning and that suicide is the rational approach: in Schopenhauer the death of the will, in the Buddha the annihilation of the self, and in Solomon a kind of oblivion of the nature of one's life generated by pleasure and a narrowing of the mind. Tolstoy concludes that one will never solve the problem of the meaning of life as long as one limits one's thinking to "reason" in this sense. One must learn to think of one's finite life as connected to the infinite and given its meaning by the infinite — by obedience to God and his commandments, and by the prospect of union with God in heaven. And such a thinking that transcends "reason" (or reconceives it as having a broader scope) seems appropriate to human beings, inasmuch as we cannot *live* satisfactorily if we do not expand our thinking in this way.

The "hidden infinity of human thought" (p. 53) is manifested, at its most authentic, less in terms of discursive, sentential thinking than in terms of deep emotions whose "logic" can retrospectively be understood in sentential form: "During that whole year, when I was asking myself almost every moment whether I should not end matters with a noose or a bullet — all that time, together with the course of thought and observation about which I have spoken, my heart was oppressed with a painful feeling, which I can only describe as a search for God. I say that that search for God was not reasoning, but a feeling, because that search proceeded not from the course of my thoughts — it was even directly contrary to them — but proceeded from the heart. It was a feeling of fear, orphanage, isolation in a strange land, and a hope of help from someone" (p. 62).[8]

---

8. Note Kierkegaard's comment that "just as no one has ever proved [the God's existence], so has there never been an atheist, even though there certainly have been many who have been unwilling to let what they knew (that the God exists) get control of their minds." *Søren Kierkegaard's Journals and Papers*, vol. 3, ed. and trans. Howard Hong and Edna Hong (Bloomington: Indiana University Press, 1975), #3606. John Calvin makes the same point: "Indeed, the perversity of the impious, who though they struggle furiously are unable to extricate themselves from the fear of God, is abundant testimony that this conviction, namely that *there is some God*, is naturally inborn in all, and is fixed deep within, as it were in the very marrow." *Institutes of the Christian Religion*, trans. Ford L. Battles (Philadelphia: Westminster, 1960), I.3.3, emphasis added.

Tolstoy concludes that the only kind of thinking a human being can truly "live with" in full consciousness of himself and his situation is one that connects the finite with the infinite, the world of everyday living with God and eternity. Every psychologically adequate answer to the question "What is the meaning of life?" or "How shall I live?" "gives to the finite existence of man an infinite meaning, a meaning not destroyed by sufferings, deprivations, or death. . . . Faith is a knowledge of the meaning of human life in consequence of which man does not destroy himself but lives. . . . If [a person] does not see and recognize the illusory nature of the finite, he believes in the finite; if he understands the illusory nature of the finite,[9] he must believe in the infinite. . . . It was now clear to me that for man to be able to live he must either not see the infinite, or have such an explanation of the meaning of life as will connect the finite with the infinite" (pp. 50-51). We are reminded of Kierkegaard's characterization of the human self, penned some thirty years earlier, as "a synthesis of the finite and the infinite, of the temporal and the eternal."[10]

9. That is, understands the unfitness of the finite life by itself to satisfy the needs of the psyche.

10. Kierkegaard, *Sickness Unto Death*, p. 13. In another passage that is highly reminiscent of Tolstoy, he writes:

Even the greatest events and the most laborious lives are whirlpools, or they are like sewing without knotting the thread — until the end is once again made fast by the fact that the unconditional is brought to bear, or that the individual, however remotely, comes to relate himself to the unconditional. To live in the unconditional, inhaling only the unconditional, is impossible to man; he perishes, like the fish forced to live in the air. But on the other hand, without relating himself to the unconditional, man cannot in the deepest sense be said to "live." He gives up the ghost — that is, he may continue perhaps to live, but spiritlessly. To stick to my subject, the religious, I say that the race, or a considerable number of the individuals within the race, have outgrown the childish notion that another person can represent the unconditional for them. . . . Very well; but for all that, the unconditional does not cease to be necessary. Rather it is the more necessary the more the individual outgrows childish dependence upon other men. Hence "the individual" himself must relate himself to the unconditional. ("My Activity as a Writer," in *Point of View for My Work as an Author*, trans. Walter Lowrie [New York: Harper & Row, 1962], p. 158)

Though Tolstoy sees clearly that it is not rational, in a broad sense, to leave the infinite out of one's thinking about human life, he continues to find strongly compelling the strictures imposed on belief by what he takes to be scientific rationality. In particular, while he feels vividly the need to be related to God and eternity, his concept of rationality makes many of the central beliefs of orthodox Christianity repugnant to him. This thralldom to a constrictive ideology of reason exists side-by-side with his hunger for God, creating strong conflicts and extreme emotional shifts:

"He exists," said I to myself. And I had only for an instant to admit that, and at once life rose within me, and I felt the possibility and joy of being. But again, from the admission of the existence of a God I went on to seek my relation with Him; and again I imagined *that* God — our Creator in Three Persons who sent His Son, the Saviour — and again *that* God, detached from the world and from me, melted like a block of ice, melted before my eyes, and again nothing remained, and again the spring of life dried up within me, and I despaired and felt that I had nothing to do but to kill myself. . . . Not twice or three times, but tens and hundreds of times, I reached those conditions, first of joy and animation, and then of despair and consciousness of the impossibility of living. (Pp. 63-64)

Tolstoy finally resolves the tension between what he takes to be "reason" and faith by trusting *both* his God-libido and his positivistically motivated repugnance for traditional Christian theology. Accordingly he rewrites the Gospels, excising from them anything that offends his "reason," but leaving enough of the "infinite" to satisfy the cravings of his spirit. We may speculate that if he had enjoyed a "postmodern" situation like our own, in which the cultural relativity of the most constricting claims of "reason" has been exposed, he could have left the Gospels unrewritten and accepted a more traditional Christianity that would have been even more psychologically satisfying than was his revision.

Tolstoy's authorship of short stories and novels of astounding psychological lucidity recommends him as something of an authority on questions about the meaning of life and the requirements of psychological well-being under conditions of very high self-transparency. And the witness of Tolstoy's need for God is all the more impressive for his intellectual resistance to religious ideas.

Freud's Interpretation

Sigmund Freud has offered an interpretation of the human need for God that is in some ways like Tolstoy's but would in the end debunk it and draw a very different picture of the basic human psyche. Freud too sees the motivation for religious beliefs in emotional needs that derive from the perceived inadequacy of the finite world. Like Tolstoy, Freud idealizes the natural sciences as the standard of reason, and uses this standard to reject religious ideas, though, again like Tolstoy, he finds it necessary to compromise this standard in his own thought: psychoanalysis is a very different kind of enterprise than the natural sciences, yet Freud thinks it yields knowledge. But our two authors are also in fundamental disagreement. While Tolstoy finds the God-libido to be a basic and ineradicable feature of the human psyche, which must be satisfied if persons are to live an emotionally healthy and yet fully self-transparent life, Freud takes the need to be transitory, one that is outgrown in the full adulthood of the individual and the culture. Religious ideas, says Freud, "which are given out as teachings, are not precipitates of experience or end-results of thinking: they are illusions, fulfilments of the oldest, strongest and most urgent wishes of mankind. The secret of their strength lies in the strength of those wishes."[11]

We human beings find ourselves in an intrinsically threatening and insecure world, in which the forces of nature place us at their mercy. But by *our* nature we want security and safety. We grow up with parents who function as means by which we get some control over our environment, and thus a reduction of our anxiety. So it is

---

11. *The Future of an Illusion*, trans. W. D. Robson-Scott, rev. and ed. James Strachey (Garden City, N.Y.: Doubleday Anchor, 1964), p. 47. Parenthetical page references in the present section are to this book.

natural that we should project personality onto nature and see in the calamities and fortunes that occur to us there the anger and the approval of the gods. Here is how we see the world in such a projection:

> Over each one of us there watches a benevolent Providence which is only seemingly stern and which will not suffer us to become a plaything of the over-mighty and pitiless forces of nature. Death itself is not extinction, is not a return to inorganic lifelessness, but the beginning of a new kind of existence which lies on the path of development to something higher. And, looking in the other direction, this view announces that the same moral laws which our civilizations have set up govern the whole universe as well, except that they are maintained by a supreme court of justice with incomparably more power and consistency. (P. 26)[12]

Monotheism arises out of polytheism "as a return to the historical beginnings of the idea of God. Now that God was a single person, man's relations to him could recover the intimacy and intensity of the child's relation to his father. . . . when man personifies the forces of nature he is again following an infantile model" (pp. 27, 31).

The motive of security, filtered through child-parent interactions, produces the concept of God:

> . . . the mother, who satisfies the child's hunger, becomes its first love-object and certainly also its first protection against all the undefined dangers which threaten it in the external world — its first protection against anxiety, we may say.
>
> In this function [of protection] the mother is soon replaced by

---

12. Freud and Tolstoy disagree, perhaps, on (a) how momentous, and (b) how eradicable, are these needs for the transcendent. Freud seems to think that the need can be pretty readily outgrown, while Tolstoy seems unable to outgrow it. Freud does not seem to think it very important to human life, while for Tolstoy it seems all-important. They may also disagree about rationality (though Tolstoy *speaks* as though he agrees with Freud); Tolstoy is perhaps more like William James, in adopting the principle that it is unlikely that human nature has in it a deep need that the universe that gave rise to the human organism refuses in principle to satisfy.

the stronger father, who retains that position for the rest of childhood. But the child's attitude to its father is coloured by a peculiar ambivalence. The father himself constitutes a danger for the child, perhaps because of its earlier relation to its mother. Thus it fears him no less than it longs for him and admires him. The indications of this ambivalence in the attitude to the father are deeply imprinted in every religion. . . . When the growing individual finds that he is destined to remain a child for ever, that he can never do without protection against strange superior powers, he lends those powers the features belonging to the figure of his father; he creates for himself the gods whom he dreads, whom he seeks to propitiate, and whom he nevertheless entrusts with his own protection. (Pp. 34-35)

So the "need" (set of urges) that Augustine and Kierkegaard and Tolstoy interpret as the indication that man is spirit, that he is in the image of God, Freud interprets as an illusion. Our question is, What can be said in favor of the one interpretation over the other? How might a dialogue go, between Tolstoy and Freud?

Tolstoy vs. Freud on Our Need for God

On Freud's account, the concept of God (and thus God himself) is a *creation* of the human mind in response to the pressures of an *infantile* need. On Tolstoy's account, the concept of God is an idea to which the human psyche is *compelled* by *self-transparency* (an aspect of human maturity) to give credence, on pain of despair.

When Freud speaks of the mind's "creating" God he means to imply that nothing in reality corresponds to the concept of God. But the mere fact that a concept is created by human beings implies nothing one way or the other about whether anything real corresponds to the concept.[13] In some sense, perhaps all concepts are

13. Freud himself admits (*Future of an Illusion*, p. 49) that "illusions" in his sense may sometimes be true. In his essay "The Will to Believe" in *The Will to Believe* (New York: Dover, 1956), William James offers some useful guidelines on when it is rational to believe something because doing so satisfies a human

created by human beings; in any case, no one will infer the non-existence of quarks from the fact that the concept of a quark is a human creation; nor will contemporary scientists, prior to the verification of quarks, accuse those who believe in them of irrationality because positing their existence satisfies a human need — the need to explain something in physics.

Freud's account of the origin of the concept is largely acceptable to the Christian psychologist. Under the pressure of emotional needs, and on the model of human parents, we come up with the idea of God (I am not saying that each of us invents the concept out of whole cloth; it is a product of tradition, of countless *generations* of human beings' thinking about their place in the universe). But instead of inferring from our "creativity" in this respect that God is only a figment of our minds, the Christian psychologist will say that God intended us to go through this developmental process by which we gain psychological access to him.

Freud's other main strategy for discounting our sense of need for God is to call it "infantile." But this too is acceptable to the Christian psychologist. Some aspects of the attitude of the child are commended in the Christian tradition as features of human maturity (Mark 10:13-16), inasmuch as denying them is dishonest and ungrateful and lacking in a proper perspective on our human situation. We are to become like little children because that is what we are: derived, dependent beings. From the Christian standpoint Freud's Stoic proposal that we accept a model of maturity that contains no transcendent comfort is the one that is unrealistic, a distortion of our nature. Freud calls our need for God infantile, and thereby denigrates it; the Christian psychologist calls our need for God infantile, and thereby commends it.

Some individuals, like Tolstoy, cannot (psychologically) live without God (Simone Weil, Kierkegaard, and Augustine are other examples). Others, like Freud, seem to adjust to atheism; they do

---

need. He suggests that it is rational to do so when (a) the options are "living" (i.e., personally real options for the potential believer), (b) the choice is "forced" (i.e., one cannot merely suspend belief/disbelief), and (c) the options are "momentous" (i.e., it makes a lot of difference what one believes). By these standards, Tolstoy's belief in God, though an "illusion" by Freud's reckoning, would be rational.

not go nutty or kill themselves. What shall we say about these two classes of persons? Tolstoy will say that the atheist is not fully conscious of self and situation. Something in his self and situation is being repressed or toned down or shaded or intellectualized or otherwise "defended" against.[14] In other words, Tolstoy accuses Freud of being immature. Freud, in response, will say that it is Tolstoy who is immature, given to wishful thinking, short on courage and resignation; he lives in his illusions, in a fantasy world. He may think that he cannot live without God, but that is either because he has not summoned enough resignation, or because he has been so damaged by religious training that such resignation is literally beyond his capacities. In either case Tolstoy's religion is a consequence of his failure to function fully as a human being. Freud leans heavily on his concept of maturity when he writes: "But surely infantilism is destined to be surmounted. Men cannot remain children for ever; they must in the end go out into 'hostile life.' We may call this *'education to reality'*" (p. 81).

Who is right? Can we adjudicate between these rival ways of conceptualizing the human need for God, which our two authors otherwise describe in remarkably similar ways? We can, no doubt, but I do not think that we can find a theoretically neutral standpoint from which to do so to the potential satisfaction of both sides.[15] The rival standpoints will continue to be occupied by reasonable people.

Rival conceptions of maturity are a fact of life in contemporary psychology,[16] so it should come as no surprise and no alarm that Christians do not fully agree with atheists about what counts as

14. For an argument that Freud was less comfortable with his atheism than biographers like Ernest Jones have represented him to be, see Paul Vitz, *Sigmund Freud's Christian Unconscious* (New York: Guilford, 1988). See also Ernest Becker's interpretation of Freud's life in *The Denial of Death* (New York: The Free Press, 1973).

15. Such "satisfaction" would of course result in one side's abandoning its position.

16. In *Taking the Word to Heart: Self and Other in an Age of Therapies* (Grand Rapids: Eerdmans, 1993), Part One, I examine the concepts of psychological maturity of six major psychotherapies, and compare them with the Christian concept of maturity.

psychological maturity and mental well-being, and in particular how the relationship to God figures in the mature personality. Personality theories and psychotherapies are based on conceptual commitments that are never fully underwritten by the data except insofar as those data are construed in terms of the conceptual commitments. It seems that psychology, as an intellectual enterprise (a science?), depends more on contestable conceptualization than such sciences as chemistry and physics. This does not stem from psychology's lack of scientific development, but rather from the nature of its subject matter: Psychology is necessarily about such issues as development and maturity, which are inextricable from moral and religious commitments. Freud's conscious commitment is to atheism and a Stoic model of maturity; Tolstoy's is to theism and an attenuated Christian model of the mature person as a trusting child of God.

To the Christian it will seem that Tolstoy is right: Freud really does need a God-relationship, and is at some unconscious level kidding himself. The Christian psychologist agrees with Freud and Tolstoy that we have a desire for God, and agrees with Tolstoy against Freud that that need is a basic drive of our nature, to deny which is to deny something fundamental about ourselves. To try to eradicate it, to class it with dispositions that we must outgrow if we are to become mature, is precisely *not* to move toward maturity, but to arrest our development and pervert our nature, to foster vice and not virtue. The Christian psychologist disagrees with both Freud and Tolstoy in their judgment that Christian doctrinal belief is irrational and incompatible with science. With positivism behind us, perhaps the major reason since the Enlightenment for thinking that Christian belief is epistemically substandard has been undermined. The Christian psychologist today is able to give doctrinally orthodox and biblically rich readings of the human desire for God and for its frequent failure to be well developed or conscious.

Religious Toleration and Human Rights

Paul A. Marshall

Strongly held and publicly expressed religious views are usually thought to be damaging to a tolerant society. As Allan Bloom put it, there is an all too common opinion that "the study of history and of culture teaches that all the world was mad in the past: men always thought they were right, and that led to wars, persecutions, slavery, xenophobia, racism, and chauvinism."[1] Richard Rorty remarks: "I take religious toleration to mean the willingness of religious groups to take part in discussions without dragging religion into it."[2] One consequence of this introverted liberal focus is a tendency to regard dissentients as mad. John Rawls suggests: "To subordinate all our aims to one end does not strictly speaking violate the principles of rational choice . . . but it still strikes us as irrational, or more likely as mad."[3] (The identity of the "us" here is not entirely clear.) Rorty proposes to "josh" his opponents and thus to dehumanize them as some kind of garrulous but senile relatives.

In this chapter I want to argue that this association of strong religious views and intolerance is misplaced and that strongly held views are in fact the sine qua non of toleration.

---

1. Allan Bloom, *The Closing of the American Mind* (New York: Simon & Schuster, 1987), p. 26.
2. "Interview," *The Times Literary Supplement,* 24 June 1994, p. 14.
3. John Rawls, *A Theory of Justice* (Cambridge, 1971), p. 554.

Discussion of toleration, especially religious toleration, has been sparse in Western political reflection in the twentieth century, since religion has been assumed to be passé. For various reasons that is now changing. In the United States there is increasing controversy over the religious freedom clauses of the First Amendment, the breakdown of cultural consensus producing the oft-noted "culture wars," and the development of postmodernism and its ilk, with its attendant concern for the "other."[4] Elsewhere, both the breakdown of the East-West polarity and the fragmentation of the misnamed "third world" have helped both to produce and to reveal national, ethnic, and religious tensions. For most human beings religion is the core of existence. For good and ill, it sustains their lives, shapes their ethics, animates their dreams, provides their hopes, and comforts their sufferings.

This increased attention to religious toleration has not always been edifying. Much discussion has assumed the form of an attack on what are called "fundamentalists" — a word dredged up from the American past, and of dubious meaning and provenance even then, and now put to use in service of a dubious psychosociology. In modern Western usage it seems merely to mean "lunatic" or, perhaps, merely someone who refuses to place material comforts above every other political consideration. They are people to be watched rather than listened to, to be psychoanalyzed rather than understood.[5] Consequently there is a continuing refusal to take religion seriously.

The Nature of Toleration

Toleration means refraining from prohibition or persecution, and so it necessarily implies disapproval or dislike of the thing tolerated. Bernard Crick describes tolerance generally as "the degree to which we accept things of which we disapprove" or "the deliberate for-

4. See James Hunter's *Culture Wars* (New York, 1991) and his more recent, more ominously titled, *Before the Shooting Starts* (New York, 1994).
5. For a good discussion of these themes see Ian S. Markham, *Plurality and Christian Ethics* (Cambridge, 1994).

bearing of power that could be used otherwise."[6] This is similar to John Courtney Murray's idea of the First Amendment as "The articles of peace": that is, they are not a new creed or articles of faith but simply the rules of disengagement.[7]

It is important to distinguish toleration, indifference, relativism, and celebration. Indifference is when we do not care about an outcome. I am indifferent as to whether someone has red hair: I simply do not care. It is no virtue that I put up with it and refrain from trying to ban it. This is the stance taken toward religion by many Westerners who would like to think of themselves as tolerant. But toleration concerns how you react to something that you really *do* care about.

Nor should we confuse relativism, assuming for a moment that relativists can exist, with tolerance. A relativist holds that all views are relative, that some other view could be as true as her own, and that views may be of equal worth. But in this case the other's view is no challenge or threat, but merely another stance. The question of disapproval or condemnation does not arise.

Celebration, or approval, is not toleration. Toleration only arises where there is already disapproval present. So spouses should not be tolerated, they should be loved. Perhaps their relatives will need to be tolerated. We do not tolerate things we love, we simply love them. This is why T. S. Eliot said: "The Christian does not wish to be tolerated." The goal was to love and be loved.

One also can practice toleration at a variety of levels. I may be socially intolerant with someone in not having them in my house and I may be analytically intolerant of their views so that I always criticize them. But at the same time I may be politically tolerant in that I have no desire that the state should try to repress them, or perhaps it would be better said that I am civilly tolerant

6. Bernard Crick, "Toleration in Theory and Practice," in *Government and Opposition* 6 (1971): 144-71.

7. John Courtney Murray, *We Hold These Truths* (New York: Sheed and Ward, 1960), pp. 45ff. The word was used in this sense in the Reformation period, with "permission" sometimes used as an alternative. Montaigne and Calvin used "tolerantia" to mean something like "endurance." In the second half of the sixteenth century *toleranz* meant something like "allowance." In any case none of these terms implied approval.

in that I do not as a citizen push the state to repress them. Similarly a church may excommunicate someone but have no desire that any civil penalties should attach to this action. Such a church could be described as ecclesiastically intolerant but civilly tolerant. It is not only possible but likely that we will at the same time be tolerant and intolerant at different levels. In a "democratic" polity different religions compete on the basis of more or less accepted ground rules (e.g., no state imposition).

The variety of levels and objects in toleration makes terminology confusing. "Religious toleration" can be used to refer to toleration *by* religious bodies, such as churches, or the toleration *of* religious practices by *another* body, such as the state. Here I will concentrate on religious toleration and intolerance *understood as the political toleration of religious bodies and views by the state,* and civil toleration by people in refraining from pushing the state to be religiously intolerant. I will not consider "ecclesiastically intolerant" behaviors by churches and similar bodies in excommunicating or otherwise disciplining members, partly because I believe that these are necessary and vital functions if genuine political toleration is to be preserved.

Currently "toleration" has something of a bad name. For some it smacks of a vague indiscriminate acceptance, of relativism, of lack of conviction. It seems merely to paper over the cracks and, in the name of openness, to take no one seriously. Years ago Herbert Marcuse spoke of a "repressive tolerance" that simply accepted the given situation.[8]

For others toleration seems to be a halfway house, a second best, a sufferance. It is treated as if it were merely grudging acceptance by a superior, a type of paternalism. Tom Paine said, "The French constitution has abolished or renounced *Toleration,* and *Intolerance* also, and has established *UNIVERSAL RIGHT OF CONSCIENCE.*"[9] James Madison pushed successfully to have the word "toleration" removed from the final draft of the Virginia Bill of

8. Herbert Marcuse, "Repressive Tolerance," in Robert Paul Wolff, Barrington Moore, Jr., and Herbert Marcuse, *A Critique of Pure Tolerance* (Boston, 1965), pp. 81-117.
9. Thomas Paine, *Rights of Man* (Cambridge, 1989), p. 96.

Rights (adopted June 1776).[10] Currently several commentators think that toleration is itself a problem, that we must move beyond toleration to real acceptance, even celebration. They demand that we not merely accept or put up with our differences, but actively rejoice in them. Tolerance is seen as fundamentally intolerant, or at least a paternalist or narrow-minded view.

This latter is a valid criticism in the case of, say, race, but not in the case of religion. Racial toleration is not a good thing, since it implies disapproval of another's race, and this is bigotry. But anyone who has never disapproved of another's religion is not open-minded but simply treats religion as trivial, as if religious differences do not matter at all. One can no more approve of all religions than one can approve of all politics. They mean something and the differences are important. If we were to accept such criticisms then we would need to say that the sentiment attributed to Voltaire, "I disapprove of what you say but I will defend to the death your right to say it," is simply a species of bigotry. Who is he to voice disagreement?

The vitally important role of toleration in the modern world is that it focuses precisely on those areas where there *is* real disagreement, but at the same time it calls for coexistence. It does not require celebration of that which we would rather not celebrate, nor does it fall into the view that all views are equal, nor does it trivialize the role of religion in the world, even in public life. But neither does it justify persecution.

For those who still find this depiction too grudging, it should also be said that toleration requires a discipline and commitment that other stances do not. They require of us nothing but what we want to do anyway. We simply follow our desires. But toleration requires a burden: It *is* a burden. Indifference seems safe, but what happens to things we are not indifferent about? Relativism seems benign, but it has no serious differences with which to contend. Celebration seems marvelous, but can we celebrate everything? If we acknowledge that there are real and important differences between human beings on religious matters, and realize that these

10. See Douglas F. Kelly, *The Emergence of Liberty in the Modern World* (Phillipsburg, 1992), pp. 133-34.

differences will not soon go away, then we need to face the strengths, and weaknesses, of toleration.

Historical Justifications of Toleration

There are three main contending justifications for toleration. The first is rooted in a type of skepticism. The second stresses the privacy of ultimate, especially religious, opinions. The third concentrates on the role of the state.

One major group to argue for a form of toleration was influenced by skepticism and humanism combined with a peculiar but common mixture of pietism. This ranged from Dutch Remonstrants such as Arminius to Polish Socinians such as their namesake, Faustus Socinus. It included influential figures such as Grotius and Coonhert in the Netherlands, John Locke, John Milton, and Jeremy Taylor in England, Bodin and Bayle in France, and, later, Wolff and Thomasius in the German states.

This view says that in important areas we cannot know the truth, or that we will always have uncertainty. But this leaves open the question of areas where we think we do know the truth, unless we are disposed to think that we do not know the truth about anything. In the post-Reformation debates it was clear that very different answers could flow from a claim of uncertainty.

Locke is often regarded as the father of toleration in the English-speaking world. His arguments for toleration were diverse, but one was an argument from the uncertainty of human knowledge. He argued that differences of opinion must be tolerated since in many areas of life answers are uncertain and no one can prove an opinion wrong.[11] Faith is a particular class of opinion and mediated revelation can only establish faith on the grounds of probability as distinct from the grounds of sure knowledge.[12] No one should try

---

11. See *Essay Concerning Human Understanding*, chap. 16, para. 4. Here Locke has in mind not the general truths of Christendom, which he thought were clear to reason, but the differences between Christian sects.

12. Chap. 15, para. 14; he argues in chap. 18 that faith can bring certainty, but this is only in connection with immediate revelation.

to enforce such views because they are not certain. And, since most religion concerns only probable things, they cannot be a secure foundation for the social order.[13]

But if something cannot be known, or if it does not matter much, then why not simply impose an answer for the sake of civil peace? Why should it be the authorities that exercise tolerance? It could equally well be demanded that the dissenters should exercise some forbearance and drop the matter. Shouldn't they just shut up, or be shut up, if they persist in pushing unknowable and troubling speculations? One danger of this more skeptical view is that it can equally well lead to the state imposing a view without necessarily making any claim that it is the true one. It merely imposes an arbitrary uniformity. Indeed this is the position that Locke defended earlier in his life in his *Two Tracts on Government*.[14] There he argued for the right of the magistrate to impose a practice in things indifferent. Since the items are "indifferent," of no great consequence, then a solution may as well be imposed if it helps civil peace. Indifference can override conscience as well as support it.

Richard Tuck[15] points out that Justus Lipsius, an ardent advocate of religious repression, was skeptically inclined. Grotius thought no one "was entitled to enforce more extensively specified religious opinions upon another merely because of their conviction that those opinions were *correct;* but neither were they entitled to resist the imposition of religious ceremonies and dogmas by the state if it believed that it was necessary to do so for *political* rea-

13. See Peter Schouls, *The Imposition of Method: A Study of Descartes and Locke* (Oxford, 1980); Thomas Spragens, *The Irony of Liberal Reason* (Chicago, 1981), chap. 2; Neal Wood, *The Politics of Locke's Philosophy* (Berkeley, 1983), pp. 171-73; D. Snyder, "Faith and Reason in Locke's Essay," *Journal of the History of Ideas* 47, no. 2 (April-June 1986): 197-213. See also P. J. Kelly, "John Locke: Authority, Conscience and Religious Toleration," in John Horton and Susan Mendus, eds., *John Locke: A Letter Concerning Toleration in Focus* (New York, 1991), pp. 125-46.

14. See Philip Abrams, ed., *John Locke: Two Tracts on Government* (Cambridge, 1967).

15. Richard Tuck, "Scepticism and Toleration in the Seventeenth Century," in Susan Mendus, ed., *Justifying Toleration: Conceptual and Historical Perspectives* (Cambridge: Cambridge University Press, 1988), pp. 21-35.

sons."[16] Hobbes was similar. Indeed Tuck describes a "combination of respect for the arguments of the sceptic, acceptance of a minimalist morality, and support for a potentially intolerant state" as "standard"; so it is not surprising to find the younger Locke expressing such a view.

Locke had another important argument for toleration, which concerned the place of religion in human life. Locke's conception of religion was as something concerned with a future life in heaven with no concerns below but the spiritual duties that would aid the attainment of this heaven.[17] Social discord could be overcome because religious differences were irrelevant to social life: "The only business of the church is the salvation of souls: and it in no way concerns the commonwealth or any member of it that this or the other ceremony may be made use of . . . religious assemblies [do not] advantage or prejudice the life, liberty, or estate, of any man."[18]

The problem with these influential arguments is that they are predicated on tolerating the socially irrelevant. Locke argues that religion should be tolerated because it has no public consequence, but this does not tell us what to do about religions that *do* have public consequence, as the vast majority do. In fact Locke is intolerant of such religions. If conflict arises then the state may step in, since "those things which are not lawful in the ordinary course of life" can be forbidden.[19] He will not tolerate those who "deliver themselves up to the protection and service of another prince" and those who "deny the being of God . . . [since] promise, covenants, and oaths . . . can have no hold upon an atheist."[20] Others that should not be tolerated are those who "will not own and teach the duty of tolerating all men in matters of mere religion."[21] In fact the law of toleration should be "so settled, that all churches were obliged to lay down toleration as

16. Tuck, "Scepticism and Toleration," pp. 30-31.
17. John Locke, *Letter Concerning Toleration,* ed. Charles L. Sherman, in *Great Books of the Western World,* vol. 35: *Locke, Berkeley, Hume* (Chicago: Encyclopedia Britannica, 1952).
18. Locke, *Letter Concerning Toleration,* p. 11.
19. Locke, *Letter Concerning Toleration,* p. 12.
20. Locke, *Letter Concerning Toleration,* p. 18.
21. Locke, *Letter Concerning Toleration,* p. 18.

the foundation of their own liberty."[22] Here Locke is intolerant of the intolerant — that is, of those who find him intolerant. There are no grounds for tolerating Catholics, Muslims, atheists, and those who will not accept Locke's view of toleration.

Locke achieves his new realm of freedom not by expanding the area of toleration but by shrinking the area of religion, and this is a move that has bedeviled the English-speaking world ever since. The result is similar to George Grant's depiction of liberal society: "As for pluralism, differences . . . are able to exist only in private activities: how we eat, how we mate, how we practice ceremonies. Some like pizza, some like steaks; some like girls, some like boys; some like synagogue, some like the mass. But we all do it in churches, motels, restaurants indistinguishable from the Atlantic to the Pacific."[23]

The third set of arguments focuses not on the nature of religion or knowledge per se but on the limited role of the civil authorities. From its earliest days, "Christendom" was divided into two realms. This had pervasive effects though it was anything but clear what the boundaries were and how the two were related to each other.[24] It became more a conceptual apparatus within which questions could be framed than any answer to those questions. Popes and Emperors used it to expand their powers and prerogatives and to assert their authority over the other.

We need also to remember what the two realms were fighting about. When they talked about religious freedom, they were not talking about retaining quaint folk customs, but about the fundamental commitments of human life. When they talked of the church they were not concerned about interference with an apparently harmless First Methodist over on the corner but with the most pervasive institution in society — one much more penetrating

22. Locke, *Letter Concerning Toleration*, p. 18.
23. George Grant, *Technology and Empire* (Toronto, 1969), p. 26.
24. One was Pope Gelasius I's view of the "two swords." He wrote to the Emperor Anastasius: "Two swords there are, august emperor, by which this world is chiefly ruled, the sacred authority of the priesthood and the royal power. . . . If the bishops themselves, recognizing that the imperial office was conferred on you by divine disposition, obey your laws as far as the sphere of public order is concerned . . . with what zeal, I ask you, ought you to obey those who have been charged with administering the sacred mysteries?"

than the putative and infant state, which had head and arms, but little body. The church was the media, since if news got out it did so via the pulpit. The church was the intelligentsia: it ran the universities and the rest of the educational system. Canon law was more pervasive than were the dictates of kings. It governed marriage, and therefore much of inheritance and property. The church ran whatever welfare arrangements there were. It was *this* institution and its relation to the political order with which they were concerned. Few modern states would relinquish control over this whole swath of the social order without a very literal fight.

Despite this confusion, or perhaps because of it, the division between these two realms is probably the single greatest contributor to the later growth of religious toleration (and of free societies) in the West. In an otherwise undistinguished book, G. H. Sabine says, "The rise of the Christian Church, as a distinct institution entitled to govern the spiritual concerns of mankind in independence of the state, may not unreasonably be described as the most revolutionary event in the history of western Europe, in respect both to politics and to political thought."[25] David Little adds, "I would underscore that statement several times."[26]

Neither the churches nor the political orders directly advocated toleration. Indeed the inquisitions were justified under such a scheme. But they always believed that there *were* boundaries and they struggled to define them. This meant that the church, whatever its lust for civil control, had always to acknowledge that there were forms of political power which it could not and should not exercise. The political orders, whatever their drive to subsume all of human life under their power, had to acknowledge that there were areas of human life which were necessarily and normatively beyond their reach. However much the boundaries were muddied, there was the abiding sense that the political order could not be identified with the order of ultimate human concern, that the core of human life, and the authority this embodied, was a realm beyond civil control. The political ruler always faced "another king." In this scheme the key ingredient in toleration was not in the first place a doctrine or

25. G. H. Sabine, *History of Political Theory* (New York, 1961), p. 180.
26. David Little, *Religion, Order and Law* (London, 1969), p. 36.

an explicit call for toleration: It was an institutional separation that imposed a civilizational warrant for limited jurisdiction.

Toward Toleration

The basis for a substantial defense of toleration in the world is a proper view of the limits of state power. That is, regardless of whether there might be certain advantages, it is simply not the state's business to interfere with certain areas of human life. We need to pick up and expand the confused history of the two realms and replace Locke's division of the civil and religious with the possibility of a boundary at a better point. Currently much American jurisprudence does the former in the pale form of the nonestablishment of religion, but it has scarcely broached the second. It is as if the "separation of church and state" were already thought to be itself the boundary marker of such a separation.

Arguments about conscience are an attempt to fix the boundaries, as are the notions of the two realms of subsidiarity and natural law in Lutheran, Reformed, and Catholic thought. Here the notion of jurisdiction and the limits of state authority is a key to toleration. In sociological terms toleration is staying in a role. In theological terms it is staying in office: It is not doing that for which you have the power but not the authority. More generally we might say that they are arguments for what are now called *human rights*. By such rights I mean a recognition that certain areas of life are off limits to the state and, conversely, that these are areas where either the individual or some other association such as a church, or union, or professional group has its own sovereignty. The key to a worthwhile view of religious toleration in the modern world is not skepticism, relativism, or indifference. Nor is it religious openness to the other. Nor is it a call to confine religion to a private realm or to take it out of politics. Nor is it a claim that religion will be allowed if it does no harm to others. Rather, its focus should be on the legal co-existence of the differing, and continuing to differ, parties predicated on the fact that they have a right to do what they are doing.

As John Courtney Murray puts it, "the public consensus . . . must permit to the differing communities the full integrity of their own religious convictions . . . it does not seek to reduce to its own unity the differences that divide them. In a word the pluralism remains as real as the unity. Neither may undertake to destroy the other. Each subsists in its own order."[27]

Some may say that this is too weak a basis for a tolerant political order, that there must additionally be an acceptance of the other, an agreement with the other, a celebration of the other: that political openness requires a skepticism, a relativism, or some epistemological forbearance. But this does not appear to be the case, and is probably just a liberal prejudice.[28] Political toleration of religious differences, like rights, addresses differences seriously enough to say that they are differences, and that some of these differences are not good. But it forswears the use of force to try to overcome them. Political and religious toleration is not necessarily tied to weak opinions on the matters at hand, nor is intolerance tied to strong opinions. Thomas Hobbes appeared to be indifferent to most religion, but disliked religious toleration. John Locke had stronger religious opinions but was more open to toleration. Roger Williams did not agree with the religious views of Muslims, pagans, papists, nor of many other Protestants, especially Quakers, and he made a point of making his disagreements known. He thought they were wrong, but he also thought that they had a right to be so.

We might hope for a world where there is agreement and acceptance, but it will not be here in the near future. In the meantime we need to find ways of living alongside one another without destroying one another and without ignoring or trivializing our differences. This is the genius of toleration. Its task is not overcoming our differences, but establishing our right to differ.

---

27. Murray, *We Hold These Truths*, p. 45.

28. A good survey of some of the social science literature is given in John L. Sullivan, James Piereson, and George E. Marcus, *Political Tolerance and American Democracy* (Chicago, 1982), chaps. 1-2. In their survey they concluded that tolerance is best seen as a political concept, with roots in political ideology and in the norms of democracy. The authors also conclude from their own work that toleration does not correlate well with education nor, necessarily, with a variety of the usual psychological variables.

Christianity, Higher Education, and Socially Marginalized Voices

Lauree Hersch Meyer

Separation of church and state is integral to the legacy of the United States. Yet from our country's beginning higher education has been deeply engaged with the church. Christians founded and taught at the nation's first educational institutions: seminaries, colleges, academies, high schools, and grammar schools. At liberal arts colleges, Christianity has played a vital role. Chaplains have been part of many state and private school staffs. Christian citizens have often sought the well-being of the nation throughout its history, and citizens who were not Christian have regularly influenced, and been influenced by, Christianity. Separation theory and rhetoric notwithstanding, the reality of American history consists of an interwoven tapestry of church and state, religious and secular influences and movements.

Given the intertwined legacy of higher education with Christianity in North American history, I will address four points in this chapter. First, I identify some dynamics common to Christian faith and higher education. This includes a commitment that all people should have access to, and be served by, their institutions — and a tendency to expect obedience, conformity, and loyalty from those served. Second, I argue that to expect those served to abandon their distinctive identities upon entry to these institutions both undermines and mis-serves the traditional vision of both higher education and Christian faith. Third, I propose that engaging "misfits" who challenge our institutions and their conventional, traditional ways of thinking and being, far from endangering, actually serves both

Christianity and higher education. I conclude, fourth, with reflections on "tenuring God."

A Common Legacy:
The Commitment to Serve All People

For two millennia, Christians have borne witness to the Christian gospel, the *evangelium*, the good news that in Christ Jesus, God is renewing all creation. *All* creation. Scripture insists that divisions along lines of nationality, politics, or religion ("neither Jew nor Greek"), of ethnicity or class ("neither slave nor free"), and of gender ("neither male nor female") cease to matter for "all [who] are one in Christ Jesus" (Gal. 3:28). People "in Christ" experience the crumbling of various "dividing walls of hostility" normally separating people (Eph. 2:14). And this raises the question of whether we can truly be "in Christ" and yet harbor hostility in our hearts. Where dividing walls of hostility remain, when we honor divisions due to religion, class, or gender, is Christ absent?

Such questions are as critical for institutions of higher education as for the church. Both usually mirror the social structures and practices of the culture around them. In this nation, dividing walls of hostility fragment people precisely along ethnic, class, and gender lines — both in the church and in the academy. A subtext running through the church's story (with parallels in the academy) concerns the struggle to establish clear, hierarchical authority[1] and truth.[2] In much Western tradition, authority has been closely tied to holding church office, while truth has been viewed as knowledge gained through education.[3]

---

1. Debates about who and what was heretical, both in the church's early years and today, are also struggles about who has the authority to say what faith, order, and practice indicate that persons are "one in Christ Jesus."

2. "Truth," referring to the church's struggle from its beginning to this day to identify (the one) true faith, order, and practice. See particularly the World Council of Churches' Faith and Order documents *Baptism, Eucharist, and Ministry* and *Confessing the One Faith*.

3. The founding of "Sunday schools" to teach religious truth indicates that reason was assumed basic (more so than spirituality?) to discerning truth.

When the church became a powerful enough institution to define and control the boundaries of the faith and practices of its members, those who made unacceptable authority or truth claims lost favor and were condemned, demonized, banished, or killed as heretics, witches, and the like. That sad tradition continues when persons and groups marginal to contemporary church consensus suffer for seeking to be heard. Vocal dissenters are too often marginalized and their reputations demeaned. Yet throughout the church's history "marginalized" voices have often positively influenced public discourse about the acceptable shape of Christian faith.[4]

It comes as no surprise that similar phenomena are visible in the academy since Western higher education has believed that the good, the true, and the beautiful are one.[5] Those who deviate from or challenge the academic consensus are in trouble. More recent Western cultural beliefs also link good education with personal

---

4. Persecuting dissenters or persons not controlled by established church authorities became a pattern; nor did the church flinch at harsh treatment of those called "heretics" who deviated from its proclamation of true dogma. Different reasons were given for heresy hunts, crusades, reformations, and persecutions of the modern era, but demonizing, persecuting, or destroying those called evil was justified religiously, and they were to be excised from public social, political, and economic life. See Elaine Pagels, *The Origins of Satan* (New York: Random House, 1995), for careful historical research and scholarly discussion on the social dynamics used to locate "other" groups and popularize them as communal pariahs. Anne Llewellyn Barstow, *Witchcraze: A New History of the European Witch Hunts* (New York: HarperCollins Pandora, 1994), traces how church leaders' fear was engaged to create popular response that supported brutal social actions. Angela Tilby, *Soul: God, Self, and the New Cosmology* (New York: Doubleday, 1992), shows how dominant philosophical understandings of the Western tradition in various epochs shaped macro- and microcosmic cultural views on divinity, humankind, and science.

5. Tilby (*Soul*, p. 25) says that "early Christians were ambivalent about Greek science and philosophy." Bishop Cyril of Alexandria influenced the mob that "tortured to death one of the greatest astronomers and mathematicians of the fifth century, Hypatia" while moderates (in this matter) like Justin Martyr "insisted that whatever truths had been grasped by the philosophers 'belonged to us Christians.'" Augustine, who most influenced the Western tradition, explained how God, truth, and good were one; that human minds are unable to grasp *how* that was so, he added, merely illumined human reason's limitations.

happiness and vocational success. Authorities in educational and religious institutions also control access to the vocational futures of those who enter them. Higher education grants or withholds academic degrees, and the church does or does not ordain to ecclesial leadership. Yet the gender-imbalance among leaders in these institutions is among the worst in the United States. And those blessed by such authorities tend to mirror those doing the blessing.

Teachers and ministers alike are expected to be properly trained and of upright character. Teachers must excel in the methods, data, and skills recognized as valid by their fields so they may teach students what and how to learn. Ministers must be properly ordained and rightly interpret the one true faith, order, and practice of God's new creation in Christ Jesus. In practice, of course, neither scholars nor church leaders agree among themselves what methods and knowledge, or what beliefs and practices, *are* true. Arguments about what constitutes *good* education and what is *true* faith and practice are as vigorous as they are diverse.

Higher education constructs knowledge by a method that determines what questions, perspectives, and data matter. Since method determines what counts as knowledge, higher education today is flooded with methodological debates, often occurring between established and newly emerging or "marginal" voices. Recently published books feature groups of writers rarely before seen in print: women, African Americans, Native Americans, Hispanic Americans, Asian Americans, and others. Such "new" writers bring a fresh angle of vision; they who were formerly objects of writing now write as *subjects* who illumine previously invisible, hidden, silenced truths. As examples, consider history and ethics.

History taught in public schools usually presents the dominant group's story as true. Should questions arise, the goodness and moral character of its people are treated as more definitive than those of others. As a result, history faithful to African, Hispanic, Native American, or women's stories is now compelled to report painful truths previously absent from public knowledge, truths inaudible in "the" story being told, American or Christian or another.[6] Neither

---

6. Three *types* of (hi)story augment familiar work. First are books telling the unrecorded "underside" of familiar stories: see Howard Zinn, *A People's*

the stories of dominant or marginal peoples tells the *whole* truth; still, church and academy choose what voices to honor, to seek out and hear, to engage or disregard, to privilege or burden.

Like history, ethics is freshly cast when considered from mujerista, feminist, womanist, or "ethnic" perspectives. Relational concerns that deal with caring and community tend to be more central to women and "marginal" peoples than the universalizations and linear logic that characterized ethical thought oriented to *polis*-centered public life ethics.[7] Academic and popular bookshops now carry diverse "voices" or perspectives on history and ethics, and vast literature from novels to biblical studies, theology, spirituality, ethnography, psychology, sociology, anthropology, and so forth.

Western tradition's legacy of "universal" thinking and speaking is both a gift and a burden in higher education and Christianity today. The agonizing need for humankind to honor one another enough to communicate and to live in peace has proved a difficult challenge to which Christianity and higher education wish to contribute. Yet what we offer and how we offer it — reflecting our long tradition of "solving" others' problems by imposing our terms upon them — often demean and disregard the agency and values of those

---

History of the United States (New York: HarperPerennial, 1990). Second are volumes presenting data simply absent from most histories. Examples are Angie Debo, *A History of the Indians of the United States* (Norman: University of Oklahoma, 1970); Robert Allen Warrier, *Tribal Secrets: Recovering American Indian Intellectual Traditions* (Minneapolis: University of Minnesota, 1995); Karen Jo Torjesen, *When Women Were Priests: Women's Leadership in the Early Church and the Scandal of their Subordination in the Rise of Christianity* (San Francisco: Harper, 1993); Riane Eisler, *The Chalice and the Blade: Our History, Our Future* (San Francisco: Harper & Row, 1987); and Robert B. Coote and Mary P. Coote, *Power, Politics, and the Making of the Bible* (Minneapolis: Fortress, 1990). Third are histories written from the perspective of peoples usually viewed as history's objects rather than its subjects. An illustration is Eduardo Hoornaert, *The Memory of the Christian People* (Maryknoll, N.Y.: Orbis Books, 1988).

7. E.g., Nel Noddings, *Caring: A Feminine Approach to Ethics and Moral Education* (Berkeley: University of California Press, 1984) and *Women and Evil* (Berkeley: University of California Press, 1989); Katie G. Cannon, *Black Womanist Ethics* (Atlanta: Scholars Press, 1988); Barbara Hilkert Andolsen, Christine E. Gudorf, and Mary D. Pellauer, eds., *Women's Consciousness, Women's Conscience: A Reader in Feminist Ethics* (Minneapolis: Winston, 1985).

who live by a truth and a good different from ours.[8] Colonialism that requires same thought is coming to be rejected in much the same way as forcing people into slavery or imposing an alien culture and religion upon them. The cost of accepting another's values is subjecting the self to disincarnate faith and experience: abandoning one's self, tradition, culture, legacy, and voice in exchange for the promise of gaining something better, in and on the terms of another's culture.

Christianity and higher education face the challenge of embodying their traditional vision of universal truth in ways that honor people from diverse cultures and contexts. The question before us is how we shall hear and honor multiple voices, learn from and teach one another, graciously sharing common living space and activities while engaging and interpreting them from our rich variety of perspectives.

This broadening of the conversation is a difficult challenge for people who have been formed to identify with some "place" in the social, academic, moral, or religious hierarchy. Learning new behavior is so crucial and difficult that Deuteronomy describes gaining a new "heart" as a divine, inner gift of grace, not achievable through external laws of decency or desire.[9] But despite the difficulty of engaging as equals those whose unfamiliar ways we find painful, or those whom we resent or find difficult, both higher education and Christianity are committed to shaping human spirits. We shape our own spirits by exercising leadership with integrity. We shape others by incarnating our values in our behavior and creating structures wherein others experience success when they internalize those values.

8. H. Richard Niebuhr called "universalizing the particular" a theological sin because in rightly affirming one's own incarnate experience, understanding, and vision, one wrongly applies that (limited particular) to all situations, places, and people. Practically speaking, projecting one's confession onto another as normative truth is also heresy: One confuses one's limited heart and understanding with God's unlimited heart and understanding.

9. Moses called Israel to circumcise "the foreskin of your heart" (Deut. 10:16), later assuring Israel that "the Lord your God will circumcise your heart and the heart of your offspring so that you will love the Lord your God with all your heart and with all your soul, that you may live" (30:6).

Commitment to such formation means living what we believe in a way that fosters in those with whom we interact the spirit that we honor as good. Times of change always bring us against the limits of our formational beliefs. "Liberals" as well as "conservatives" in higher education and in the church have internalized hierarchical assumptions — for instance, that certain (types of) people have a "place" in the social order. Those with a higher place (audible in the "we" of "What should *we* do?") usually also have power to give or withhold benefits like degrees, privilege, and place.

"Backlash" emerges from a fundamental grief over disorientation, power loss, and diminished ability to grant or withhold privilege. People formed in classist societies know how to function in "their" place. Within their familiar classist structure, they can also imagine how one should function in a place superior or inferior to theirs. But they feel disoriented and lost in social arrangements that disregard familiar class distinctions. An exodus from domination is experienced as liberation by those who are set free — but it may reduce to angry hostility those who have lost social proof of their superiority. Members of both groups are refugees without adequate language, experience, or ability to navigate the contours of the new terrain. Grief and loss burden former owners while delight and hope energize former slaves. From different experiences they "create" different worlds.[10]

Much as method determines what counts as knowledge in higher education, cultural context and expectations shape what terms are experienced as life-giving and acceptable for Christian gospel proclamation. Education, *educare,* calls for leading or drawing persons out so that they may make meaningful lives. Similarly, *evangelium,* the gospel good news, proclaims that God is renewing all creation — always in specific, particular, incarnate contexts.

10. Classist hierarchies prevail in most contemporary cultures: top social status is usually enjoyed by white males. Privilege then moves "down" to white females, males of color, and females of color. Further subdivisions of rank exist among different peoples of color or ethnic groups. People raised to identify with the heirs-apparent to privilege (notably white males) are more apt to feel threatened and/or become hostile when change recasts the norms governing who receives privilege or power.

Social Location and Power:
Mainline and Marginal Voices

Our nation, our society, and our world are undergoing a social upheaval restructuring the economic, cultural, political, and religious shape of human communities.[11] After the upheaval of World War II, vast energy was directed toward correcting some global and national social injustices. "Liberal" people and institutions advocated for and made common cause with marginalized, colonized, poor, and dispossessed peoples. Recognizing the deep prejudice and hostility internalized by people in our nation, leaders sought legal support to assure such human rights as equal access to public transportation, shops, schools, jobs, vocations, and other socioeconomic opportunities. Many knew that while laws could not change hearts, just behavior could be required even of bitter hearts.

Educational and religious leaders pressed the nation to embody the American equal opportunity myth. A world was envisioned in which the evils of prejudice, brutality, and hostility might wither away as legal structures of inequity were replaced by legally protected access to equal opportunity. It is now clear that those laws failed to give birth to the vision of a changed society. Even those who gained entry into the equal opportunity world remained subject to classist values.

Mainstream institutions helped birth the self-consciousness of marginal peoples — though the latter came to realize that dependence in some form was the normal price for receiving a "better place" in the equality franchise. Nevertheless, thoughtful examination of reality and reflection on experience "raised the consciousness" of many who were viewed as socially, morally, culturally, or in some other way inferior. Among groups considered "marginal" (e.g., African-, Native-, Hispanic-, and Asian-Americans, as well as women, gays, lesbians, bisexuals, the differently abled), many per-

11. See Tilby, *Soul*, and Jacob Neusner, *Self-Fulfilling Prophecy: Exile and Return in the History of Judaism* (Boston: Beacon, 1987). Tilby tracks major cultural shifts in Western economics and philosophy, noting how those shifts influenced Christian life and thought. Neusner discusses how Judaism's religio-socio-political self-understanding changed by epochs each time Jewish experience significantly changed.

sons reassessed and then turned away from the equality star they once followed. Many became convinced that "equality" was but a doubtful reward for good behavior controlled by those in power. They faced a new choice: whether to compete with one another to please those in power for whatever spaces might be opened for "others" — or to enter the unfamiliar terrain of discerning and then publicly expressing their own minds and hearts, knowing the uncertainties of such a choice.

Many persons identified with marginal groups chose risky freedom independent of patrimony.[12] Previously invisible, silent people began speaking from their own experience, in their own voice, saying, for one thing, that their socially inferior status was invalid. They knew their inferiority was not "the way things are," but a social construction that served those who control power. Socially marginal people saw how those among them who got good jobs felt pressured to "cross over," to identify or align with authority-holder benefactors and to distance themselves internally from their people. Yet those who identified with their benefactors usually became isolated and lonely: They rarely acquired sufficient power to become peers with those to whom they owed their new status, and they were often alienated from their community of origin. The price of achievement seemed to be anger, isolation, shame, self-betrayal.

Although in a dominance-subordinance hierarchy, marginal peoples were ranked by alien cultural measures and they learned that no one could remove from them the freedom to reject dependence and to behave as spiritual peers. Some who were marginal to the nation's social franchise believed the price of participation in the "center" to be dependence and identity loss that undermined spiritual integrity and power, and found that price too high. Being "inside" mainstream social structures in return for receiving faint praise and material perks at the price of relinquishing one's histori-

---

12. The terms "marginal" and "mainstream" are problematic in that peoples who honor themselves and their communal identity all think from their center, creating as many mainstreams and margins as there are peoples with clear identity. The terms are also perspectival: e.g., peoples who are economically marginal becoming numerically dominant though not socially mainstream.

cal identity and values was too costly. In the price of social enfran-
chisement, intellectual or religious obedience and loyalty, they recognized a subtle but powerful form of cultural slavery. Depending
on the favor of those advantaged in public life meant risking loss
of privilege unless they continued to please. Seeking identity meant
inquiring into identity "roots" and the shape of integrity.

Thinkers who honored their lives-in-context without demonizing others saw that all thought is based on experience. This insight
gave rise to a new question: *Whose* experience informs what one
believes normative? Marginal people, like mainline people, preferred living from their own values and choosing when to challenge
actions that demeaned them. No longer was their mantra "How
can we make it?" A new question — "What are my goals and intent?" — often led to self-affirming identity, speaking in their own
voice, finding and cherishing their spiritual legacy, and nurturing
interpersonal and communal well-being.

People from marginalized groups gained an excellent education, took good jobs, and remained connected with families, friends,
and communities who remained "stuck." Newly freed voices with
novel questions and perspectives gave rise to new literature and
academic disciplines. Many particular truths danced together where
the myth of one universal truth once dominated perception. People
spoke their own story, interpretation, and appropriation as the
marginalized groups' voices spoke out alongside of those in socially
dominant positions. Diverse voices began to emerge from people
often thought of as a monistic unit. As the myth that equality has
a universal face collapsed, it gave birth to commitments to engage,
rather than to hide from or simply to accept one's situation — to
learn one's legacy and voice, to exercise one's authority and vision,
and to intentionally shape one's identity.

As marginal peoples take initiative to exercise their identity
and spiritual power, previously dominant educational and religious
communities must choose how to respond to this enormous be-
havioral paradigm shift. One measure of how difficult this has been
is that mainstream people now complain of *not* being heard!
Genuine empowerment of marginalized peoples results in their
speaking for themselves, including challenging mentors' academic
methodologies and/or religious values. Resistance remains to open-

ing the social, intellectual, and religious franchise to riffraff.[13] Backlash is sometimes energetically mounted, and financial support arranged, to undermine those thought to challenge existing structures.[14] The question is: Who decides who "should" have a voice, who "should" speak and be heard, whose view "should" be valued? How, and by what (whose) criteria are such decisions made? Since the socially and politically marginal often endanger themselves if they speak openly and publicly, of what significance is it that people speak and act, hear and engage, when their voice is not valued or they are demeaned? More specifically, what is the relation of Christianity and higher education to marginalized voices?

Learning from Marginalized Voices

Leaders in institutions of higher education and the church often refer to people who challenge them as trouble-makers, irritants, misfits. Yet the historical vision and mission of both institutions suggest that "misfits" are central to their legacies. God-with-us in the biblical story was regularly present in misfits who provided life-giving sustenance for the spirit's growth and faith's transformation. Eccentric thinkers have often proved over time to have given brilliant insights to the world of learning. As Christian faith is incarnational, an understanding of "misfits" is the theological key to an understanding of God and self, and illumines one's psychological and spiritual life as well.

Commitment to live faith means engaging internalized contradictions and tensions and choosing whether and/or how to take responsibility for them. For example, if I wish to grow spiritually while harboring hostility in my heart, I am at a spiritual crossroads. My proclaimed intent is at odds with the spirit I keep alive in my heart. I may overlook, deny, excuse, reinterpret, or blame my inter-

---

13. The term is taken from Donald Dayton's article, "Yet Another Layer of the Onion: Or Opening the Ecumenical Door to Let the Riffraff In," *Ecumenical Review* 40 (Jan. 1988).

14. See Susan Faludi, *Backlash: The Undeclared War against American Women* (New York: Crown, 1991), for unnerving specifics.

nalized fragmentation on someone or something else. All of these moves (perhaps unintentionally but, in fact, really) nurture the growth of hostility in me. On the other hand, I may recognize and acknowledge my inner tension, fear, fragmentation, and anger, accepting them as worthy adversaries capable of teaching me the contours of my inmost spirit.

My intent guides my attitudes, behavior, and understandings. I open my heart to the spirit or spirits or Spirit that I embrace. My intent is basic; it is not simply what I wish for, desire, am drawn to, or how I think things should be. My intent is my choice to take responsibility for my behavior and belief. If my intent is to learn from and honor all whom God loves, my feelings of inner discomfort with or resistance toward misfits or marginal people put me on notice to examine the match between my feelings and actions and my educational understandings and theological confessions.[15]

I find my confessions far easier to speak than to live. Yet lived faith is central in higher education and Christianity, as is affirmation of change and a tenacious hold to continuity.[16] On one hand, the continuous curriculum revisions of higher education and Christianity's trail of reformations bear witness that both expect renewal to arise in the exquisite diversity of particular experience. Neither accepts a "one-size-fits-all" universal view of truth. Yet, on the other hand, people entrusted with places of privilege are often offended when their actions, vision, leadership, or perspectives are ignored

15. I believe that "misfits" are not genetically "born" so much as communally created: as lives are shaped by suffering, twisted by anguish, demeaned by hostility, and limited by pain. Yet misfits have spiritual resources not limited to or shaped by the spirit prevailing in the society that dominates their social experience. I wrote a brief confession to clarify my faith understanding relative to misfits: I confess

- that I tend to view and/or treat others as misfits when I feel concern for my safety, status, or "place" in existing psychospiritual, politico-religious, and/or sociocultural arenas;
- that God loves people I dislike, resist, find irritating; is incarnate in people I reject; and addresses me in and through people I judge; and
- that people and communities "create" misfits "in the image" of their internalized experiences and self-perceptions.

16. Not so stability. Indeed, an ancient spiritual and ethical challenge is to discern how things become more what they are as they change.

or resisted. Those who raise critical questions but lack social power are apt to pay for their independence by being dishonored or scapegoated.[17]

Leaders in higher education and Christianity are called to be open to new experience, new understanding, and new realities because we cherish inquiry and curiosity, and because we worship a God who cherishes all people and all creation. A legacy central to both religious faith and educational growth is that the finest leaders embody as well as teach the strength and compassion of global citizens. We seek leaders with the inner confidence, power, and freedom to cherish as companions precisely those people who may struggle with, irritate, or alienate many. We expect leaders to affirm people who press up to, and beyond, familiar intellectual or spiritual terrain into discomforting arenas. Teachers in higher education want to hear, examine, and understand unfamiliar methods, perspectives, views, data, and values carefully so as to more fully know truth and understand reality. Christians want to love as God loves, to live as members of God's body in this time and place.[18] Thus educators and believers seek fuller understanding and life — daily reimagining reality as we walk in others' shoes, see through others' eyes, hear with others' ears, and engage that life and reality which opens us more fully to God's amazing, whole truth.

Should God Get Tenure? Constructing Identity

One who honors another without being honored in turn, suffers. To be denied access to the normative (i.e., socially dominant) economic, educational, religious, or social franchise is a harsh, painful aspect of such suffering. Those seen as apart from, rather than a part of, society's dominant group face a painful choice. They may

17. Cf. as illustrations Rene Girard, *The Scapegoat* (Baltimore: Johns Hopkins University Press, 1986); Raymund Schwager, S.J., *Must There Be Scapegoats? Violence and Redemption in the Bible* (San Francisco: Harper & Row, 1987); Pagels, *Origins of Satan*; and Riane Eisler, *Sacred Pleasure* (San Francisco: Harper, 1995).

18. Roberta Bondi chose to title her book, learning from early Christians seeking to live God's presence on earth, *To Love as God Loves: Conversations with the Early Church* (Philadelphia: Fortress, 1987).

affiliate with the dominant group, of which they can never be a genuine part (unless that dominant identity and behavior changes); or they may deepen inner identity with their "own" group and remain spiritual "resident aliens" to the dynamics, values, and structures of dominant religious, social, and cultural bodies.[19] If the pain is great enough, members of nondominant groups may try to "make it" on others' terms, but then feel spiritually closeted for accepting a life that demeans their legacy and identity.

Desire to be accepted easily leads people from marginal communities to thinking they may "get ahead" if they identify with the dominant culture. The "good" is then reduced to material benefits, and a harsh choice between seeking acceptance or being demeaned seems unavoidable. Both higher education and Christianity betray themselves when they contribute to the sense that such a choice is necessary. As an "incarnate" faith, Christianity bears witness that God is alive in all people and in each age and place. God looks as they do, speaks their language, is subject to their experiences, feels their joys and anguish, suffers their "fate."

Whether or not we think God should get tenure in institutions of higher education, the Christian song of salvation says that God already *has* tenure in human life. God's ineludible presence with us is our source of life and breath, of pleasure and joy, of hope and compassion. The name of the human capacity for love and faithfulness, for transformation and forgiveness, for mutual care and changing our minds and hearts, for new possibilities, new beginnings, new life, is God. Even when leaders or institutions betray themselves and live by control and abuse rather than by compassion and faith, God's divine energy indwells the clay vessels of ordinary lives and multiple cultures.

Alongside the legacy that God is present with and for all is a cultural legacy that identifies God as with "us" and against or apart from "them," demonizing the "other."[20] Socially marginal persons

19. This was St. Augustine's name for Christians, whom, if in their hearts they were citizens of heaven, he saw as residents yet aliens in earthly life.

20. In *Origins of Satan*, Pagels traces changes in how hostility towards "others" was expressed in the Bible, and shaped communities influenced by biblical faith.

and groups who internalize such demeaning cultural attitudes learn to hate, betray, and harm themselves and others.[21] Similarly, the values, legacy, and identity of Christians and leaders in higher education may be at risk. For example, those in higher education may identify competitive capitalist professional success with goodness; church language and iconography may, in imaging God as white and male, reinforce social assumptions that it is white males' "place" to hold positions of greater authority and power than people of color or women.

Inasmuch as identity is socially constructed, it is "created" as people and groups internalize specific experiences and self-understandings as social, religious, political, cultural, class, and gendered beings. People do indeed identify with and/or against a particular nation, class, race, gender, religion, church, theology, ethics, biblical understanding, and so forth. But higher education and Christianity are committed to nurture in people the delight, courage, clarity, and compassion to live without honoring or obeying dividing walls of hostility, protective hierarchical structures, or self-protection that demeans persons and groups who challenge their values. "Tenuring" God is integral to our mutual legacy, as God is the source and end who values and calls us to value all people.

Addendum

I value misfits. My biblically schooled faith knows that God-with-us as Jesus was a social and religious misfit who associated with misfits. It was largely misfits who believed he rose from death. Since we justify how we treat others by referring to our views of God, confessing that God restores and makes us whole in Jesus raises the question of whether we believe Jesus is today bodily present in God's "Kindom" (Ada Maria Isasi-Diaz's word echoing God's gracious non-hierarchical authority and life-giving blessing with and for all humankind).

Where God is with us, God's incarnate misfit Jesus is likely to

---

21. See particularly Arno Gruen, *The Betrayal of the Self* (New York: Grove Press, 1988), and *The Insanity of Normality* (New York: Grove Press, 1992).

challenge believers now as then. And then as now, people who identify with misfits are apt to be seen and treated as misfits. Liberation theologians remind us that God is present in the faces of the poor and abused; God is suffering in the lives of people battered or demeaned; God is denied in people hated or scorned; God is incarnate in those on life's "undersides." My discomfort quickly finds a voice: There are plenty of misfits utterly *unlike* Jesus. Indeed. But asking whether God always, or never, acts in misfits changes the subject so that we can avoid asking whether dislikable misfits are life-giving faces of God-with-us.

Discussing misfits inclines us to judge others rather than to ask how to recognize God's presence when faced with unexpected, alien, and repugnant situations — such as the one Mary and Joseph faced expecting Jesus' painfully timely birth. "Son of God" was not written on Jesus' forehead any more than we find "member of Christ's body" written on those who appear as moral or religious misfits.

My Church of the Brethren legacy, like Scripture, is replete with stories of divine misfits. Protestants and Catholics alike considered us heretics and cooperated to destroy us. During the Revolutionary and Civil wars, as pacifists we again misfit our neighbors' religious values and were judged disloyal. I believe that God is present in many people my church and nation dub misfits. At times I fear saying so publicly, lest I be associated with "them." Then I think of Nicodemus who came to Jesus by night. Or of the Danish king who, when Hitler invaded and commanded Jews to wear a yellow star to identify themselves, was next seen with a yellow star on his clothing. Then the populace did likewise, and Denmark was the only country where Jews were not taken by droves to the camps and ovens.

Higher education and Christianity rightly seek for integrity and truth. It is a task that requires tenacity, strength, and courageous willingness to examine even what we always took for granted. Religious people know God transcends our understanding and continuously calls us to be converted, to reform our views and actions, to be(come) a new creation. Educated people know what we perceive as true is limited, dependent on our angle of vision, our lived context, experience, and formation: our unspoken assumptions, starting points, assumptions about understanding self, other, God. *How* Jesus Christ is experienced in higher education influences whether God "gets tenure" in our lives. People's experiences with church leaders and with administration, faculty, and staff in higher education in turn indicate what kind of God is tenured in our hearts.

Diversity, Christianity, and Higher Education

Robert G. Clouse

Diversity and multiculturalism are among the hottest topics in higher education today — right up there with the cost of tuition. All too often, however, the debate about diversity has become contentious and polarized. There are good human, political, and theological reasons to reform higher education in the direction of greater openness, receptivity, and respect for other voices. Unfortunately, many currents in the push for diversity risk becoming as oppressive as the regime they wish to replace. How we define diversity and how we ground our arguments and reforms will, in the end, decide whether we will achieve an authentic and constructive result.

Recently a professor of education at a midwestern university challenged the academy by pointing out that

> The historic response of dumping everyone into a simmering melting pot intended to boil us down into a common essence is being challenged. Research findings suggest that many students from African-American, Spanish-speaking American, Native American, and certain Asian-American populations are receiving a substandard education that does not meet their needs or empower them to participate fully and equally in the emerging global community of the twenty-first century. The initiatives which focused on holidays, heroes, and other superficial aspects of cultural diversity have been replaced by affirmative action. This aggressive

103

pursuit of diversity has resulted in cries of reverse discrimination by whites as well as deepening polarization along racial and ethnic lines among people of color. This phenomenon brings us to an important question: If the academic community cannot overcome the social and intellectual separations that currently influence the quality of campus life, what then can we expect from society at large?[1]

The crisis brought on by diversity, to which she refers, has challenged the entire spectrum of university opinion. Conservatives and traditionalists attack liberals for their thinking and their betrayal of historic university ideals. A writer on the left has indicated that conservatives view every radical suggestion no matter how trivial or ephemeral as the coming of the four new horse riders of the Apocalypse — Speech Codes, Multiculturalism, Sexual Correctness, and Affirmative Action.[2] Those on the left point out that conservatives have certainly become late converts to First Amendment rights in the light of their history of McCarthyism and censuring of radical thought and action on the campuses.

Diversity and Its Critics

Christianity, one hopes, can offer a more moderate and kindly approach to this highly charged debate. Before one can propose a more balanced view, however, it is necessary to trace the development of the diversity controversy. The situation was brought to national attention by the best-selling book, *Illiberal Education: The Politics of Race and Sex on Campus,* written by Dinesh D'Souza.[3]

1. W. 'Dene Andrews, "Visions and Illusions of Accepting and Celebrating Ethnic Diversity," *Contemporary Education* 67 (Fall 1995): 4.
2. See John K. Wilson, *The Myth of Political Correctness* (Durham: Duke University Press, 1995), esp. pp. 1-62.
3. D'Souza, *Illiberal Education: The Politics of Race and Sex on Campus* (New York: Free Press, 1991). By having his book excerpted in *The Atlantic Monthly* D'Souza avoided the conservative label, but his earlier highly laudatory *Falwell, Before the Millennium: A Critical Biography* (Chicago: Regnery Gateway, 1984) certainly demonstrates his extreme right-wing bias.

Politicians such as George Bush, popular magazines including *Newsweek*, TV news-talk shows, and the editorial pages of major newspapers joined in denouncing what they felt were dangerous new attitudes and teachings on the nation's campuses.

Most of the early attacks on diversity were made by neoconservatives, but liberals and many individuals on the left later joined them. They believed that a new postmodern generation from the 1960s had taken control of the major American universities by promoting a radical ideology that condemned Western civilization as oppressive, prejudiced, and reactionary. This new view began in the field of art by undermining standards of quality and taste. Later it was taken up by postmodernist professors in the humanities and literature departments. Conservatives believed that these individuals reduced literary studies to political questions and matters of gender. They encouraged their students to read cheap, ephemeral works that promote Marxism rather than read the great masterpieces of literature.

The diversity or multicultural approach is not confined to the classroom but is forced on everyone in the university. In order to be a sensitive person one must adopt the speech and behavior of the postmodern radicals or else be denounced as a sexist or racist. Professors outside of this movement must be very careful not to call people "Indians" but rather "Native Americans" and "women" must never be referred to as "ladies" or "girls."[4]

New curricular developments resulted from the emphasis on diversity, especially Afrocentrism, which traces most of the major achievements in human civilization to Africa. When extended to the story of other minorities this approach began to wear down the bonds that hold American society together.[5] This emphasis on minority cultures also puts in question the way different people learn. Certain "learning styles" are appropriate to particular ethnic or racial groups and cannot be used by others. For example,

4. For a hilarious look at this "newspeak" note H. Beard and C. Cerf, *The Official Politically Correct Dictionary and Handbook* (New York: Villard Books, 1992).

5. For a brilliant substantiation of this charge see Arthur M. Schlesinger, Jr., *The Disuniting of America* (New York: W. W. Norton & Co., 1992).

European or Western thought and language is basically inadequate for women and non-Western minorities because it is phallocentric, racist, competitive, and scientific. Above all, students of other cultures are to think well of themselves, because if a person has adequate self-esteem he or she can excel at most tasks.[6]

It is difficult to express in a succinct manner all that is included in the multicultural and diversity creed. This is due to the origin of these ideas in the works of several French writers such as Jacques Derrida, Michel Foucault, Jacques Lacan, Pierre Bourdieu, and Claude Levi-Strauss. Drawing on thinkers as diverse as Marx, Nietsche, and Freud, these scholars taught that the individual is not free to make his or her own decisions but rather is under the control of hidden, giant, impersonal structures. The major force that permeates everything is language. We fool ourselves by believing that language is a tool, for, in reality, it is our master and we are the tools. Perhaps if one recognizes the existence and power of structures, it would be possible to overthrow them in an apocalyptic moment. A feeling of millenarian expectancy permeates these ideas.

French radical thought came to America at an opportune time because the revolt against liberalism in the 1960s needed an ideology. American radicalism was essentially a practical, rather than a theoretical, reaction to the "liberal" war in Vietnam and to a growing conviction that traditional liberalism could never solve the problems of African-Americans. Radicals turned away from liberal democracy and the labor union movement. They focused instead on "identity politics" and formed organizations for women's rights, for various ethnic revivals including black nationalism, and for gay and lesbian liberation. Although this radical left faded in the 1970s, these identity political groups remained. They proved to be quite

6. As one author points out, "In fact, the relationship between self-esteem and achievement might almost be inverse — 'almost' because a serious lack of self-esteem leads nowhere. Yet insecurity and self-doubts also stoke achievement and hard work; and they place self-esteem on a real basis. The relationship between self-esteem and achievement may, at the very least, be reciprocal. The way to achieve self-esteem is through skills and accomplishments, not through self-esteem workshops and lectures." Russell Jacoby, *Dogmatic Wisdom: How the Culture Wars Divert Education and Distract America* (New York: Anchor Books, 1995), p. 89.

adaptable and were able to find a political home in the Democratic Party, thus becoming part of the general culture.

Through footholds in the humanities departments of a number of major universities during the 1970s and 1980s, these French ideas were adopted by those who believed in identity politics. This resulted in a belief that in cultural affairs the most important way to classify individuals is by gender, race, and ethnicity. Thus one person is defined as a white male, someone else is a Latino lesbian, while a third is an Asian female.[7] With this general framework in mind they adopted, from Derrida, the idea that language and literature determine the nature of society and, from Foucault, that cultural change is a way to achieve political power. From Marxism came the view that marginal social groups can lead the general society to beneficial change. Lacan and the Freudians encouraged these radicals to emphasize the erotic and male domination. Third World writers led them to a bias against Western culture.

As one writer summarized this union of French and American radical thought:

> Voila: the great new melange. Its name is, or ought to be, "race/class/gender-ism," since "race, class, and gender" is the phrase that dominates its analyses. . . .
>
> It pictures culture and language as the giant hidden structure that permeates life. But culture and language are themselves only reflections of various social groups, which are defined by race, gender, and sexual orientation. (The word "class" is invoked only for the purpose of conjuring a slight aura of Marxism.) Groups, not individuals, produce culture. Every group has its own culture, or would, if oppressors didn't get in the way. Thus we have the

7. The ridiculous lengths to which this can be taken include, "A feminist professor [who] identifies herself as a woman, a teacher, a daughter, a mother, a feminist (should I add a heterosexual, a Jew, an immigrant, middle class, an only child, a mother of sons?), within the institutions of patriarchy, of motherhood, of literary studies, of feminist studies, of the university in the United States (should I add of marriage, of divorce, of the Ivy League, of Comparative Literature and French Studies, of the development of Women's Studies?). A person becomes a series of groups, less an individual than twenty agendas." Jacoby, *Dogmatic Wisdom*, p. 145.

cultures of white men, of black men, of women, of black women, of homosexuals, of Hispanic women.

The different cultures are engaged in a struggle for power. The culture of white males (specified . . . most popularly as Dead White European Males or DWEMs) has pretty much won this struggle, and thus has achieved domination over the rest of the world. But by shining the light of race/class/gender analysis upon it, this success can be revealed as the power play that it is. . . .

The American idea even offers something of the old Apocalyptic spirit . . . the feeling that a new intellectual revolution is at hand, something monumental like the invention of modern physics at the beginning of the century.[8]

Institutionalizing Diversity

It is difficult to determine just how widespread these teachings are in American academic life. However, they have become an official part of most institutions through an organized multiculturalist bureaucracy including assistant deans, assistant provosts, diversity directors, social equity programmers, and affirmative action officers who monitor the institutions and hold seminars and programs on diversity. They are trained in psychology, social work, and education and use a vocabulary that includes expressions like "internalized oppression" and "psychological captivity" and words such as "problematize" and "impact" (as in " 'white culture' negatively impacts the lives of people of color").

Diversity leaders have been given great influence by certain interpretations of the law. They claim to believe in "equal employment opportunity," yet they emphasize affirmative action to such an extent that it leads to setting of quotas for the hiring of women and minorities, thus making it nearly impossible for a white male to be selected. This attitude has tainted the civil rights movement and has even been accepted by such prestigious leaders as the late Thurgood Marshall, who replied to the argument that discrimina-

8. Paul Berman, *Debating P.C.: The Controversy over Political Correctness on College Campuses* (New York: Dell, 1992), pp. 14-15.

tion against whites was just as unconstitutional as discrimination against African-Americans with the comment, "You guys have been practicing discrimination for years. Now it is our turn."[9]

The actions of diversity bureaucrats extend to almost every aspect of campus life and lead to a coercive environment. Several examples of such activities on one university campus were noted by the editor of a well-known educational journal. They included the condemnation of a professor for mentioning Christianity in her class, charges of "sexual harassment" against a professor for displaying old motion picture advertisements on the office wall, complaints that another professor used the term "rug rats" when referring to children, the citing of an administrator for asking a candidate for a flex-time clerical position as to exactly what hours she would be able to work, and the admonishing of another administrator for having a copy of a Christian book on moral development on his shelf.[10] The editor might have added that on the same campus the Affirmative Action Officer has tried to ban the mention of Christian holidays such as Christmas or Easter and symbols of the seasons such as Christmas trees and even Santa Claus.

Exclusion, Division, and Relativism

Incidents such as these reveal a basic anti-Christian bias in the diversity movement. Perhaps this is because of the exclusive claims of the gospel (John 14:6; Acts 4:12), or the identification of Christianity with Western civilization. The prejudice against Christianity on the part of the multiculturalists is unfortunate because of their reliance on Western Christian ethical ideals of human dignity. In fact, by denying their intellectual and moral debt to the Western

---

9. Quoted by Lillian and Oscar Handlin in "America and Its Discontents, a Great Society Legacy," *The American Scholar* 64 (Winter 1995): 29. If this were only an isolated cynical remark by an individual in his dotage it could be forgotten, but attitudes such as this have actually caused research to be hampered. See Sandra Scarr, "Race and Gender as Psychological Variables," *American Psychologist* 43 (Jan. 1988): 56-59.

10. These instances are cited in David A. Gilman, "Politically Correct Meets Death by Cheeseburger," *Contemporary Education* 67 (Winter 1995): 68-69.

outlook they fail to fulfill their goal to respect and cherish what is valuable in all cultural groups. The diversity perspective seldom awards the same respect to the majority American culture that it demands for minority groups. Thus one reads statements such as: "Racism is a basic and integral part of U.S. life and . . . all Whites are racist whether knowingly or unknowingly."[11] These assertions are seldom qualified by the recognition that racism and ethnocentrism are commonly found in all cultural groups and therefore present a challenge to the entire human community.

Another problem associated with the multicultural approach is its paradoxical emphasis on increasing the distance between ethnic groups by demanding separate college dorms and eating areas. Reacting against the melting-pot ideology of assimilation, proponents feel that intercultural distance is necessary because of fear that the Western European culture will overwhelm minority groups. Yet this isolation undermines the dialogue that is supposed to enrich life for everyone. For how can one's outlook be enriched by others' points of view if constant defense is necessary against real or imagined threats? Such an attitude loses sight of the power of minority cultures to define themselves and to influence the main culture. Two examples of this in recent American history include the widespread acceptance of African-American jazz, blues, and spiritual music and the importance of Native-American inspiration for the environmental movement.

A further difficulty with multiculturalism comes from its insistence that all cultures be recognized for their unique and equally valuable contribution to humanity. Although on the face of it this appears to be a commendable goal, some cultures may not deserve respect. Shall we affirm the Serbian Nationalists who engage in ethnic cleansing or the ethnic slaughter in Rwanda? Ever since the Holocaust it is clear to most people that there are cultures and nations such as the Third Reich whose internal workings are evil.

As two eminent psychologists recently pointed out, "What would multiculturalism recommend in response to practices such as involuntary virginity tests in Turkey or 'female circumcision' in

11. D. W. Sue and S. Sue, *Counseling the Culturally Different* (New York: Wiley, 1990), p. 113.

Africa? If we . . . tolerate these practices in the name of the dignity we wish to accord another culture, we seem to condone the subjugation and brutalization of women. If we condemn such practices as inhuman and insist that they be stopped on the basis of supporting human dignity and basic human rights, we are clearly imposing our standards of behavior on them. . . . Multiculturalism seems to be impaled on both horns of this dilemma, for many cultures' ideas about human rights and dignity are not even remotely similar to ours."[12]

This leads to the recognition of a crucial, self-defeating aspect of multiculturalism, namely, its futile attempt to combine relativism with basic ethical principles. The equality of all cultures necessitates a radical relativism in which each culture can be understood only in its own terms. This neutrality seems to require the abandoning of any standard with which to judge other cultures. At the same time, diversity relies on certain universal principles such as respect, equality, and tolerance to insure the integrity of cultures. These values cannot be defended from a relativistic point of view. In fact, many religious and communitarian groups find relativism destructive to their culture. "The Amish, Hasidic Jews, and other well-defined subgroups in our society could not tolerate the view that the identity of their subculture is merely another expression of human diversity — unique, but no more or less valid than any other. Their sense of deep commitment and mission would be impossible without seeing their way of life as clearly superior in a moral and spiritual sense."[13]

However, in recognizing the above problems one must not move too far in the neoconservative direction, because that can lead to a materialistic, worldly success orientation that is as foreign to true Christianity as are many of the goals of the multiculturalists. As historian Russell Jacoby points out:

> The Free Enterprise Institute, the American Heritage Foundation, and the Olin Foundation all fund the conservative education critics; and the foundations bless the free enterprise system.

12. B. J. Fowers and F. C. Richardson, "Why Is Multiculturalism Good?" *American Psychologist* (June 1996): 51, 615.
13. Fowers and Richardson, "Why Is Multiculturalism Good?" p. 616.

Students get the same message everywhere: go for the money
. . . the steady dismantling of the curriculum is an old story. It
predates leftist professors and feminist theorists. It has more to
do with the professionalization of labor, consumerism, utilitari-
anism, and market forces. Earlier conservatives, less enamored
with capitalism, knew this. More recent conservatives are not only
more timid but more ambivalent; they worship the market and
bemoan the education it engenders. They blast BMW radicals, not
a BMW society.[14]

A Christian Alternative

Despite the condemnation of Christianity by numerous diversity
spokespersons, the faith is admirably suited to support a genuine
multiculturalism. Although it began in the Middle East and has
spread to Western Europe, Christianity is really based on a personal
relationship with Jesus Christ that exists independently of any
philosophy or ideology. When the early Church Fathers needed to
defend their faith from attacks by pagans they used the concepts
and categories of Greek thought. These have been elaborated
through the years by theologians and scholars of the faith, but there
is nothing inherent in the Christian message that demands an
Aristotelian approach. One need not identify the liberating, global,
cosmic Christ with DWEMS! In fact the Apostle Paul suggested that
in Christ neither race or nationality nor gender or social class should
make any difference (Gal. 3:28). One can express the faith in a great
variety of ways.

It is not necessary to accept all of the practical consequences
or the philosophical basis of the modern diversity movement to
agree with some of its basic points. Christians should realize that
it is wrong to exclude people because of gender, ethnicity, and race
from decision-making roles in society. Because of love for our neighbors we should recognize the common humanity shared by all
groups. The prophecies of the Old Testament and their reflection
in the visions of John indicate that people who follow Christ from

14. Jacoby, *Dogmatic Wisdom*, p. 11.

every tribe and nation will be part of the kingdom of God (Isa. 66:18; Joel 3:23; Rev. 5:9; 21:24).

It is the believer's duty to anticipate this final glory as much as possible in today's world. Thus there is much within multiculturalism that ought to be affirmed. For example, the countercultural analysis of history is often more accurate than conservative critics care to admit. African-Americans, Native Americans, other minorities, and women have too often been subjected to slavery, genocide, rape, and cruel oppression. Their voices have been ignored, their contributions overlooked. These things should not have happened according to the standards of Western European Christian culture. The tragedy is that often such activities have been blessed with a text or a shrug of indifference by the Christian church.

This is in sharp contrast to the attitude of Jesus who, as sociologist Stan Gaede points out, "lived in a world of differences, a world where bigotry and hatred and injustice ran rampant. And how did he respond? His approach to the Samaritan woman at the well was typical. In talking with her, he crossed all kinds of cultural boundaries. He was a man who shouldn't have been talking with a woman. He was a Jew who shouldn't have been involved with a Samaritan. He was a religious teacher — a rabbi — who shouldn't have been seen with a sinner. Yet he crossed all these barriers to talk with her, to include her in his world."[15]

Some of the apostles reluctantly followed their Lord in this new multicultural approach. Peter, for example, had to be challenged by a vision to go to the Gentile Cornelius' home and share the gospel with him (Acts 10). However, Paul more eagerly embraced the mission to the Gentiles. As the church developed it came to include individuals from all of the various racial groups in the Empire, and they formed a corporate unity. Despite this unity an individualism still existed, because admittance to the group was through a personal commitment to Christ. This diversity within a

---

15. S. D. Gaede, *When Tolerance Is No Virtue: Political Correctness, Multiculturalism and the Future of Truth and Justice* (Downers Grove, Ill.: InterVarsity Press, 1993), p. 60. Note also the thoughtful study by a leading evangelical, Tom Sine, *Cease Fire: Searching for Sanity in America's Culture Wars* (Grand Rapids: Eerdmans, 1995).

unity is one of the marvelous paradoxes of the faith. The church to which the early followers of our Lord ministered was part of a group that extends through all ages to the consummation and that consists of people of all colors, sizes, and ages; women and men, speaking different languages, following different cultures but all worshiping the same Lord.

Such an outlook has important consequences for the entire society. For example, Paul joined Jesus in shattering social norms when he sent Onesimus the slave back to his master "no longer as a slave, but better than a slave, as a dear brother" (Philem. 16). In essence he was encouraging Philemon to take a social revolutionary action and free Onesimus.

Perhaps the clearest passage in Scripture that calls Christians to multicultural action is the remarkable address of the Apostle Paul to the Athenians (Acts 17:22-31). Athens was the most racially, ethnically, and culturally diverse city in the Roman Empire. Paul addressed the question of their differences in the sight of God and emphasized four points. First, he affirmed the unity of humanity because God is the Creator, Sustainer, and Father of all humankind. Consequently, racism and sexism are not only foolish but evil, as they violate the creative purposes of God.

Second, Paul acknowledged the diversity of ethnic cultures. Despite the fact that God made all nations from one person, "he determined the times set for them and the exact places where they should live." Scripture acknowledges that cultures enrich the total picture of human life, so Christians must affirm both the unity of humankind and the diversity of ethnic existence.

Third, although the apostle accepted the richness of the various cultures, he did not carry this over into the realm of religion. He did not accept the idolatry on which other religions were based because God does not tolerate any rivals to his Son Jesus Christ, the only Savior and Judge of humankind. Of course, Paul was content to *argue* this point in the forum and to *appeal* for conversion — he had no interest in *coercing* conversion.

Finally, the apostle declared the importance of the church, which would be a new and reconciled community to which all may belong (Acts 17:34). Once again Paul's statement in Galatians 3:28 comes to mind: In Christ "there is neither Jew nor Greek, slave nor free, male nor female." The church is intended to be a model of diversity and unity in a world that makes diversity grounds for separatism.

John R. W. Stott sums up the appropriate Christian attitude toward diversity: "Because of the unity of humankind we demand equal rights and equal respect for racial minorities. Because of the diversity of ethnic groups we renounce cultural imperialism and seek to preserve all those riches of inter-racial culture which are compatible with Christ's lordship. Because of the finality of Christ, we affirm that religious freedom includes the right to propagate the gospel. Because of the glory of the church, we must seek to rid ourselves of any lingering racism and strive to make it a model of harmony between races, in which the multiracial dream comes true."[16]

Finding a Better Way

If the university is to be a servant of society (with its growing diversity and global interconnectedness), if it is to be true to the best of its traditions of humane, liberal learning — then there is no going back to a narrow, elitist model of higher education. If Christians, for their part, are to contribute to the debate over diversity in higher education, then it must be the notion (and accompanying practice) that the passionate search for truth and the faithful commitment to distinctives are necessarily accompanied by respectful, open, critical, two-way conversation with those of different convictions.

A diversity or multiculturalism that excludes Christianity (no less than Islam, Marxism, or feminism) is a hypocritical contradiction in terms. A diversity that blesses separatism or a competitive tribalism is a grave disservice to our strife-torn world. A diversity that fails to explore common ground or that timidly avoids questions of truth and ethics is an educational and social failure.

16. John R. W. Stott, *Decisive Issues Facing Christians Today* (Old Tappan, N.J.: Revell, 1990), pp. 225-26. Also, an excellent presentation of the multicultural aspects of the Christian faith is Robin Keeley, ed., *Christianity: A World Faith* (Oxford: Lion, 1986).

Evangelical Civility and the Academic Calling

Richard J. Mouw

When I set out a few years back to write a book about civility, I was motivated by a concern about some of the more news-worthy examples of incivility in contemporary life.[1] I was especially interested in situations where religious intolerance is a major factor: Catholic versus Protestant in Northern Ireland, Christian versus Muslim in Bosnia, Jew versus Arab in the Middle East, as well as the American "culture war" conflicts over abortion and homosexuality. In interviews and talk-show discussions after my book appeared, though, I discovered that many people are distressed over a more everyday kind of incivility: They want to talk about a mean-spiritedness that they encounter regularly in parking lots, supermarket aisles, and expressway traffic lanes.

The academy has not escaped this new wave of incivility. Colleges and universities these days often seem to be occupied by very angry people. In the much analyzed educational environs of "political correctness," scholarly communities often reveal this same uncivil spirit when they debate about admission criteria, hiring practices, reading lists, curricular philosophies, research agendas, and labeling systems.

I want to pay some attention here to the topic of academic civility, especially as it constitutes a challenge to Christians who are

1. Richard J. Mouw, *Uncommon Decency: Christian Civility in an Uncivil World* (Downers Grove, Ill.: InterVarsity Press, 1992).

committed to the academic enterprise. How are they to understand the current mood of incivility? And how are they to respond in ways that are faithful to the Christian calling? Given the nature of Christian commitment as it bears on academic issues, will Christians in academia inevitably be a part of the problem? Or can they possibly point the way to some solutions?

Let me say at the outset that I am convinced that the Christian life should motivate its followers in the direction of civility, including academic civility. While being civil is not the be-all and end-all of the Christian life, it is a way of relating to other human beings that displays many of those characteristics that are listed in the New Testament under the heading of "the fruit of the Spirit": "love, joy, peace, patience, kindness, generosity, faithfulness, gentleness, and self-control" (Gal. 5:22). Needless to say, none of these characteristics can be divorced from a concern for the truth of the Bible's vision of reality. For the Christian, civility must be integrally linked to Christian conviction. The Apostle Peter succinctly stated the correct way of bringing the two together. "Always be ready to make your defense," he counsels, "for the hope that is in you"; then he quickly adds: "yet do it with gentleness and reverence" (1 Pet. 3:15-16).

Correcting Evangelical Incivility

It will seem strange to many people to think about the ways in which evangelicals might help to promote academic civility. Evangelical Christians have not been known for their civility; and the situation has not improved much when they have specifically focused on the academic enterprise. In dealing with matters of the mind, evangelicals have often wavered back and forth between anti-intellectualism and intellectual arrogance. Each of these attitudes must be dealt with if evangelical civility is to be promoted in academic contexts.

The patterns of evangelical anti-intellectualism have been given careful attention in Mark Noll's much-discussed book, *The Scandal of the Evangelical Mind*. Evangelical Christians, Noll insists, have not done well in matters of the mind, and he probes for the most important causes of this failure. For the most part he paints a rather sobering picture. It is interesting, though, that in the final analysis he does offer grounds for hope. Evangelicals have a lot of catching up to do intellectually but they may also bring some distinctives to the life of the mind. A personal commitment to Christ, a sense of spiritual urgency, a love of the authoritative Scriptures, even a tendency toward activism — these evangelical traits and emphases have the potential for strengthening and re-shaping the intellectual task.[2]

A much more optimistic assessment of the intellectual state of evangelicalism is offered by Oxford theologian Alister McGrath, in a book published around the same time as Noll's. Indeed McGrath credits his own conversion to the intellectual vitality of the evangelical movement. McGrath worries that the "increasing intellectual sophistication" of evangelicals could lead to an unhealthy rationalism. As an antidote, he emphasizes the need for continued attention on the part of evangelical intellectuals to the experiential dimensions of evangelical spirituality. This will make it possible, he insists, to maintain a vision of Christian wholeness "in which theologians are evangelists and evangelists theologians."[3]

Both Noll and McGrath arrive, then, from two rather different angles, at an emphasis on the need for evangelical scholarship to be grounded in a strong spirituality. This is a point of consensus that deserves careful attention in the present context. The promotion of academic civility requires a recognition of an intimate connection between spirituality and scholarship. If evangelical anti-intellectualism is to be avoided, there must be a recognition of the need for a genuine spirituality to be grounded in careful thinking. And if evangelical intellectual arrogance is to be avoided as well, there must also be a recognition of the need for a healthy scholarship to be rooted in a spirituality that cultivates the fruit of the Spirit.

My own sense of the situation — which places my reading of recent evangelical history closer to McGrath's than to Noll's — is

2. Mark Noll, *The Scandal of the Evangelical Mind* (Grand Rapids: Eerdmans, 1994), pp. 250-51.
3. Alister McGrath, *Evangelicalism and the Future of Christianity* (Downers Grove, Ill.: InterVarsity Press, 1995), p. 189.

that evangelicals have made significant gains in fostering a creative and careful scholarship in recent decades. However that may be, I will simply assume that the case for an evangelical intellectual life does not have to be made here. Instead, I will focus on the need for intellectual activity to be undergirded by a spirituality in which civility is a central feature.

Academic Spirituality

If evangelicals could develop an integrated academic spirituality, it would be of benefit to more than the evangelical movement. The lack of a spiritual undergirding for the academic enterprise is an important feature of the present crisis in higher education.

Mark Schwehn has made the case for academic spirituality with much eloquence in his recent study of the crisis in academic vocation. Academic activities are not performed by isolated individuals, Schwehn argues; they are functions of academic *community*. The great universities that were founded on European and North American soil were established and sustained over the centuries by people who believed that the academic calling had a profound religious significance. Consequently these intellectual communities were undergirded by such "spiritual" virtues as humility, faith, self-denial, and love. These qualities have been sustained in past academic settings by affections, liturgical practices, and symbol systems that are intimately intertwined with religious convictions; and, as Schwehn boldly states his case, "their continued vitality would seem to be in some jeopardy under wholly secular auspices."[4] Indeed, Schwehn strongly suspects that "most of our present-day academies" are "living off a kind of borrowed fund of moral capital."[5]

The virtues featured in Schwehn's account are not a mere pious gloss for academic life. They provide the cement that gives cohesiveness to the academic enterprise. Humility translates in very

---

4. Mark R. Schwehn, *Exiles from Eden: Religion and the Academic Vocation in America* (New York: Oxford University Press, 1993), pp. 50, 56-57.
5. Schwehn, *Exiles*, p. 53.

concrete ways into a spirit of critical self-examination that is necessary for a healthy intellectual quest. Faith builds the trust and reliance on others that is foundational to a community of scholars. Self-denial and love of other people — and love of one's subject matter — reinforce the patterns of scholarly teaching and dialogue.

Schwehn does not shrink from pointing out that in the past these spiritual virtues were themselves grounded in practices of communal worship in the academic setting. It is unreasonable to expect, of course, that such practices can be reintroduced into the present-day academy on a widescale basis. It is not unreasonable to contemplate, however, that some groups of scholars — those who have not abandoned the religious convictions that were once widely accepted in the academy — could bear witness in their own scholarly lives to the connections between academic tasks, spiritual virtues, and communal worship. This is one of the key strategies that Schwehn proposes: those religious academic institutions in which worship and the spiritual disciplines can still be openly encouraged must keep the connections alive, resisting the secularizing forces that have already caused widespread academic disintegration.[6]

It is possible to hear in Schwehn's discussion some echoes of the somewhat more apocalyptic scenario sketched out in the concluding paragraph of Alasdair MacIntyre's *After Virtue*, where MacIntyre calls for "the construction of local forms of community within which civility and the intellectual and moral life can be sustained through the new dark ages which are already upon us." This time around, MacIntyre insists, "the barbarians are not waiting beyond the frontiers; they have already been governing us for quite some time." Our only hope is to wait "for another — doubtless very different — St. Benedict."[7]

Apocalyptic scenarios have a certain attractiveness for evangelicals, and it is tempting to link the call for intellectual civility to MacIntyre's "Benedictine" option: Since the rest of the academy has lost its moorings, why don't Christians withdraw into strong, faith-

6. Schwehn, *Exiles*, p. 81.

7. Alasdair MacIntyre, *After Virtue: A Study in Moral Theory* (Notre Dame, Ind.: University of Notre Dame Press, 1981), p. 245.

based academic communities where they can maintain patterns of civility in their internal communal lives? But such an alternative is defective in at least two ways.

First, it fails to recognize the historic intent of the actual "Benedictine" option. The monastic tradition in Roman Catholicism was never seen simply as an abandonment of everything that existed beyond the boundaries of the abbey. Monastic communities existed to keep certain communally based virtues alive in a manner that would strengthen the larger church, and even the larger human community. Monastic communities formed a subset of a broader system of "orders," all of which were seen as making a contribution to the overall scheme of things.

Religiously based academic institutions have an important role to play. Schwehn makes a forceful case for their existence in the present-day confusions of academic life. But he also rightly observes that this is only one of several strategies that need attention. And this is precisely the point where it is helpful to think of the formation of separate religious "orders" in the academy. Maintaining academic communities that are organized around a common set of beliefs and spiritual practices is one very important strategy. The sustaining of networks of Christian scholars who work in other, more "secular," academic settings is also crucial — especially when good patterns of communication and mutual edification are established between those scholars who are pursuing their vocations in the context of diverse "orders."

A second defect in a thoroughgoing academic separatism is that it is simply not good for evangelicals. It is not enough to concentrate only on intra-evangelical civility. We must also work at being civil in broader academic contexts.

Expanding Pluralism

An important obstacle must be faced, though, in thinking about how scholars with strong Christian convictions can work at promoting civility in the larger academy: Such persons are often not very welcome in the secular academy, in which the resistance to religious conviction is rather pronounced. George Marsden has given careful attention to both the historical background and the present shape of this attitude in his magisterial study, *The Soul of the American University.* Marsden concludes by suggesting that room be created in higher education for the consideration of "substantive religious concerns" in scholarship by broadening the scope of pluralism and academic freedom — much-celebrated themes in secular education.[8]

Marsden wants typically secular faculties to be more welcoming to committed religious scholars. However, he rightly questions whether the secular emphasis on pluralism can be expanded in the way he would like. His worries are legitimate. In spite of the widespread advocacy of pluralism in contemporary life, the pluralistic patterns of thought are often not very consistent. For one thing, present-day pluralists are not usually committed to any sort of *ultimate* pluralism. They themselves place significant limits on a thoroughgoing relativism — even if only implicitly — in their attempts, for example, to give favorable notice to a variety of contingent "social constructions." Such limits are clearly necessary if these perspectives are to be taken seriously. No relativist viewpoint could really do justice to the points of view represented by Anglo-American women, African-American slaves, Native Americans, and Peruvian shamans — points of view that, it is rightly contended, have often been ignored by elite classicists. A relativistic pluralism cannot account for the sense that previously marginalized viewpoints have something that ought to be given due consideration. Relativism can only perpetuate their marginalization by continuing to deny them the right to make truth-claims.

This also means that pluralistic arguments often mask deeper nonpluralistic commitments. If that is the case, it is not likely that Christian scholars will get very far simply by asking for more consistent pluralism. Or if they do get anywhere by this ploy, it will be because they have been successful in exposing the underlying commitments of those who advocate a surface pluralism.

Genuine success on this level requires that Christians argue

8. George M. Marsden, *The Soul of the American University: From Protestant Establishment to Established Nonbelief* (New York: Oxford University Press, 1994), pp. 436-40.

from a detailed understanding of the fundamental theoretical issues that are at stake — and in a manner that will elicit the respect, even if only grudging, of the secular academy. To possess this requires, in turn, a collective Christian scholarly enterprise in which Christian intellectuals operate with a clear sense of what a Christian worldview is all about. Marsden points to this need in his insistence "that religiously committed scholars who are already present at many universities will have to overcome their own long-standing inhibitions about relating faith to scholarship and establish academic credibility for expressed religious viewpoints."[9]

This is to point to the importance of a strategy mentioned in passing above: the formation of Christian intellectual networks and caucuses, that is, organizations of Christians representing existing institutions who band together for the purpose of regular scholarly exchange in the context of a variety of academic disciplines. Actually, some of this is already occurring. Several such organizations — such as the Society of Christian Philosophers, the Conference on Faith and History, and the American Scientific Affiliation — have flourished in recent decades. Strengthening such organizations is an important part of the overall picture as we think about promoting Christian civility in the academy.

Cultivating Civility

How do we actually go about cultivating civility? In what ways can efforts in this area benefit the larger academy? Suppose, contrary to current patterns, the secular scholarly community were to encourage Christian scholars, and other persons of substantive religious convictions, to work, as a part of the pluralistic mix, at explicitly relating their faith commitments to the intellectual enterprise. How could this be done in a way that would serve the cause of civility? The subject is a large one. I will attempt to offer here only some reference points for our ongoing efforts.

9. Marsden, *Soul*, p. 439.

Respect for the Academic

Efforts at academic civility must be approached with a clear sense of the integrity of the academic project as such. Civility requires that we acknowledge the norms and characteristics that are proper to our context. This means that we must respect the academic enterprise for what it is: a context for teaching, learning, and research.

This is not a trivial point to make. Too often religious people see academic activity in functional terms: teaching, learning, and research are seen simply as means to other ends. They see their presence in the academy primarily as, say, an opportunity for evangelism or as an exercise in apologetics. Neither of these goals is bad. There is nothing wrong in hoping that the occasion might arise in an academic setting for speaking to another person about Christ; neither is it misguided to hope that scholarly efforts will demonstrate to other persons the intellectual attractiveness of a biblically grounded worldview.

What is confused, though, is when the activities of teaching, learning, and research are seen *simply* as occasions for working toward these goals. From a Christian perspective, teaching, learning, and research have value quite apart from their evangelistic and/or apologetic benefits. Even if there were no people around to evangelize or to convince of the intellectual strengths of a Christian outlook, it would still be a good thing to engage in academic activities. Teaching others about God's creation, learning about that creation, conducting research into the complexities of created reality — all of these have intrinsic value in the Christian scheme of things.

An "Invitational" Spirit

Again, there is nothing wrong with hoping that our involvement in academic activity will also be the occasion for evangelization and intellectual "missionary" activity. But even here it is important to think about the appropriate way of engaging in such activities in an academic setting. The Christian teacher, for example, must not use the pedagogical podium as a bully pulpit or an ideologist's rostrum. This applies, of course, not just to Christians or other religiously committed professors but to all of the ideologically committed.

What can be done, however, is to invite others to consider possibilities that they may have previously ruled out because of their own secularist or anti-religious biases. I mean to emphasize the word "invite" here. An academic course is an invitation to students to investigate areas of inquiry. Conversionist tactics have no place in the classroom. But this does not mean that we cannot work hard, in very self-conscious ways, at eliminating the kinds of prejudices, misconceptions, and stereotypes that often serve as stumbling blocks to conversion. As a Christian I want to open up possibilities for non-Christians that they might have otherwise missed. But this invitation must be issued and acted upon in conformity to the very norms mentioned above: clarity, reasonableness, fairness, and truthfulness.

A Love of Reality

One very important way of bearing witness to a biblically grounded worldview in the academic setting is to demonstrate what it is like to *love* the reality that we are studying. The academy is devoted to the investigation of what Christians understand to be the rich complexity of God's creation. "The earth is the Lord's and all that is in it, the world, and those who live in it" (Ps. 24:1). This profound sense of God's loving lordship over the reality that we are investigating can serve as a corrective to many regrettable features of contemporary academic life.

The present-day academy often operates with a very disconnected view of reality. Not only do people in different disciplines not know how to talk to each other about their scholarly interests, the lack of any real basis for communication also occurs *within* disciplines. Christians have a deep interest in keeping the lines of communication open because they are convinced that there is an underlying unity to the reality being studied by diverse disciplines and subdisciplines: Jesus Christ "is before all things, and in him all things hold together" (Col. 1:17).

This conviction of the cohesive character of reality does not justify a simplified understanding of interconnectedness. Rather, it should inspire a sense of appropriate *mystery* as evangelicals conduct their investigations — but a mystery that is undergirded by a deep conviction that reality is ultimately a cosmos and not a chaos.

A Healthy Pluralism

The contemporary advocacy of pluralism is often, as I mentioned earlier, set forth in a manner that is inconsistent and arbitrary. But when secular pluralism is followed out to its consistent conclusion, it results in a thoroughgoing relativism. None of this is very satisfactory from a Christian point of view. But that should not make Christians insensitive to the merits of the pluralistic impulse.

It is difficult for Christians to be for or against pluralism as such. Much depends on what "plurals" are being celebrated.[10] For example, one kind of pluralism that has received much attention in recent years stems from a positive appraisal of the fact of cultural diversity. Christians ought to be especially appreciative of this emphasis. The church is a community of people drawn from the diverse tribes, nations, and peoples of the earth (Rev. 5:9). Within a Christian context, the exploration and celebration of cultural diversity is an important — indeed an essential — activity.

It is crucial that Christians draw on their own uniquely communal resources for demonstrating to their secular colleagues that it is possible to foster a healthy cultural pluralism without slipping into relativism. A self-conscious awareness of their actual involvement in the worldwide, multicultural body of Christ can provide them with access to a cross-cultural conversation intensified by a degree of spiritual bonding that is seldom available to secular scholars whose global sensitivities are nurtured by the normal academic dialogic opportunities. The fact of this extensive Christian network seems to me to provide an important argument for en-

---

10. For an extensive discussion of the complexities and varieties of pluralism, see Richard Mouw and Sander Griffioen, *Pluralisms and Horizons: An Essay in Christian Public Philosophy* (Grand Rapids: Eerdmans, 1993).

couraging Christian scholars to maintain a strong churchly identity. Such an involvement has a crucial bearing on the contribution of evangelicals to the academy.

Hopeful Humility

Arthur Holmes has argued that the Christian faith provides important spiritual resources for the complex challenges of the intellectual life, even though only the Creator has a clear and comprehensive knowledge of all things. This should inspire a strong sense of humility. In addition, Christians have received the promise that God will eventually lead them into that mode of perfect knowing that is proper to human creatures. This should provide a significant measure of hope.[11] If evangelicals effectively appropriate these attitudes, they can display the kind of patience that is capable of tolerating complexities and living with seemingly unconnected particularities without giving in to despair or cynicism. To show forth this kind of approach to intellectual complexities is to perform an important ministry in the present-day academy.

A passage that occurs about mid-point in Plato's *Meno* provides a valuable clue as to how this can be done. Socrates' friends are discouraged at this stage in the discussion, because they have been looking for a unified definition of virtue — but instead, all they have come up with is a "swarm" of virtues. Do not get discouraged by swarms, Socrates tells them. In spite of appearances to the contrary, "all nature is akin." This means, he says, that there is nothing to hinder us, having tackled just one small assignment in the epistemic quest, from going on to find out about all of the rest, as long as we do "not weary in seeking" (*Meno* 81A).

Christian scholars can take heart from similar sentiments — but with even better reasons, I think, for not getting disillusioned in the important process of attending to the complex details of the intellectual quest. Jesus Christ has created all things and "sustains all things by his powerful word" (Heb. 1:3). Because he is the One

---

11. Arthur F. Holmes, *Contours of a World View* (Grand Rapids: Eerdmans, 1983), p. 128.

in whom all reality coheres, Christians can explore that reality with a profound love for that which they are studying.

Christian scholars can also love those co-explorers with whom they have significant disagreement. In humility they can acknowledge to their colleagues that they have not yet arrived at an adequate understanding of reality. But they can also look for opportunities to show them what it is like to face the exciting challenges of scholarship in the confidence that this too is an area where Jesus Christ exercises his lordship. In this mix of humility and hope can Christian civility be born and nurtured.

Ethics With and Without God

David W. Gill

There are two reasons why ethics (morality, values, etc.) has become such a hot topic in both the academy and the larger society over the past twenty years or so. First, the inventory of difficult ethical dilemmas has been growing exponentially, largely because of the development of technology in various domains. We are faced with many new quandaries for which there is no, or inadequate, moral guidance about right and wrong. Often the stakes, in terms of potential harm as well as benefit, are extraordinarily high.

Take health care and medicine as an example. New medical technologies have raised acute questions about our tampering with human life, especially at its beginnings and endings. Genetic research and therapy pose challenging new issues. The AIDS epidemic, and the general, growing problem of basic health care for the poor and underinsured, raise questions about the just allocation of health care resources. Political and legal issues — about patient self-determination, rights, privacy, and confidentiality, about public health concerns such as smoking and sexually transmitted disease, and about malpractice judgments — are laden with ethical values. Modifications in health care delivery institutions and in the roles and relationships of health care providers are also morally problematic.

What is happening in health care has parallels in the business world, in entertainment and the media, and in information technology, to mention only some of the most obvious domains. The question is "What is the right thing to do?" — not just "What is possible?" or "What is legal?" How do we decide questions of right and wrong; of good and evil; of justice and compassion? How do we resolve differences of moral values and convictions? Still more profound than the search for resolution of our quandaries and dilemmas are questions about our moral character. What kind of people are we? From what stance, with what vision, from within what communities — do we live out the moral life?

Much of our contemporary ethical challenge arises, then, because of this plethora of novel problems for which we have no inherited or intuitively obvious moral wisdom. Today's moral landscape is extraordinarily complex. The sheer number of problems can be overwhelming; the consequences of our actions can be horrifying if we do not choose wisely.

The second reason for the surge of interest in ethics is the lack of consensus about basic moral values in our culture (or even in a given profession or business or neighborhood). Many of our modern issues are global and international; locally, we live and work in what have become very diverse, multicultural communities. Thus, our inventory of ethical dilemmas does not present itself to homogeneous communities with long traditions of shared values and agreed-upon structures and processes for moral guidance and resolution. We are not all Italian Catholics, or Russian Jews, or Kantian males, or Ivy-league-trained Democrats, or anything else. Our ethnic and cultural identities, our extended families, and our social or religious group affiliations still matter to many of us. But today's moral challenges usually present themselves to diverse communities that lack agreed-upon, shared ethical starting points. Diversity can be illuminating; often, though, it is an impediment to dilemma resolution. We cannot apply our moral wisdom to a given problem if we cannot agree on what is that moral wisdom.

There are, of course, other factors beside these two great challenges (so many new problems, so little consensus) that add to our difficulty. The speed and intensity of modern life conspire against deep study, reflection, and conversation — exactly the elements necessary for wisdom. The omnipresent messages of mass culture usually appeal to (and shape) a rather simplistic, self-centered set of values. Geographic (and other forms of) mobility tends to detach people from whatever moral resources might have assisted them in families and communities left far behind. Moral formation of children by parents has been undermined by economic and other trends.

All of the foregoing is old news, at this stage. Vigorous efforts are being undertaken to respond to our ethical crises. In the world of business and the professions, ethics codes are being elaborated and revised, ethics committees and experts are put in place, and the character of the corporate culture and its participants is being examined. Conferences, colloquia, and workshops address such questions and issues on a regular basis. In the academic world, ethics courses and centers have proliferated. Ethics-across-the-curriculum is now a common program in many schools. And before this there was "values clarification" to help with personal moral identity. Books and journals on ethical subjects are churning off the presses at an amazing rate.

As far as it goes, then, the current resurgence of interest in ethics is an encouraging feature of academic and vocational life today. Better to face our issues directly than to avoid them and/or simply muddle through, guided only by legal, individual, technical, economic, or pragmatic judgments.

However, many of today's ethical efforts are undermined by a conscious attempt to bracket out religious perspectives. "Values" courses often insist that students leave religion outside of the study. Applied ethics textbooks often argue that morality is not dependent on religion. Ethics codes normally do not invoke religious authority. Political and educational leaders have urged or required us to keep church and state separate — often improperly extending that to mean a separation between religion and public life.

I wish to argue here that this strategy is a mistake. Ethics is best pursued alongside of religion, *with* rather than *without* God. The choice of our gods inevitably affects or even implies the choice of our goods. Bracketing out the god-question is a serious if not fatal impediment to our resolving the questions of good and right. Historically, most ethical values have been inextricably embedded in a religious texture. What was good had everything to do with what was God. Even with the philosophers (not just the theologians) this was usually so. Reason was not a sufficient basis for Plato's ethics in the *Republic;*

the "myth of Er," with its reincarnational themes, provides a religious context. Philosophers since the Enlightenment, such as Kant, Hume, and Nietzsche, have diverged from this tradition and tried to ground ethical values in something human or natural rather than in God and religion. But since philosophers do not rule the world, it is all the more important to pay attention to the ways real people actually do, in practice, link their goods and their gods, their ethics and their religion. Ethics without God (or religion) is an interesting philosophical exercise; ethics with God (and religion in some form or other) is about life and reality among the people.

Ethics Without God

In his recent study of religion and American education, Warren Nord sums up our contemporary position: "The conventional wisdom now is that morality can be understood and taught without religion. But the problem is not just that religious accounts of morality are ignored, it is that they are rendered suspect at best, and matters of superstition at worst, by the secular worldview that pervades modern education."[1] British philosopher Peter Geach has written: "In modern ethical treatises we find hardly any mention of God; and the idea that if there really is a God, his commandments might be morally relevant is wont to be dismissed by a short and simple argument that is generally regarded as irrefutable."[2] Ethics is typically studied in a way that banishes God and religion from the discussion. But as Stephen Carter has noted, "the truth — an awkward one for the guardians of the public square — is that tens of millions of Americans rely on their religious traditions for the moral knowledge that tells them how to conduct their lives."[3]

1. Warren Nord, *Religion and American Education: Rethinking a National Dilemma* (Chapel Hill: University of North Carolina, 1995), p. 341.
2. Peter Geach, "The Moral Law and the Law of God," in *Divine Commands and Morality*, ed. Paul Helm (Oxford, 1981), p. 165.
3. Stephen L. Carter, *The Culture of Disbelief: How American Law and Politics Trivialize Religious Devotion* (New York: Basic, 1993), p. 67. Carter says that "roughly half of Americans" report that their "religious tradition is very important in reaching moral decisions" (p. 56).

At a college I recently visited, the capstone "Senior Values Studies" course specifically stated in the orientation material, for both students and the faculty teaching team, that religious perspectives were not to enter the values discussions. A widely used business ethics textbook devotes one page to the subject "Morality Needn't Rest on Religion" and concludes: "You cannot justify a moral principle simply by appealing to religion — for that will only persuade those who already agree with your particular interpretation of your particular religion . . . so it is human reason to which you will have to appeal in order to support your ethical principle."[4] These are relatively tame but typical examples of what Nord, Geach, and Carter describe.

Why is ethics approached in higher education without God or religion? Certainly part of the reason is a fear of encroaching on the separation of church and state: The church can teach religion but state-sponsored or -funded schools cannot. The fear of appearing to "establish" or privilege one religion over another, or over those who adhere to none, has led to the preclusion of all religion from the classroom. Further, since multiculturalism and diversity have become both facts and values in society and in higher education, we have become more concerned than ever that partisan religious convictions should not rear their divisive heads.

This reaction is a mistake, however. A distinction must be made between *avoiding the establishment* of official churchly authority where it should not occur and *preventing the free exercise* or expression of religious conviction by the people. A distinction must be made between *teaching* religion in the sense of indoctrination or propaganda and *teaching about* religion. Furthermore, if education is preparation for real life and work, students will be entering a world in which they and others *will* (according to the data cited by Carter and others) often bring (or encounter) religiously based

---

4. William H. Shaw and Vincent Barry, *Moral Issues in Business,* 6th ed. (Belmont, Calif.: Wadsworth, 1995), p. 11. Shaw and Berry, whose otherwise fine textbook I have often used, are arguing against the necessity and sufficiency of religiously based ethics for a pluralistic business environment. They have a point but it needs to be nuanced to allow that for many individuals in business, and for some companies, religiously based ethics is relevant and even indispensable within this pluralistic mix.

values to the table — but they will have been prepared in college only by ethics and values courses that *refused* to examine the religion/morality connections.

A deeper reason why the religion and morality connection has been severed is philosophical. Since the Enlightenment, the philosophical (and hence ethical) authority of religion has been marginalized or eliminated. A nonreligious foundation for ethics has been sought in nature, in reason, in social contracts, and in the intuition, feeling, or will of the individual. Ethical values and principles must be justified by their logical relationships, by their rationality, by their universalizability. Ethical norms that are embedded in traditions, in particular communities, or in the irrational or supernatural have been found wanting by these standards.

Probably the most aggressive modern philosopher opposed to the link between ethics and any sort of theology is Kai Nielsen, the author of *Ethics Without God*. Nielsen argues that "no reality, no force or being or world ground, no matter how powerful or eternal, would be called 'God' unless that reality were taken to be good by the agent making that judgment. . . . This shows that our concept of goodness and our criteria for goodness are prior to and not dependent on our belief in the existence of some 'world ground' or 'transcendent being.'"[5] How would we recognize the God who is good if we did not already have a notion of goodness? Thus, Nielsen argues, morality is prior to, and not at all dependent on, religion or theology; in fact, the converse is true — religion is dependent on morality.

Nielsen repeats the same argument over and over in his text. But his point, finally, is not just that religion is insufficient or unnecessary or secondary to ethics — it is flatly false. "The fact [is] that these religious concepts are myths — sources of illusion and self-deception." "We have no evidence at all for believing in the existence or love of God." "The plain fact is that we do not have any grounds for believing that God exists or for believing that his purposes are good."[6] For Nielsen everything can be, and must be,

5. Kai Nielsen, *Ethics Without God*, rev. ed. (Buffalo, N.Y.: Prometheus Books, 1990), p. 31.

6. Nielsen, *Ethics*, pp. 84, 98-99.

explained within a naturalistic, rationalistic worldview, and that includes our ethics.

It is fair to say that *most* philosophers since the Enlightenment have given up on any sort of divine command or theologically based ethics. They have generally rejected both the character of God and the structure of nature ("natural law" — sometimes given a theological spin as God's "general revelation") as bases for ethics. Often this rejection is on logical grounds: Even if you could describe God or nature, you cannot logically derive an "ought" from an "is" (the "naturalistic fallacy"). What we are left with is ethics as a system of duties created and accepted by a social group (a social compact or contract) to order its survival and promote its flourishing. Or, more cynically, we are left with ethics as a purely personal intuition or preference. Modern philosophers often commend rationality, logic, universalizability, coherence, and/or personal authenticity as criteria for the construction or justification of ethics.

This rather breezy sketch does not do justice to the sophistication and variety of post-Enlightenment moral philosophy. Nevertheless, it is this sort of philosophical picture that lies in the background, implying much of the modern search for an ethics without God or religion.

It is not my agenda to argue that *only* God or religion provides moral guidance. It is foolish to deny that there are secular, non-religiously based ethics. Nor can we say that religious commitment and ethical performance are coordinated. Many nonreligious ethical arguments are admirable and persuasive; many nonreligious persons exhibit salutary moral behavior. Many theological ethical arguments are weak and unpersuasive; many religious persons behave shamefully. These are not the issues.

Our question is whether ethics *must* always proceed *without* God, as Kai Nielsen argues forthrightly, and as our ethics and values courses often suggest in practice. To this the answer is No; philosophically and historically, God and ethics, religion and morality, can be, and have been, legitimately linked together. The worldview of a dogmatic philosophical naturalism is clearly one obstacle that must be addressed. But it is impossible to conclusively, logically prove to all rational persons that God (or the supernatural) exists or does not exist — or that a supernatural God could (or has) in some way broken into our natural order with divine moral guidance. Any decision on these matters is a product of more than simple logic; it depends on our reason but also on our presuppositions, our temperament, and our experience.

Theories (metaphysical, theological, naturalistic, or otherwise) relate to life like shoes to feet: they need to "fit" the "facts" as carefully as possible. More than one style of shoe will fit the same foot; but ultimately the test is not logic and abstract measurement but "walking." Many (most?) people find it best to wear a "shoe" with a religious/theological dimension: it fits their life best; it is most comfortable; it facilitates their movement and work; it protects them best; they like best its aesthetics and style. Does our academic "dress code" ban "religious shoes" from the ethics classroom?

Another way to approach arguments like Nielsen's is to point out that moral reasoning does not normally occur as he specifies (and it rarely will except in certain ivory tower enclaves). This is the historical argument. The moral life does not consist of a series of discrete logical exercises, abstracted from life. We do not begin with a major premise, add a minor premise, and seek a logical conclusion. We are not isolated, a-historical atoms confronting a tabula rasa on which we sort through abstract statements. Our premises are connected to the messy-ness of life, to persons and communities; our logic or reasoning is affected by our interests and our stories. Nielsen's argument is interesting and important; it is not, however, an adequate account of ethics — or of the complex relations of religion to morality. In an adequate account of how people's moral lives actually are lived, religion will often play an integral role.

Philosopher William Frankena has argued: "Those who think that morality is dependent on religion need not and do not always mean that it is logically dependent on religion. They may mean only that it is *causally* or *historically* dependent on religion, or that it is *motivationally* or *psychologically* dependent on religion."[7] While

---

7. William K. Frankena, "Is Morality Logically Dependent on Religion?" in *Religion and Morality*, ed. Gene Outka and John P. Reeder, Jr. (Garden City, N.Y.: Anchor, 1973), p. 296. Outka and Reeder's collection of essays remains an outstanding resource for this discussion.

for Frankena the *logical* dependence of morality on religion is un-proved, "it may still be that no adequate ethics can be developed without the help of religious beliefs as premises. . . . Ethics may rely on religion for the development of its working rules and conclu-sions, or at least some of them."[8]

The philosophical door that Frankena shows to be open has been walked through by moral philosophers such as Iris Murdoch, Richard Mouw, Robert Merrihew Adams, Peter Geach, and Dewi Z. Phillips — each of whom, in their various ways, has proposed philo-sophically responsible accounts of a constructive relation between God and ethics. Banishing God from our discussions of ethics and values is not a philosophical requirement.

Ethics With God

Perhaps the best-known way of representing the religion/morality option has been to speak of "divine command" theories of ethics. In this model, ethical principles concerning right and wrong, ob-ligation and prohibition are supplied their authority and their con-tent by God's word to us. The Ten Commandments are a famous example. It will surprise no one that for multitudes of people today, God's commandments (generally meaning those given in sacred Scripture although other variations are possible within this theory) remain crucial, foundational, and even decisive for the moral life.

It is unlikely that very many adherents to the "divine com-mand" approach will give it up because of Kai Nielsen's arguments! What is possible, and I believe necessary, is to assist such moral agents to explore their traditions more carefully and deeply, to consider how their various commands may relate or even conflict with each other, to practice the application of their commands to specific cases, and to discuss how their moral perspective would interface with the convictions and practices of others not sharing their perspective. These are not negligible tasks and it is tragic to

8. Frankena, "Is Morality Dependent?" p. 315. Frankena does not argue that religion *is* necessarily connected to ethics in these ways, but that it *may* be. Such openness is the point of my chapter.

think that such work is excluded from the academic study of ethics, leaving such moral agents to go it alone outside of class.

A second way that God and religion are related to ethics is in terms of the formation of moral character. Stanley Hauerwas, Gilbert Meilander, Peter Kreeft, and others argue, I think rightly, that the relationship to God and to the story and contemporary experience of the community of faith transforms moral character. God and religion affect one's disposition and stance, one's vision and orientation, one's traits and habits. Edmund Pincoffs criticizes the reduction of the moral life to "quandary ethics." "If my personal ideals and my conception of myself as a moral agent are to be excluded from consideration as merely personal; if nothing is to remain but considerations which have to do with the situation as it would appear to anyone regardless of his former character; then the decision-process has been distorted in the interest of a mistaken conception of ethics. The legal analogy has been taken too seriously."[9]

Thus, religiously based ethics do not just provide principles for deciding what to do; they often affect even more vigorously who we are and what our communities are like. Despite the "quandary-," "dilemma-," or "case-orientation" of so much ethical study today, there is a growing movement to restore some emphasis to personal character and to corporate culture. For many of our students, such moral identity is closely related to their relationships to God and communities of faith. How tragic if we insist that this go unarticulated and unexamined in our universities because God-talk is prohibited.

A third way that God and religion are related to ethics has to do with justification and motivation. The questions are, "On what grounds, by what authority, for what reasons, are these values (virtues, duties, etc.) morally obligatory and true?" and "Why should I be moral, why should I cultivate these virtues or follow these principles of right and wrong?" These are two distinguishable

9. Edmund Pincoffs, "Quandary Ethics," in *Revisions: Changing Perspectives in Moral Philosophy*, ed. Stanley Hauerwas and Alasdair MacIntyre (Notre Dame, Ind.: University of Notre Dame, 1983), p. 100. Alasdair MacIntyre (*After Virtue*, 2nd ed. [Notre Dame, Ind.: University of Notre Dame, 1984] and *Three Rival Versions of Moral Enquiry* [Notre Dame, Ind.: University of Notre Dame, 1990]) is the moral philosopher leading the rediscovery of character/virtue ethics.

but related sets of questions. Even if Kai Nielsen were right that the content of our ethics cannot be derived from God and religion, the latter might well be what justifies and motivates ethical behavior.

Most religious people believe in some sort of accountability to God, sometimes expressed in terms of punishments and rewards. Often they also believe in accountability to a community of faith. Our discussions of why we accept certain moral values, and why we choose to live according to them, need to make room for the justifications and motivations brought to class by religious students. Alongside other answers to these questions, the religious answers deserve some critical attention.

Glenn Tinder's *Atlantic Monthly* article, "Can We Be Good Without God?" raises the justification and motivation questions in a provocative way. "The question that secularists have to answer is whether these values can survive without these particular roots. In short, can we be good without God? Can we affirm the dignity and equality of individual persons — values we ordinarily regard as secular — without giving them transcendental backing? Today these values are honored more in the breach than in the observance."[10] Iris Murdoch argues the motivation issue in her *Metaphysics As a Guide to Morals:* "Religious belief may be a stronger motive to good conduct than non-religious idealism. . . . High morality without religion is too abstract, high morality craves for religion. Religion symbolizes high moral ideas which then travel with us and are more intimately and accessibly effective than the unadorned promptings of reason. Religion suits the image-making human animal."[11] Whether or not one agrees with Tinder and Murdoch, they raise an important point for discussion. If we do not have God or religion, what or who will motivate our goodness?

10. Glenn Tinder, "Can We Be Good Without God?" *The Atlantic Monthly,* December 1989, p. 70. Actually Tinder's article would be a good class reading in ethics and values classes.

11. Iris Murdoch, *Metaphysics As a Guide to Morals* (New York: Penguin, 1992), p. 484.

Substitutes for God and Religion in the Moral Life

Another, more controversial angle of vision on the subject of religion and morality has to do with our definition of religion and God. David Little and Sumner B. Twiss, Jr., argue that "religion 'functions' to resolve certain distinctive problems in the lives of individuals and social groups . . . anxieties about certain 'boundary situations' in human life and experience." This includes trying to make sense of the natural world — its existence, purposes, processes, and events — trying to cope with suffering and death, and trying to manage the ambiguities and puzzles inherent in human conduct. "Religion copes with these problems in three ways: conceptually, emotionally, and practically." While a specific notion of "God" cannot be required (Buddhism has none) in the definition, they like the notion of "sacred authority" to distinguish religion from other personal and social philosophies of life.[12]

Social philosopher and critic Jacques Ellul argues that human beings always have or create a more-or-less integrated combination of (1) something treated as "the sacred," (2) moral duties that spin off from that sacred, (3) a system of explanatory myths, and (4) religious rites and practices. In our secularized post-Christendom epoch, Ellul argues, technology and the nation-state are the most prominent loci of the sacred, although many other religious phenomena continue to be popular.[13]

Robert Bellah and others have made the term "civil religion" common in our vocabulary. In this context, we could say that the nation serves as the sacred; historic texts such as the Declaration of Independence, the Gettysburg Address, or the Communist Manifesto serve as the "Bible" to which appeal is made for ultimate values, for mission, and for authoritative direction. Great patriots or revolutionary heroes of the past serve as saints, national holidays become holy days for festivals, political leaders serve as a priesthood,

---

12. David Little and Sumner B. Twiss, Jr., "Basic Terms in the Study of Religious Ethics," in *Religion and Morality,* ed. Gene Outka and John P. Reeder, Jr. (Garden City, N.Y.: Anchor, 1973), pp. 60-62.

13. Jacques Ellul, *The New Demons,* trans. C. Edward Hopkin (New York: Seabury, 1975).

and hymns like the "Internationale" and "The Star-Spangled Banner" help us voice our worship and give us the requisite chill up the spine.

Thus, a functional/structural definition of religion raises provocative questions: What do we worship? That is, to what do we do sacrifice and what do we treat with holy respect at the center of our lives? What receives our praise? To what do we look for salvation from our problems and perplexities? What inspires in us both awe and fear, attraction and devotion? What gives unity, meaning, and direction to our lives? This, one can argue, is whatever occupies the "god-place" in our existence. Some are polytheists, with several gods in their pantheon. And certainly, in traditional religions as well as their substitutes, we sometimes disagree with or disobey our gods. We profane our sacred from time to time; but all the same, each of us has something that functions as our sacred.

And if religion consists of doctrines (and myths) as well as practices, don't we all in effect have, in greater or lesser degrees of development, religious doctrines and practices? We make sacrificial offerings, develop rituals, consult sacred literature, revere saints, revile devils and the reprobate, and, often enough, enjoy something that serves as sacred music, dance, and festival. And we have "church" — we belong to communities of "fellow-believers" where we can share our life-transforming commitment to the same sacred, teach one another, experience approval and discipline, share our sorrows and comfort one another, and renew our hope.

It is in such a frankly "religious" context that our moral values and identities are formed and shared. Our values spin out of our religion, our ethics from our god. The point is that *functionally* and *structurally* human beings are religious: Something occupies the places of the sacred, myth, and ritual, and our fundamental moral and ethical values are directly related to this. Therapeutic and "recovery" groups such as Alcoholics Anonymous often take on this religious role. Any ideological "ism" (feminism, environmentalism, racism, and sexism in their multiple forms, etc.) can fill the void left in the absence of traditional religion. The technophiles of our era are one of our most religious groups. All one has to do is pay attention to the value-laden judgments of members of these various groups to see how morality is linked to religion.

In this perspective, refusing to call these phenomena religious gets us nowhere. Refusing to acknowledge our gods is disingenuous. If something or someone is treated as the sacred center of existence, the object of devotion, the focal point of knowledge, salvation, truth, and meaning, the inspiration and guide of life — it is a god. Just "take its name in vain" in the presence of one of the true believers — just debunk it, doubt it, or profane it, and see what happens. Listen to its "evangelists" and "prophets" earnestly come after you (you pagan unbeliever!), if you doubt its worthiness. As the saying goes, "If it walks like a duck, quacks like a duck, looks like a duck. . . ."

Against this perspective, philosopher William Frankena rejects the argument that "every ethical system or moral code depends on some set of ultimate beliefs about man, the meaning of the universe, and his place in it; therefore every ethical code or system depends on a religion of some kind." It is a "ploy" to be "claiming that any such basic commitment or postulate is *ipso facto* an act of religious faith, concluding that therefore every ethics rests on religion." Frankena's problem is with "defining 'religion' in a very wide sense — in such a wide sense that any basic ethical or value commitment is by definition an act of religious faith."[14] Frankena wants to retain a "theistic" connotation to religion.

Interestingly enough, atheist philosopher Annette Baier argues the opposite of Frankena. "I shall suggest that the secular equivalent of faith in God, which we need in morality as well as in science or knowledge acquisition, is faith in the human community and its evolving procedures — in the prospects for many-handed cognitive ambitions and moral hopes. . . . It will be faith, not knowledge, which will replace religious faith . . . faith in a community of just persons."[15]

In summary, it is, I think, unacceptably arrogant and imperialistic to *require* that those who reject conventional or traditional religion accept the label of "religious" in the ways permitted by the definitions of Little, Twiss, Ellul, Bellah, Baier, and others. If some-

14. Frankena, "Is Morality Dependent?" pp. 310-11.
15. Annette Baier, "Secular Faith," in Hauerwas and MacIntyre, eds., *Revisions*, pp. 204-5.

one wants to be recognized as "secular" or "nonreligious" or "atheistic" we must respect those choices. Nevertheless, there is a rich and potentially productive and illuminating discussion possible about what sorts of ultimate commitments and values, what kinds of practices, and what kinds of communities fulfill the human needs met for others by God and religion. This discussion bears powerfully on the way we do ethics and construe our moral identities.

Teaching Ethics With, and Without, God

As Warren Nord has recently written, "we are deeply divided about how to think about and justify moral judgments; a good education should take the alternatives seriously. Students must be taught something of religious positions on controversial issues and, more important, religious ways of making sense of morality just as they are (inevitably) taught something of secular positions and ways of understanding morality." However, "contemporary American education betrays a want of moral seriousness. . . . Education is first and foremost a moral enterprise. . . . The idea that students can be educated about how to live, what kind of a person to be, and how to act, *without* taking religion seriously is at last illiberal and quite possibly absurd."[16]

Three recent introductory textbooks on ethics exemplify a more adequate approach. Lawrence M. Hinman, in *Ethics: A Pluralistic Approach to Moral Theory*, argues that "one of the central moral issues that we all face, whether we espouse religious beliefs or not, is how we ought to deal with the diversity of religious beliefs."[17] Hinman makes four suggestions for our teaching goals: (1) respect (not necessarily approval) for others' religious beliefs, (2) understanding of religious worldviews and comparative clarification of our own, (3) seeking common ground, and (4) exploring how we will deal with possible conflict and disagreement.

Christina Sommers and Fred Sommers, in *Vice and Virtue in*

16. Nord, *Religion and American Education*, pp. 342, 351.
17. Lawrence M. Hinman, *Ethics: A Pluralistic Approach to Moral Theory* (New York: Harcourt Brace Jovanovich, 1994), p. 99.

Everyday Life: Introductory Readings in Ethics, have assembled a great collection of brief readings on good and evil, virtue and vice, moral education and motivation, moral doctrine and theory, character and society. Their sources include not only philosophers such as Aristotle, Kant, Nietzsche, Singer, and Foot, but the Bible, Melville, Augustine, Tolstoy, Camus, the Bhagavad-Gita, and other examples of ethical reflection and insight.[18] Gabriel Palmer-Fernandez's *Moral Issues: Philosophical and Religious Perspectives* argues for a robust pluralistic approach to ethics, and brings together an outstanding, diverse collection of essays on foundations (Kai Nielsen gets his say along with others!), and on topics ranging from abortion to euthanasia, sex, war and peace, hunger, and justice.[19]

In classroom settings, therefore, I am arguing that we should *invite* students, even *require* students, to reflect on the religious question, understood in the broadest possible sense of what is treated as sacred, what is at the interpretive and meaning center of worldviews and lifestyles, and what basic presuppositions and faith assumptions are held. First of all, how are these questions answered by students in their own personal existence? What do they treat as god in their life — and why? What, in other words, is their ultimate purpose in life? Who or what do they wish to serve with their life, energy, and talents? Some may say Jesus Christ. Others Allah. Still others may say humanity or their ethnic community or their family or even their self. Why do they make this choice? And how will they prepare themselves to best serve this god? What are the moral principles, virtues of character, and methods of moral discernment and action that grow out of these fundamental stances? These are questions of faith as well as of reason, of theology as well as of philosophy. They are fundamental to an adequate education in ethics.

Since we do not live and work in religiously homogeneous communities, it is then essential to raise these "religious" questions with respect to those with perspectives different from our own.

---

18. Christina Sommers and Fred Sommers, eds., *Vice and Virtue in Everyday Life,* 3rd ed. (New York: Harcourt Brace Jovanovich, 1993).

19. Gabriel Palmer-Fernandez, *Moral Issues: Philosophical and Religious Perspectives* (Upper Saddle River, N.J.: Prentice-Hall, 1996).

Learning to listen to how others in class answer these questions is a start. Reading and encountering representatives of other faiths and other philosophies extends this learning process in preparation for the real world. A basic understanding of Islamic ethics, for example, is just as important as an understanding of Kant or Mill.

When we discuss cases (quandaries, dilemmas) in ethics, we need to hear how these might be analyzed and resolved within a Jewish or Buddhist or Christian moral framework — as well as how we might approach them with a deontological or utilitarian or egoist perspective. Our discussions of public ethics, of moral education in the public schools, of ethical challenges in business, health care, law, politics, and the mass media, need to address the possibilities for common ground and united action. They also need to discuss how we can best deal with our differences of opinion, especially those differences that are deeply held and appear to be nonnegotiable.

The role of an ethics teacher is not to indoctrinate a captive audience. But neither is it to deny one's own religious/moral identity and pretend to be above all normative conviction. Much better for the instructor to share his or her own perspective when appropriate and engage in careful self-critical analysis as a model for the students. We need to educate students to be self-critical, to articulate their convictions and reflect on their grounding and consequences. We are not just sponsors and referees in class, we are models.

If the "gods" and ultimate "goods" of our colleges and universities are such things as truth, knowledge, skills, personal growth, and social justice and peace, then it is unethical for us as professors to disallow an appreciative and critical examination of the ultimate commitments that in one way or another undergird all morality. As a Christian I can say that, for me, ethics without the God of Jesus Christ seems a pale and weak substitute for the Jesus-centered approach. That is my viewpoint and I think it is true. But as a professor who teaches students of all types and persuasions, I always stress that many people disagree with my personal perspective — but that everyone has *something* that functions in much the same way Jesus does for me. And we cannot study ethics without paying attention to, and critically examining, what this is.

C. S. Lewis on Eros as a Means of Grace

Corbin Scott Carnell

C. S. Lewis may well be the best-known and best-loved avowedly Christian university professor of the twentieth century.[1] While some of his Oxford University colleagues may have been put off by his Christianity (or his popularity!), his biographers attest to the great affection and appreciation of his students. Scores of visitors and hundreds of correspondents tell stories of Lewis's generous attention. Many scholars continue to praise his works of literary criticism — such as *The Allegory of Love* (1936), *A Preface to Paradise Lost* (1942), and *An Experiment in Criticism* (1961). Children (and their parents) around the world love C. S. Lewis for his many works of fantasy and fiction — such as *The Chronicles of Narnia*. And no Christian author in our century has provided more helpful, intriguing, and enduring essays on theological topics than has C. S. Lewis. His great little books *Mere Christianity, The Problem of Pain,* and *Miracles,* and those on so many other subjects, continue to be easily available in bookstores everywhere.

Although C. S. Lewis was a bachelor until the last few years of

---

1. This essay appeared in an earlier form in *Imagination and the Spirit: Essays in Literature and the Christian Faith Presented to Clyde S. Kilby* (Grand Rapids: Eerdmans, 1971) and is reprinted here in this revised form by permission.

For some general introduction to the life and writings of C. S. Lewis, see Chad Walsh, *C. S. Lewis: Apostle to the Skeptics* (Folcroft, Pa.: Folcroft Library Editions, 1974), and Clyde Kilby, *The Christian World of C. S. Lewis* (Grand Rapids: Eerdmans, 1964).

his life, he wrote profoundly on a subject with which our culture is greatly preoccupied, the love relation between man and woman. Sex and romance are inescapable in modern culture — they are omnipresent themes and images in our entertainment, advertising, and daily life. And in the world of research and teaching, sex, romance, and love also receive a great deal of attention. In our colleges and universities these topics are approached, in one way or another, by many of our academic disciplines — as well as, of course, in the nonacademic aspects of college life.

Undeniably, our knowledge of sex, romance, love, and human relations has been augmented in various ways over the past few decades. In particular, quantitative and scientific data have been multiplying at an incredible rate, but how much such growth contributes to our knowledge of how to live — and how to truly love — is another matter. C. S. Lewis, whose intellectual roots were in the classical and medieval world, was generally uneasy about the social sciences on the grounds that they were new subjects, at times too brash to know their limitations.

Lewis's greatest disagreements were not with the natural and physical scientists but with the social scientists and social engineers who assume too readily that people can and should be conditioned in the light of "new discoveries." He would have been the last to advocate sending out questionnaires or using interviews to analyze attitudes and problems with any depth. Yet he understood much about the causes of our discontents in this century. His perspective owed much to the insights of Plato, Augustine, Chaucer, and Milton.

In *The Four Loves* Lewis refers to the state that we call "being in love" as Eros. It includes the animally sexual element, which he calls Venus; but he points out that sexual experience can occur without Eros and that Eros includes other things besides sexual activity. Eros causes the lover to center his thoughts on the Beloved. He is full of desire for her; but the sexual interest is only part of a total desire to contemplate, possess, and give pleasure to his beloved. There have been those from Lucretius down to Orwell's Winston Smith in *1984* and Hugh Hefner's *Playboy* who want the physical sensation above all. They theorize that emotional involvement and talk of love will dull the sheer physicality of Venus. Yet the majority of human beings sing songs, write verses, give gifts and otherwise behave as if sexual activity should *mean* something. This meaning may be outrageously sentimental, but meaning is sought — witness almost any of the week's "Top Twenty" tunes.

Lewis points out that without Eros sexual desire becomes simply a fact about ourselves, that the most beautiful mountain view is "killed" when one begins to locate it in his "own retina and optic nerves."[2] But he is quick to challenge the view that Eros is noblest when Venus is reduced to the minimum. Though some of the Church Fathers depreciated sexuality, they did not see the greatest danger in soul-destroying surrender to the senses but rather in seeking to please one's partner to the neglect of "waiting uninterruptedly upon God."[3]

Lewis goes on to say that the Scriptures do not speak disparagingly of the marriage bed. In fact, St. Paul discourages prolonged abstinence from Venus in 1 Corinthians 7. Lewis might have added at this point that Luther commended marriage as a way toward chastity, for since the sexual impulse is so strong and few have the power to sublimate it completely, a married man may be more chaste than a monk in that he is free from the obsession of sex. Luther here stresses the remedial nature of marriage, for which Lewis does not settle. In our era it has become fashionable (1) to *detach* sexual love from the marriage relationship, and (2) to *reduce* the meaning of the sexual relationship to physical gratification. Lewis's perspective, a salutary gift to our confused times, relocates sexual love back into the marriage commitment and then broadens and deepens our understanding of it.

The Disciplined Awareness of a Unique Other

There are four basic emphases in Lewis's thought concerning the benefits of married love. First, in marriage one has the opportunity to develop a disciplined awareness of another person, to get to know that person in his or her uniqueness. In this respect, marriage is like friendship, and it is risky to marry someone with whom you

2. C. S. Lewis, *The Four Loves* (Harcourt Brace, 1960), p. 89.
3. See Roland Bainton, *What Christianity Says About Sex, Love, and Marriage* (New York: Association Press, 1957).

have had no real friendship. But the marriage relationship is mediated by a constancy of association and a physical closeness not to be found in friendship.

In *A Grief Observed,* writing anonymously on the death of his wife, Lewis says, "The most precious gift that marriage gave me was this constant impact of something very close and intimate yet all the time unmistakably other, resistant — in a word, real." He speaks of the "rough, sharp, cleansing tang" of the otherness of one's beloved. He says that even after she died, there rushed upon his mind "her full reality . . . not . . . foreshortened and patheticized and solemnized by my miseries but as she is in her own right." He finds this awareness, even when it is accompanied by grief, a "good and tonic" thing.[4]

It is good and tonic because you cannot love another until you have given that person the right to be himself or herself in his or her uniqueness (this is Erich Fromm's definition of love). We are commanded to love our neighbor and, as Luther taught, one's spouse is one's nearest neighbor. One loves her when she is attractive and when she is not, because one has discovered and affirmed her in her otherness. In this sense then, Eros can teach us to be self-giving, for as Lewis observes in *The Four Loves,* Eros is not prudential. Even a lawless love can teach a person something of the uniqueness of another.

In speaking of prep school homosexual affairs Lewis says in *Surprised by Joy* that for some boys it was the "only chink left through which something spontaneous and uncalculated could creep in. Plato was right after all. Eros, turned upside down, blackened, distorted, and filthy, still bore traces of his divinity."[5] Lewis here and elsewhere follows Dante and Aquinas in believing that sins of the body are the least bad of all sins. They arise, he says in *Mere Christianity,* out of the "Animal self"; and though they may become involved with the "Diabolical self," such pleasures as "putting other people in the wrong . . . back-biting . . . the pleasures of power, of hatred" are worse. They are worse because the mind and the will conspire in their gratification.[6] This view, of course, is in marked

4. C. S. Lewis, *A Grief Observed* (Faber & Faber, 1963), pp. 18, 45.
5. C. S. Lewis, *Surprised by Joy* (Geoffrey Bles, 1955), pp. 109-10.
6. C. S. Lewis, *Mere Christianity* (New York: Macmillan, 1953), p. 80.

contrast to the current American tendency to reduce "morality" to sexual morality.

Celebrating a "Pagan Sacrament"

Lewis finds a second gift bestowed in marriage in the opportunity it affords to celebrate sexuality as a kind of pagan sacrament. Good sex thus offers a way to be more physically and intensely alive; it brings a sense of well-being, of unity with the world of living things. I have wondered how much of the illicit sexual activity of our time reflects precisely a quest for this quality of aliveness. People who live and work in insulated high-rise capsules, surrounded by cement and smog, lose contact with the earth and living things. Such people are bound to feel less and less alive, less and less male or female. Perhaps sex and violence are the two most available ways for city-dwellers to be aware of their physicality.

Lewis believes Christianity to be "almost the only one of the great religions which thoroughly approves of the body — which believes that matter is good, that God Himself once took on a human body, that some kind of body is going to be given to us in Heaven and is going to be an essential part of our happiness, our beauty, and our energy."[7] In this connection he observes that nearly all of the greatest love poetry in the world has been produced by Christians.

In the light of these facts it is curious that Christianity has generally avoided the celebration of human sexuality in its teachings and ceremonies. Highly rhythmic music, dancing, and scant clothing have generally been taboo in Christian worship. Perhaps the best explanation is seen in the fear that practices associated with paganism would lead to idolatry. For example, the early Christians buried their dead, partly because of the belief in bodily resurrection but partly because their pagan neighbors cremated their dead. It would have been equally undesirable to celebrate Easter with liturgical dancing, which called to mind Bacchanalian rites, or to glorify

7. Lewis, *Mere Christianity*, p. 77.

the female form in any way, a practice too reminiscent of the cults of Venus and Diana.

It is regrettable that church history gives ammunition to those who find in Christianity a suspicion about sex and a tendency to connect the transmission of original sin with sexual function. Though this uneasiness about sex is not without sound reason (Eros can be badly perverted by the Diabolical self or the Animal self), it is unfortunate in that it obscures the thing that pagan cultures have glimpsed by means of what theologians have called "general revelation." Observing the rejuvenation of the earth in spring, sensing heightened powers in sexual relationships, and experiencing the amazement of parenthood must have led various pagan societies to their celebration of sexuality. Lest we disparage their insight we should remember that "pagan" comes from the Latin *pagani,* which literally means "worshipers in the fields." Better to be a worshiper in the fields than to worship at the altar of militarism, race, or even the American way. The Psalms and the Epistle to the Romans remind us that there is a revelation of God in nature.

Lewis's fictional and theological writings are filled with images that capture the joy of maleness and femaleness. Knowing that sex is not something we do but something we are, he celebrates it in descriptions that relate to the totality of our being (the Green Lady in *Perelandra,* Mark Studdock in *That Hideous Strength,* the tribute to femininity in *A Grief Observed:* "a nest of gardens, wall within wall, hedge within hedge, more secret, more full of fragrant and fertile life, the further you entered").[8]

Such an approach causes much of the glorification of intercourse, so frequently encountered today, to appear tawdry and mechanical. With respect to sex as with other subjects (government, art, worship), Lewis had a way of discovering profound insight in pagan cultures, for he did not believe that divine truth came only through the Hebrews and the Christians. Lewis finds in the phenomenon of myth-making itself evidence of a divine reality. Clyde Kilby's summary of Lewis on this point is important: "What is the cause of myth-making? There is a great, sovereign, uncreated, unconditioned

8. C. S. Lewis, *Perelandra* (New York: Macmillan, 1944); *That Hideous Strength* (New York: Macmillan, 1946); *Grief Observed,* p. 50.

Reality at the core of things, and myth is on the one hand a kind of picture-making which helps man to understand this Reality and on the other hand the result of a deep call from that Reality. Myth is a 'real though unfocused gleam of divine truth falling on human imagination' which enables man to express the inexpressible."[9]

In teaching literature I have found that students generally have difficulty with the relation of the Christian myths and symbols to other myths and symbols. They either want to say one is as good as another, leveling everything out, or they cannot fit Christian and pagan insights together. Perhaps the church has directed too much energy against paganism and not enough against the idolatries in our own culture, including those in the churches.

Lewis says that in the "pagan sacrament" of sex the man plays the Sky-Father and the woman the Earth-Mother. But, he adds, we must give full value to the word "play" — it is "play" in the sense of playing a part in a larger whole and also in the sense of happy abandon, as in a game. Lewis quotes Charles Williams in *Arthurian Torso:* "The maxim for any love affair is 'Play and pray; but on the whole do not pray when you are playing and do not play when you are praying.' We cannot yet manage such simultaneities."[10]

In *That Hideous Strength* Ransom warns Mark and Jane against that daintiness in love that would intellectualize the bodily instincts away. In *The Four Loves* Lewis says, "The highest does not stand without the lowest. A plant must have roots below as well as sunlight above and roots must be grubby. Much of the grubbiness is clean dirt if only you will leave it in the garden and not keep on sprinkling it over the library table."[11] A gloss on this statement appears in *Mere Christianity* in the warning against confusing propriety with chastity.[12] Primness has nothing to do with virtue and bodily functions do not in themselves connote anything immoral.

Perhaps our confusion here comes from the zeal of two extremes: one saying, with the Victorians, that the body must some-

9. Kilby, *Christian World of C. S. Lewis,* p. 81.
10. C. S. Lewis, *Arthurian Torso* (Oxford: Oxford University Press, 1948), pp. 58-59.
11. Lewis, *Four Loves,* p. 20.
12. Lewis, *Mere Christianity,* p. 74.

how be disowned or at least ignored (nineteenth-century girls did not have "legs," they had "limbs"); the other extreme saying, with the sex cultists, that human sexuality is far too magnificent to be associated with domesticity, pregnancy, or mundane body functions. Both groups need to be reminded of St. Francis's name for the body, "Brother Ass," which in Lewis's view strikes just the right note theologically.

The Victorians and sometimes the pietists before them treated human love in vague and airy terms, exalting "ideals" at the expense of any mention of the body. On the other hand, a composer like Wagner or novelists like D. H. Lawrence, Hemingway, and Norman Mailer expect too much from Eros. They make it carry much more of life than it is able to bear. The same may be said of television serials and Hollywood films whose subject is the constant toying with love and the search for the perfect love. These dramatic fantasies are produced through the talents of small armies of cosmetologists, costumers, script writers, musicians, and camera specialists — all aiming to create images of desirable man and woman, in impossible Technicolor in the case of the films and with omnipresent tremolo organ accompaniment in the case of the TV series. While the Christian interpretation of sex fully appreciates its pleasures, it has in it a profound sanity and humility that refuse to make sex an idol.

Perhaps only in this way can the perils of romantic love be avoided. Denis de Rougemont argues in *Love in the Western World* that romantic love by its very nature must be thwarted and unfulfilled, that the only "happy" fruition is for the lovers to die together. This is true because romantic love promises more than can be given in this world, as Emma Bovary and Anna Karenina discovered. De Rougemont observes that "love ceases to be a demon only when he ceases to be a god."[13]

Healing and Completing One Another

Lewis finds a third gift in marriage in the way one person completes the other, helping to heal the wounds encountered in living, help-

13. Quoted by Lewis in *Four Loves,* p. 17.

ing to overcome the limitations of being one person sealed in one skin. Here we can be kinder to the Victorians, who inherited from their Puritan forebears a genuine understanding of the companionable aspects of marriage. The Victorians had a special appreciation for these least exciting and least glamorous aspects of the relationship; and perhaps many of them understood that if Eros included falling in love, it also included the contemplation of the beloved — not simply over candlelight on the wedding trip but on humdrum journeys when a couple who have been long married can communicate by sharing the care of children or, occasionally, good silence.

This total relationship involves many common experiences in a total commitment. And this is precisely what is wrong with premarital or extramarital coition — it is an attempt to have part of the relationship out of context. It is not simply on whim that illicit lovers like to make breakfast for each other or in some way play at keeping house.

Stressing the companionable side of marriage may seem to favor the idea of the platonic marriage or the marriage of convenience. But because sex may not be to the fore does not mean that it has not been crucial in sealing the relationship. Venus need not, however, be as magically blissful as it was during the first year of marriage when the couple were young and unencumbered. In Lewis's thought it is the touchstone of lust to want "to have it again," whatever it may be — sexual ecstasy, money, or praise.

Lewis assumes that only in focusing on persons can we expect to avoid thing-centered lust. He would not go so far as some, however, in arguing that we should never love things; there is a legitimate love of things — for God's sake, as St. Augustine urged. For someone to love a beautifully tended garden that no one else ever saw might be immoral in the eyes of those who argue that we must use things and love people, never the reverse. But in Lewis's context the gardener might be responding, in a dim way perhaps, to the love of God and cooperating in the work of creation.

The role of memory is also important in understanding the difference between longing and lust. In *Out of the Silent Planet* Ransom discovers that to the unfallen *hrossa* on Malacandra, longing is not painful. "A pleasure is full grown only when it is remembered," they tell him. Thus the things that come only once in a *hross's* life, such as mating, are not only enjoyed in anticipation but are remembered and "boiled inside" and made "into poems and wisdom."[14] And in a letter he wrote as a young man while on vacation in southern England, Lewis says: "I still feel that the real value of such a holiday is still to come, in the images and ideas which we have put down to mature in the cellarage of our brains, thence to come up with a continually improving bouquet."[15]

Thus it may take many years of living and remembering to make a marriage. The traditional Christian stand against divorce reflects not only the belief that two have sacramentally become one but that it takes a lifetime to know some of the uniqueness of another person. And not the least value of the discovery of the other is the degree to which his or her being complements, challenges, and enlarges one's own being. "Five senses; an incurably abstract intellect; a haphazardly selective memory; a set of preconceptions and assumptions so numerous I can never examine more than a minority of them — never become even conscious of them all. How much of total reality can such an apparatus let through?"[16] Lewis argues that when two become one flesh their capacities for hearing and feeling and tasting the multitudinous variety of creation are enhanced.

There is still the temptation to mold the other person, to deny his or her "personhood"; but there is help in sexual and companionable incentives to expose oneself, to enjoy the otherness of one's spouse. It is in the nature of Eros to promise loyalty and constancy.[17] To that extent, Lewis would accept Luther's understanding of marriage as remedial. But agents used to alleviate human ills — the legal doctrine of equality, depth psychology, the peace efforts of the United Nations — are medicines, not foods. If we try to make them into systems that will in themselves provide nourishment, we commit the error of trying to make medicines into foods. The wellsprings of law and health and peace lie deeper than remedies. And so it is

14. C. S. Lewis, *Out of the Silent Planet* (New York: Macmillan, 1943), p. 76.
15. C. S. Lewis, *Letters,* ed. W. H. Lewis (Geoffrey Bles, 1966), pp. 71-72.
16. Lewis, *Grief Observed,* p. 51.
17. Lewis, *Mere Christianity,* p. 83.

with love, whose springs are deeper than domestic comfort or sexual sublimation.

Reflecting Divine Love

This leads to a final insight about marriage that Lewis crystallizes so memorably in climactic passages in several books and essays: earthly love as a reflection of divine love. Others before Lewis have explored the first three benefits that I have discussed (though seldom with as much clarity as Lewis brings to the subject). In dealing with these earlier points he focuses and synthesizes much that theologians, literary scholars, and others have said. But with respect to the last point he seems to me to be breaking fresh ground. Plato, St. Augustine, Dante, and St. Teresa have surveyed this land, but no other writer that I know has communicated as much about Eros as a preparation for heaven; many of the saints who have glimpsed this either lapse into mystical raptures (St. Teresa) or seem to renounce the body (St. John of the Cross).

Lewis had first become interested in the ideological implications of Romanticism when he was a student at Oxford, as we discover from *The Pilgrim's Regress* and the edition of letters compiled by his brother. *The Allegory of Love,* published in 1936, applied Lewis's thinking on the rise of romantic love to the development of literature. And then in *Surprised by Joy* he tells, autobiographically, how nameless longing and "Joy-Melancholy" entered into his religious pilgrimage.

A fairly subtle point emerges when we trace Lewis's treatment of romantic questing and longing: there are many good things to be enjoyed in this life, among them beauty, friendship, and love, but they are never quite what we anticipate nor quite what we remember. We are beckoned on continually toward that which will satisfy our hearts. This may sound like only a paraphrase of Augustine's "We are restless till we rest in Thee." But Lewis says somewhat more, with more careful analysis. He is arguing that God is present in every good but is not to be identified with that good. To echo Ingmar Bergman's Isak in *Wild Strawberries,* he woos us in "the twilight . . . an ear of grain and the fragrance of flower . . . in every sign and breath of air his voice is there. His voice whispers in the summer breeze."

Augustine shies away from sexual imagery in speaking of the vision of God, perhaps because in Augustine's experience sex was associated with a bondage that kept him from God. But Lewis celebrates the fact that in Hebrew-Christian thought God is always *he*, that God is definitely male in relationship to us. Before him we are all feminine, in physical strength, in dependence, and in needing him to define our being. It is significant in this connection that many psychologists now believe that a woman is fulfilled most completely not in sex itself but in motherhood. (This does not necessarily mean literal maternity — I have met nuns who were fully feminine and motherly in a most winsome way, though their willingness to give up conventional motherhood is not to be taken lightly.)

We are not only dependent upon God to define our being, but we look forward expectantly to union with him, though it is not to be a Nirvana sort of union in which our selfhood is lost. Lewis is quick to point out, however, in *The Problem of Pain*, that the sexual analogy of divine-human relationship is not one that can be pressed too far. The analogy has a long history; there is evidence of it in the early church response to *The Song of Songs* and in the continuing metaphor of the church as the Bride of Christ; it is also a consistent thread running through much of devotional literature. But the analogy cannot be pressed because there are no adequate analogies for the divine, and the erotic inevitably suggests that God has a body, an idea that has no real basis in Scripture.

While he does not press the erotic analogy, Lewis does make a strong case for Eros as a way to learn love for both God and other people. As he reasons in *The Four Loves*, we have no metaphors for the resurrection or heaven except as we find images in nature. As nature offers images for heaven so Eros offers images for love. He presents the different kinds of love as intermingling, each leading toward Charity, which is God-directed love (directed toward God — and by God toward others). Lewis is not disturbed by the idea, which Freud endlessly adumbrated, that there is an erotic element in friendship, religious experience, and many sorts of affection. Lewis in several books offers some telling rebuttals to Freudian arguments, but in *The Four Loves* he is content to stress the intermingling of our various loves.

Love is not the same as unselfishness. It may proceed out of an ample ego, but it develops in the person who learns to bend, to be vulnerable, and at times to be silent in order to affirm the well-being of the other person. This sort of behavior reflects a fidelity to God in that it involves loyalty to the realm of being — in fact, to very concrete other beings.

The fact that human loves can be images of divine love does not assure anyone salvation through Eros or Affection or Friendship, even at their highest. Proximity of likeness is not the same as proximity of approach.[18] Just as one does not need a college education to respond to God's love, so one need not to have deeply experienced Eros. There are many ways to know God. It is remarkable that Lewis as a rationalist and a scholar could recognize so humbly that reason is not enough, that simple "need-loves" can lead some people to God when their minds do not. Lewis's understanding of Eros does justice to the sacramental, companionable, and romantic aspects of marriage. Yet what is most helpful to me in his approach is that he rejects any concept of grace that abolishes nature.[19]

I do not recall Lewis commenting on that troubling passage in Matthew 22: "For in the resurrection they neither marry, nor are given in marriage, but are as the angels of God in heaven." At first Jesus' reply to the Sadducees appears to set aside earthly relationships and even sexuality — as if some of the earth's goods would be lost to heaven. But the context indicates that the basic issue is not the extent of a continuum between earth and heaven (the Sadducees did not believe in the resurrection). Jesus' reply to their mocking question about the woman who was married seven times seems to be about love, rather than about legality and institutions. Perhaps Christ is saying that in heaven there is no marrying or giving in marriage in the sense of exclusive, possessive love, but there is rather a mutuality of loves. Perhaps these will complete rather than set aside those loves that were growing on earth.

18. Lewis, *Four Loves*, p. 20.
19. Lewis, *Arthurian Torso*, p. 175.

Divine grace therefore does not set aside the creation. This world is real and human loves are real harbingers of a love that draws us toward a dance of life. In his memorable conclusion to *The Problem of Pain* Lewis describes this gamelike dance, which he envisions as a part of heaven. There the "golden apple of self-hood" is not an apple of discord for which the greedy scramble. Every dancer must by all means touch the ball (i.e., they must not deny their selfhood) and then pass it on: "To be found with it in your hands is a fault; to cling to it, death. But when it flies to and fro among the players too swift for eye to follow, and the great master Himself leads the revelry, giving Himself eternally to His creatures in the generation, and back to Himself in the sacrifice of the Word, then indeed the eternal dance 'makes Heaven drowsy with the harmony.' All pains and pleasures we have known . . . are initiations in the movements of that Dance."[20]

20. C. S. Lewis, *The Problem of Pain* (New York: Macmillan, 1947), p. 153.

Faith and Imagination

Jill Peláez Baumgaertner

On a steamy summer evening I found myself searching for a parking place on a Chicago street I would not ordinarily be driving down after dark. I had accepted an invitation to read my poetry at a place in Chicago called "Hothouse." When I agreed to do this, I did not know exactly what Hothouse was, but poets are always in search of audiences voluntarily cornered, so that is why I found myself walking into what was, to put it bluntly, a dive.

During the open-mike portion of the program, before my scheduled reading, I began to get nervous. The poems I was hearing were angry. The readers were artsy and unkempt. Soon, I realized in despair, I would have to make my way to the stage and read my poems, which were, in comparison, positively suburban.

It is always gratifying for a writer to feel that she has reached an audience — but this time I knew it would not happen because I did not fit here. I am not referring to the bar or to the seedy street in Chicago. I am referring to the character of the audience — the avant garde — those who dress entirely in black. I had read my poems before — but always to audiences filled with my friends — students, colleagues, people interested in the connections between the arts and Christianity — in short, to groups of people who would be naturally sympathetic to my conviction that there was such a reality as absolute truth. This audience at Hothouse? I had met versions of it many times before. One would not necessarily call Modern Language Association conventioneers part of the avant garde, or particularly artsy or necessarily urban — but as far apart as scholars and artists might be in American culture, still there are attitudinal similarities — a certain pack mentality that says to the casual observer what I often in sheer desperation say to my bull terrier: Hey! I am the master — and you are the dog. My years of graduate training, followed by the requisite years of nontenured, terror-induced, frenetic productivity, followed by another decade of the mad scramble through the professorial ranks had allowed me to master the process of writing the MLA paper — feverishly finished the day after Christmas to be delivered the day after that in that happiest time of year for everyone on earth except for English professors attending MLA in the no man's land between the Nativity of our Lord and New Year's Day. But this time, at Hothouse, I did not have a paper on John Donne or Flannery O'Connor in my hand. I had my poems. And it is very hard to adopt a pose or be anyone other than oneself when one is pronouncing the words of one's own poems.

In his essay "What Are Poets For?" the philosopher Martin Heidegger described the people in these audiences (wherever one meets them — MLA or Hothouse). After contending that "the appearance and sacrifice of Christ mark the beginning of the end of the day of the gods," Heidegger continues: "Night is falling. . . . The evening of the world's age has been declining toward its night." Heidegger calls this a "default of God" — God stepping back, dissociated from the world. He goes on to describe the world as having "grown so destitute, it can no longer discern the default of God as a default."[1] In other words, modern men and women have become so separated from God that they do not even recognize that any separation has taken place. The memory of union with God is so vague that the possibility of it does not exist even in the imaginations of the people. This is certainly the failure of clear vision, in addition to the collapse of the imagination. Outside of English classes (and increasingly even *inside* many English classes) the acknowledgment that the imagination is a necessary component of the fully lived life is usually as nonexistent as are references to God.

---

1. Martin Heidegger, *Poetry, Language, Thought* (New York: Harper & Row, 1971), p. 91.

I must say right now that I did not preach the gospel in the poems that I read that evening at Hothouse. I also realize that the poems I read about Fidel Castro's Cuba or my father's return from the Korean War are inherently political subjects, not completely suburban. But I nonetheless made an important discovery about audiences. Audiences, like children before bed, want neither poses nor polemics, either political or theological. What they really want is story, and if you give them that, you do not have to be wearing black. I learned that one should not be surprised if suddenly, on a warm night in a bar in Chicago, the glasses stop clinking and the room becomes very quiet.

I was greatly encouraged by this very promising indication that the imagination is always ready to be set in motion. And if the imagination is alive, well, of course, faith can be, too. In fact, it is in the imagination that faith begins. How could it possibly be otherwise? Believers believe in what cannot be seen. They accept the miraculous as fact. They must have imaginations to be people of faith.

What happens when the imagination fails? When that happens, faith is no longer a possibility. When the imagination fails, the writer can no longer write. When the imagination fails, even the nonwriter is cut off from the future and can do no more than live the present moment as if there were nothing else. And living that way, it is true: There is nothing else. The poet Sherod Santos says, "It may be we've wandered so aimlessly, so unsure of why or where we're going, because there's no longer anywhere to wander to, not even the future."[2] Our writers often reflect this, and it is helpful to point our students to the writers who grapple with this dilemma, writers whose imaginations collide with the grim implications of life in a culture that has forgotten the future. Martin Amis's novel Time's Arrow is a pilgrimage in reverse.[3] It is the story of a man's life played backward. It begins with the moment of his death and follows him as he lives his life backward, ending with his birth — but a birth that is also

2. Sherod Santos, "Into the Unknown to Find the New: Baudelaire's Voyage into the Twenty-first Century," The American Poetry Review (July/August 1995): 41.
3. Martin Amis, Time's Arrow (New York: Harmony Books, 1991).

backward, resulting not in a baby, but in a baby sucked back into his mother. Because everything works in reverse in this novel, the characters walk backward, drive backward, speak backward. Eating is particularly unattractive. They remove their food from their mouths, put it back onto their plates, walk backward into the kitchen, put it back into the pots and pans where after stewing for a while, it emerges fresh and uncooked and goes back into the refrigerator, later even taken back to the store in bags that are unloaded into grocery carts, the contents placed one by one back on the shelves, the cashier having already paid for its unloading.

In this kind of a universe, lived backward, everything is perverse. Physicians, for example, are no longer healers, but the evil creators of pain and injury. The narrator is a surgeon who must fit tumors back into the human body. "You want to know what I do?" he asks. "All right. Some guy comes in with a bandage around his head. We don't mess about. We'll soon have that off. He's got a hole in his head. So what do we do? We stick a nail in it. Get the nail — a good rusty one — from the trash. And lead him out to the Waiting Room where he's allowed to linger and holler for a while before we ferry him back to the night."[4]

The narrator is, understandably, in despair. How could this kind of world make any sense to anyone? His dishwasher, for example, works perfectly until a repair man comes and fools around with it a while and leaves after he has broken it.

As we move backward through this man's life, we realize that he was, in the early years of his medical career, a doctor who worked in the medical section of Auschwitz Concentration Camp — and once we discover this, we begin to realize that the "inversions of chronology in this novel seem perfectly in keeping with the Nazis' inversion of morality."[5] In this universe of the Backward, it is only in the medical wards at Auschwitz that doctors heal — since murder, at reverse speed, appears to be the giving of life. Out of ashes, the Jews are assembled. Gold is restored to the corpses' teeth, and bodies return to life in the gas showers.

4. Amis, *Time's Arrow*, p. 76.

5. David Lehman, "From Death to Birth," *The New York Times Book Review*, 17 November 1991, p. 15.

Return for a moment to Heidegger, who ironically, or maybe not so ironically, had his period of Nazi allegiance: "Not only does the holy . . . remain concealed; even the track to the holy . . . seems to be effaced." Martin Amis, in a strange way, an ironic way, points out the tracks and shows us how easily we head in wrong directions. How intensely he relies upon his imagination and upon the reader's sense of play to make this point.

We live in a culture in which people travel many miles and never arrive because, quite frankly, they do not know that they should have a destination. Our culture — and this is particularly true in the academic world — values "process over product"; it values "the means of making over and above what the making means."[6] And so we trivialize outcomes. We talk about critical thinking, but we often do not have anything worthwhile to think about. In literary theory this means that phrases such as "the deferral of meaning," or "refusal of closure," or "the poetry of indeterminacy" thrive because they describe a poetry that has rid itself of narrative structures to dwell solipsistically on itself.

Recall Bunyan's famous work, *The Pilgrim's Progress* — and pay careful attention to the title. A pilgrim is always someone on a journey to a goal; Bunyan's pilgrim, Christian, progresses through life on his way to the Heavenly City and union with God. There is *something* at the end of the journey, and it is something better than the journey itself. This journey of many steps and stages is a progress, an unfolding, an advancement. I am not suggesting that Christian always learns from his experiences or that he becomes a better and better person as a result. In many ways he does learn as he matures, but he also possesses the human tendency to lapse into doubt and error, to make mistakes, to commit sin. He cannot shed his flesh. But he is on his way to a goal, and that is what makes his journey important. Without a final destination, or a direction, his trials and tribulations would have no meaning because, frankly, at the end of his life he is still experiencing some of the same melancholic tendencies he showed at the very beginning of his journey — before he had encountered the cross. His experiences are important, but not in and of themselves. They are important because they are taking him somewhere.

6. Santos, "Into the Unknown," p. 41.

Perhaps this is the key difference between the seventeenth-century worldview and our own. Since 1976 a group of writers called the Language Poets have published over two hundred books of poetry and criticism. These language writers — including Charles Bernstein, Susan Howe, P. Inman, and Hannah Weiner — contend that language itself is the focus of their writing. They say that for them language is not something that explains or translates experience. Instead, it is the source of experience. They see writing as a political action in which the reader is not merely required to read or listen to the poem but is asked to participate with the poet/poem in bringing meaning to the community at large. This requires a new kind of reading in which meaning is not self-contained but is inseparable from the language in process.

What these poets are saying, essentially, is that the reader, as a participant in an interpretive community, creates the meaning of the poem. This idea has been around for a long time — and I believe it has some credibility — but only with the Language Poets do we find poets writing poems in which meaning is immaterial. In other words, the poet's goal is not communication of a specific truth or experience. Narrative and image are unimportant. It is the process of interpreting that is important, not any truth it might lead to, because, after all, "What is truth?"

Reflecting the disorder and unbelief of our time *is* something art does, but it is not enough. Once again, one sees imagination's failure operant — even in the world of poetry that should elevate it. The Language Poets do write the occasional stunning poem. But we need to be careful about embracing this school with uncritical minds. The duty of the writer is to reveal the disorder — and then, unlike the Language Poets, to push beyond it, to make connections, to put human experience into its varied, fascinating, and proper contexts.

How to capture the attention of a world in which traditional scriptural truths no longer have meaning was Flannery O'Connor's dilemma. Her fiction, grounded in this concrete and fallen world, has been called the fiction of the grotesque. The word is descriptive of her characters who are often unlovable, caricatured, and distorted. O'Connor is, of course, showing us ourselves. We cannot dismiss any of her characters as unworthy of grace without dismissing ourselves, too. Sin has done its job with even the most righteous. Accordingly, usually the most self-righteously moral of O'Connor's characters turn out to be the blindest, needing God most desperately and often capable of recognizing God only in the oddest, most distorted forms. Again, these characters are ourselves, the readers of O'Connor's fiction — and to read O'Connor is to enter a world laden with religious artifacts that demand our response.

A few images from her stories give a picture of the world to which O'Connor demands that her readers respond. After studying the heavens for days with a telescope, scrutinizing them carefully for the location of his mother who has died, a child hangs himself in order to get to the other end of the telescope so he can be with her in heaven. In "Greenleaf" a selfish and self-righteous woman is gored by her own bull, and finally, as she bends over his horns, receives revelation. In another story, "A Good Man Is Hard to Find," an entire family is shot by the side of the road, and in her final second on earth, the grandmother begins to act out the gospel. After her murder, the criminal carefully wipes his glasses and says, "She would have been a good woman, if it had been somebody there to shoot her every minute of her life." How odd these stories are — and how offensive. In this last story a criminal, the Misfit, complains to a woman he is about to shoot: "Jesus was the only One that ever raised the dead and He shouldn't have done it. He thrown everything off balance. If He did what He said, then it's nothing for you to do but throw away everything and follow Him, and if He didn't, then it's nothing for you to do but enjoy the few minutes you got left the best way you can — by killing somebody or burning down his house or doing some other meanness to him."

The grandmother he is about to kill says, "Maybe He didn't raise the dead," and the Misfit answers, "I wasn't there so I can't say He didn't. I wisht I had of been there. It ain't right I wasn't there because if I had of been there I would of known. Listen lady, if I had of been there I would of known and I wouldn't be like I am now."[7]

How odd that the Misfit's doubt has — at its center — belief.

7. Cited in Santos, "Into the Unknown," pp. 131-32.

"If I had of been there I would of known and I wouldn't be like I am now."

The grandmother spouts pious clichés to the Misfit in an attempt to flatter him and to save her skin. The Misfit does not resort to the dishonesty of clichéd language. He speaks the truth in both belief and in doubt. His denial of Christ is by his own admission a failure of his imagination. He cannot believe because he cannot see that story is inseparable from truth. Stories create the environment for the imagination to work — and no one who lacks imagination can have faith.

We usually see so little. How unaware we are of what is around us. The writer helps us to see what is there — and then helps us to see that that is not all there is — that amid the cacophony, the chaos, the backwardness of our time, if one listens hard enough, one can also hear a still, small voice and know that though "our life is hidden with Christ in God," it will finally be revealed with him in glory.

How unaware we are, usually, of God's orchestration. The novelist Paul Auster says,

> I believe that the world is filled with stories, that our lives are filled with stories, but it's only at certain moments that we are able to see them or to understand them. Most of us, myself included, walk through life not paying much attention. Suddenly, a crisis occurs when everything about ourselves is called into question, when the ground drops out from under us. I think it's at those moments when memory becomes a most powerful force in our lives. You begin to explore the past, and invariably you come up with a new reading of the past, a new understanding, and because of that you're able to encounter the present in a new way.[8]

Auster claims that his work comes out of "a position of intense personal despair, a very deep nihilism and hopelessness about the world, the fact of our own transience and mortality, the inade-

---

8. Mark Irwin, "Memory's Escape: Inventing *The Music of Chance* — A Conversation with Paul Auster," *Denver Quarterly* 28 (Winter 1994): 114.

quacy of language, the isolation of one person from another." And yet at the same time, he says, "I've wanted to express the beauty and extraordinary happiness of feeling yourself alive, of breathing in the air, the joy of being alive in your own skin. To manage to wrench words out of all this, no matter how inadequate they might be, is at the core of everything I've ever done." And then he tells a story of something that happened to him. He describes how over a number of months he came into contact with a series of individuals who had been strangers to him but who knew each other. He transforms a series of unlikely but true coincidences into a sign of some deep orchestration, some profound order, and a rich interconnectedness of human experience and spirituality. From most angles of observation, Auster seems to be an unbeliever, but when one looks closely at his stories and at the experiences that seem to trigger those stories, one realizes that he is portraying a world that appears chaotic and unplanned on the surface, but reveals mysterious structures to the person with the eyes and the imagination to see them.

And the poet or fiction writer who is also a member of a faith community? Sometimes in our communities of faith, as in the rest of life, we are overwhelmed with clichés and formulae, and a required faith language that masks rather than reveals. But, I ask you, how is this actually any different from our lives as English, theology, or history professors? Sometimes it is difficult to find the connections, but a writer must find connections. In our communities of faith and our communities of learning a writer's mandate is to see clearly enough to make those connections, to revitalize the language, to push beyond surfaces, to avoid the mindless banalities of culture (including those of religion), to resist cheap commercialism that always opts for the superficial — and to dare to see the truth, which is sometimes hidden and mysterious.

The writer in this situation may often feel that she does not fit perfectly into her community — but in actuality this uncomfortable position is also a position of privilege, and it gives the writer a unique angle of vision. And of course it is not just chance that has put her there.

We dream dreams. And in that sense we are all believers, we

are all visionaries, we are all poets. We require a vision — of something else — of something beyond the mundane to which we are so inextricably attached. And the way we escape the mundane is not by walking backward, but by walking forward into the dark. Christ did this. He did not reverse his life when he saw the cross in front of him, even though in the Garden he wanted to. Nor can we reverse our lives, even though sometimes we may want to. What he did in history, he did, and as he said when his time in history was over, "It is finished." What we have done, we have done. Our past is over. We live in the present moment. But the present for us is a moment that stretches forward into a future that only our imaginations allow us to glimpse, just as the present for Christ stretched forward into the Resurrection.

The imagination needs careful cultivation. Heidegger described the postmodern plight when he said, "The time of the world's night is the destitute time, because it becomes ever more destitute. It has already grown so destitute, it can no longer discern the default of God as a default." Heidegger did not stop there. He went on to say, "The poet in the time of the world's night utters the holy." The poet is able to sense the divine and to trace its tracks. One must recognize the danger of romanticizing the "Cult of the Artist," but at the same time that Heidegger veers in a dangerous direction (and his life was filled with such veering), he also fingers the truth. The writer, speaking from his or her position of privilege on the fringe, tied to images, to characters, to narratives as linear or circular as life itself, making connections, speaking not in abstractions but telling stories, provides, as Dennis Ford has noted, "the necessary means of giving shape to the moral life." Ford contends further that as a culture "we are not storyless because we are nihilistic; we are nihilistic because we are storyless."[9] The imagination and its image-making, word-creating, storytelling functions afford us life-giving glimpses now and then of the transcendent.

The greatest gift any professor can give to students is the freedom to see the truth of story and the absolute necessity of poetry

---

9. Dennis Ford, *Sins of Omission: A Primer on Moral Indifference* (Minneapolis: Fortress, 1990), pp. 65, 68.

in the fully lived life. A bureaucrat who loves poetry will never be just a bureaucrat. A physician who understands the importance of story in a patient's life, a lawyer who knows Shakespeare, a pastor who reads *The Brothers Karamazov,* will be encouraged to live life as if it mattered, and then to step through the pointless mundane to another level of reality.

Prayer and Higher Education

Carnegie Samuel Calian

Americans have a propensity to pray. According to a recent Gallup Survey, 91 percent of women indicated they prayed; 85 percent of men said they did. One could almost say that the United States is a praying nation. Most college students, however, are not encouraged to develop the practices of prayer. This may be due to the prevailing secular environment, campus restrictions, or a general lack of enthusiasm among administrators, faculty, and the student body for such behavior. Whatever the reasons, this is a tragedy!

Clearly, our public and secular universities and colleges ought not to serve up some "lowest common denominator" official prayers for general consumption as an answer to this need. Coerced piety cannot be religiously faithful, pedagogically effective, or politically acceptable. Nevertheless, just as our political science departments respect political activism and our sociology departments look with favor on social activism, so our religious studies programs ought to look with favor and appreciation on religious practice, central to which is prayer. Religious commitment has been at the foundation and at the heart of the historical development of higher education. Appreciatively, critically recognizing this in the classroom — and generally encouraging such commitment in individual student lives and among various campus groups — is true to our educational tradition.

Among the hundreds of church-related colleges and universities in America, the situation is, if anything, more tragic. Despite their roots (and often their ongoing support by Christian individuals and churches), too many such colleges are either passively or actively secularizing life and learning on their campuses. In many cases, there may be a "chapel" vs. "classroom" struggle going on within the college psyche, revealing the fact that we have yet to integrate these two experiences harmoniously. Consequently, many church-related college campuses are no longer communities of expectation. Prayer life has become sterile. We are too busily engaged in cognitive learning, neglecting the spiritual dimension that complements our intellectual pursuits. The educational agenda of our colleges is not yet sufficiently holistic. At worst, the atmosphere is hostile to religious practice and prayer. What spirituality is cultivated (or tolerated) is then left to outsiders and parachurch movements. Unfortunately, denominations today have tended to restrict and reduce their limited resources to campus ministries. This is sad, and the prospects for its improvement seem dim.

The simple and plain truth is that prayer and spiritual development are essential to the well-being of every college student. This is the argument of this chapter. At the very least, I am contending that all of our colleges and universities should welcome such prayer (expressed in appropriate, noncoercive contexts, of course) — and that our church-related colleges and universities should take active steps to reestablish prayer in their communities of learning. In what follows, I want to sketch out the meaning and importance of prayer for college students so that even "nonprayers" and "nonbelievers" among faculty and administrators might understand its significance for the "prayers" and "believers" on their campuses.

Everyone, I contend, is on a personal journey of faith — in search of authentic relationships worthy of trust during their lifetime. We are also in pursuit of our self-interest, but are often too myopic to see what is in our best interest. Prayer is the process of discerning our self-interest in the light of God's will. In other words, prayer can be described as everyone's earnest conversation with God to ascertain the Divine will, knowing in our heart of hearts that following it is in our best interest. True prayer is not asking God to do our bidding, but rather discovering what God's will is for us and then doing it. Most responses to prayers are seen in retrospect. Prayer is God's way of saving us from ourselves. In the final analysis, the person of prayer knows that God alone offers the peace that surpasses all understanding leading to personal fulfillment.

This is why prayer should be encouraged and cultivated in the student's self-development. The practice of prayer is an important exercise in character building within our lives. The depth of our prayer life measures the progress of our faith journey. College education can provide perspective and substance to our prayers; but there is no guarantee that "educated prayers" are more effective than the prayers of a novice. During college years we often sidetrack the development of our prayer life for the information and stimulation provided in our courses. We may know that there is no need for division between prayer life and intellectual pursuits; however, when we analyze where we spend most of our time, the classroom and library often overshadow the college chapel or other venues and occasions for prayer.

Clarifying the Meaning of Prayer

I recently asked a former classmate if the understanding of prayer he brought to college and his present understanding of prayer were different. His immediate response was "Yes, there has been a change." He went on to say that his present understanding of prayer has benefited from an additional thirty-six years of experience. "And what does this mean?" I asked. His response was less clear at this point. "I guess," he said, "prayer is an expression of my private, personal struggle to gain a greater grasp on the meaning of life. Prayer enables me to be open with God; it is an expression of my ongoing trust in God." "But were you less trusting," I asked, "less open earlier in your life when you conversed with God in prayer?" He had a confused look on his face; perhaps I had been unfair in pressing for further clarity in what was obviously an ambiguous situation. I wonder, for that matter, what progress any one of us has made in our prayer life since our pilgrimage of faith commenced? If we would confess to one another, I suspect we might admit that we have even regressed, or at best that our journey of faith reveals a zigzag pattern with little progress. Of course, we have read more books, heard more lectures, and have more scars to show for our added years of experience.

Many within our college communities are in a better position today to articulate their struggles with God than when they first entered the hallowed halls of ivy. After all, the college community is where critical interpretation takes place — we interpret not only the text and context, but also our range of experiences — learning to place tragedies as well as joys within perspective. Prayer for many of us is a means of reviewing the text and context of our experiences in dialogue with God. Colleges are indeed acute arenas in which to practice the hermeneutics of prayer — allowing us space for our doubts, skepticism, and suspicions.

To pray is to engage simultaneously in many aspects of dialogue with God — at one moment we are expressing adoration and praise, in another thanksgiving and confession, announcing our sorrows as well as blessings, and presenting further petitions and supplications before God. All prayers are premised on God's grace and freedom to respond to us. The believer trusts that God has our best interest at heart; it is for this reason that every prayer is uttered in the spirit that God's will, not ours, be done. The Psalms and Lord's Prayer are our models for praying.

Eugene H. Peterson, well-known writer and translator of Scripture, in his recently published modern rendition of the Psalms informs us that "the impulse to pray is deep within us, at the very center of our created being, and so practically anything will do to get us started — 'Help' and 'Thanks!' are our basic prayers." Frankly, there is no "insider" language to prayer. "Prayer," he points out, "is elemental, not advanced, language. It is the means by which our language becomes honest, true, and personal in response to God. It is the means by which we get everything in our lives out in the open before God."[1]

It is not surprising then that we have the Pauline admonition to "pray without ceasing" (1 Thess. 5:17). On the Pittsburgh Theological Seminary campus, the presence of a prayer room, regular chapel services, prayers before classes, at times in faculty and ad-

---

1. Eugene Peterson, *The Message* (Colorado Springs: NavPress, 1995), pp. 646-48.

ministrative offices, and at the beginning and close of committee meetings are ways in which institutionally we attempt to follow through on the apostolic admonition to "pray without ceasing." On a personal level, we are tempted to ignore this praying attitude toward life; we are too busy trying to make it on our own. Even as we study the sacred subjects of the curriculum including classes on spirituality, we know there is a gap between where we are and where we need to be in our communion with God.

Prayer and Learning

To say that prayer ought to be at the heart of college education is to emphasize that we need prayer institutionally and individually. Every campus (at least, Christian campuses!) ought to have a sacred place for prayer and meditation. To pray "without ceasing" is both an activity and a state of being that engages our hearts, minds, and souls. Within such a composite outlook, we can foster an atmosphere of expectation and excitement to energize our studies and community life together. We must learn to pray with our eyes open as well as shut. Open to the facts and insights gathered in our classrooms; and shut in meditation and awesome wonder before the mysteries of God, which defy absolute definition.

John Calvin often referred to the world around us as a "theater of God's glory." To transform this world into the kingdom of God calls for praying with our eyes open as well as with our eyes shut. In Christian history there are two traditions of prayer and theologizing — apophatic and kataphatic. Apophatic prayer is "praying with eyes shut," centering on the Divine in silence knowing that all human expressions of conceptualizing are inadequate. Kataphatic prayer is "praying with eyes open," seeking to express in a limited way the majesty of Divine grace experienced. Both approaches, at their deepest levels, view prayer as listening for God's peace and presence, beyond words and images, as we enter into a unifying moment of ecstasy and tranquillity. Being at one with God (John 17) and listening to the murmuring of the Spirit within the silence of our hearts are the essence of prayer.

To pray is a universal exercise among all religionists of every persuasion. Every tradition in its own way fights against turning prayers into form without substance. The late distinguished Rabbi Abraham Joshua Heschel has said, "To pray is to bring God back into the world . . . to expand His presence." But for Heschel, talking *about* God, which is what religion professors do, can become idle chatter unless one first learns to talk *to* God. Real prayer seeks to address God through silence, not chatter.

Unless we are dialoging prayerfully with God, academic study can indeed become arid. Prayer needs to be foundational to all college education if the excitement and enthusiasm for studying the sacred is to flourish. William James has rightly said, "Prayer is the very soul and essence of religion." Prayer is the religious experience *par excellence* that is available to each of us. It is much more than the human attempt to bend God's will to our will. Prayer is more than the human manipulation of Divine providence — a form of spiritual lobbying for our desires. Prayer instead quickens our sense of social responsibility and stewardship before God. Without fear we ask for God's will to be done in our lives, believing in a loving and gracious God.

What we pray for and what we think about are closely interrelated. Prayer is the fundamental way that we approach God. Prayer reminds us that we come from God; we are sustained by God and our destiny is to be with God. Prayer is our way of expressing trust in God, finding affirmation as we move closer to the Divine purpose and meaning of our lives. As Augustine has said, we are restless until we find our rest in God.

Prayer and Empowerment

Prayer is also our means to combat the demons and dinosaurs in our midst. Theologian Karl Barth, in his insightful book *Prayer,* uncovers from Luther's *Large Catechism* the fact that prayer is necessary in our demonic struggles. According to Luther,

> we know that our defense lies in prayer alone. We are too weak to resist the Devil and his vassals. Let us hold fast to the weapons of the Christian; they enable us to combat the Devil. For what

has carried off these great victories over the undertakings of our enemies which the Devil has used to put us in subjection, if not the prayers of certain pious people who rose up as a rampart to protect us? Our enemies may mock at us. But we shall oppose both them and the Devil if we maintain ourselves in prayer and if we persist in it. For we know that when a Christian prays in this way: "Dear Father, thy will be done," God replies to him, "Dear child, yes, it shall be done in spite of the Devil and of the whole world."[2]

Jesus also used prayer to counter Satan when taken to the desert (Matt. 4:1-11). He was tempted following his forty days in the wilderness where he had fasted. Jesus was vulnerable at that moment and Satan knew it. Each Satanic gesture was an offer of food, power, and wealth. Jesus, empowered through praying, responded each time with the aid of Scripture.

Not only is prayer useful in fighting off demons, but also in sidestepping the dinosaurs that wish to drag us down into the tar pits of irrelevance. Under the guidance of the Holy Spirit we need inspired and visionary prayers to lead us. To many, our prayers seem to restrict us to the status quo, missing our need to relate to an increasing hostile and hurting world undergoing rapid change. As William Easum has recently written in his provocative book, *Dancing with Dinosaurs,* we cannot afford to be insensitive to the accelerated pace of change around us; otherwise we are drawn dangerously close to "dancing with dinosaurs" before the tar pits of doom. Churches and academic institutions "with a slow pace of change are no longer adequate in a fast-changing world. In an age of computers, we cannot express truth in the language of a chariot age. The time has come for new wineskins."[3]

Today, institutional long-range planning is confronted with tough choices as schools seek to clarify priorities. The call is out for a new reformation within our academic institutions that is future

2. Karl Barth, *Prayer, According to the Catechisms of the Reformation* (Philadelphia: Westminster, 1952), pp. 9-10.
3. William Easum, *Dancing with Dinosaurs* (Nashville: Abingdon, 1993), p. 13.

oriented and realistic. Unless we plan strategically and wisely, we will become a museum of dinosaurs. Canadian writer Douglas Coupland, author of *Generation X*, already anticipates Dinosaurland in his recent book intentionally entitled *Life After God*.[4]

The practice of prayer will not only help us to resist demons and dinosaurs, but it will help us to develop our "fourth instinct." According to Arianna Huffington in *The Fourth Instinct: The Call of the Soul*, the first three instincts are survival, power, and sex. The fourth instinct within us is the urge to find meaning, transcendence, wholeness, and truth.[5] Prayer makes a difference in life by changing our view of the world and our understanding of ourselves. Prayer gives us a cosmic outlook beyond our limited horizons. Through prayer, this fourth instinct is given an opportunity to express itself; the channels of prayer can lift us to new levels of authenticity and fulfillment beyond our imagination.

In her book *The Body of God*, theologian Sallie McFague suggests that all of the world is "God's body"; we are all interconnected.[6] Playwright John Guare indicates that there exist only "six degrees of separation" between any two persons on this planet. We are a network of humans who can empower one another by the grace of God through prayer. Spirit-led prayers are essential in quickening the pulse of our college communities, enabling us to fulfill our mission.

Religiously related colleges carry the responsibility to support the transforming of society under God. Prayer is essential in this transformation, and the cultivating of prayer ought to be at the core of the church-related college's education and vision. Nonreligious colleges and universities are also a part of the transformation of society. Adopting a tolerant, appreciative stance toward the practices of prayer by individuals and communities related to their campuses can have a salutary impact on their overall mission in today's world.

4. Douglas Coupland, *Life After God* (New York: Simon & Schuster Pocketbooks, 1995).

5. Arianna Huffington, *The Fourth Instinct: The Call of the Soul* (New York: Simon & Schuster, 1994), p. 14.

6. Sallie McFague, *The Body of God* (Minneapolis: Fortress, 1993), pp. 210-11.

What We Can Learn About
Higher Education from the Jesuits

W. Ward Gasque

One of the most dynamic educational forces in the world over the past 450 years has been the movement founded by Ignatius Loyola and six brilliant young theological students in Paris in 1534.[1] Eleven years earlier, the Spaniard Ignatius had experienced a profound religious conversion followed by a series of mystical experiences. In 1534 he was both the eldest and the least well educated of the group that founded the Jesuits. But he was a religious and organizational genius, and an extremely charismatic personality. The vision of Christ and his kingdom that Ignatius later formulated in his celebrated and influential handbook (entitled simply *Spiritual Exercises*) found a home in the hearts of his youthful companions.

Ignatius's six younger friends (Peter Favre of Savoy, Francis Xavier of Navarre, Simon Rodriguez of Portugal, and Diego Lainez,

---

1. For some general introduction, see William A. Bangert, *A History of the Society of Jesus* (St. Louis: The Institute of Jesuit Sources, 1972); Philip Caraman, *Ignatius Loyola: A Biography of the Founder of the Jesuits* (San Francisco: Harper & Row, 1990); John W. Donohue, *Jesuit Education: An Essay on the Foundations of Its Idea* (New York: Fordham University Press, 1963); Allan P. Farrell, *The Jesuit Ratio Studiorum of 1599* (Washington: Conference of Major Superiors of Jesuits, 1970); George E. Ganss, *The Jesuit Educational Tradition and Saint Louis University* (St. Louis: The Institute of Jesuit Sources, 1969); George E. Ganss, *Saint Ignatius' Idea of a Jesuit University* (Milwaukee: Marquette University Press, 1956); Ignatius Loyola, *The Constitutions of the Society of Jesus*, trans. George E. Ganss (St. Louis: The Institute of Jesuit Sources, 1970); Robert Schwickerath, *Jesuit Education: Its History and Principles*, 2nd ed. (St. Louis: B. Herder, 1904).

Alphonsus Salmeron, and Nicholas Bobadilia of Spain) were among
the most gifted university students of their day. They bound themselves together by a common commitment to poverty, chastity, the
evangelization of the world, and a fierce desire to serve Christ and
the church. The name they took for themselves was "The Company
of Jesus." Ignatius, a former military man, used the Spanish term
compania to express their soldierly loyalty to their Captain, Jesus.
This was Latinized to *societas* or Society. Their aim as a company
loyal to Jesus was "not only to seek with the aid of God's grace the
salvation and perfection of [their] own souls but with the aid of the
same to labor for the salvation and perfection of [their] neighbor[s]"
(from the opening declaration of the *General Examen*).

After several false starts, they came to the conclusion that the
best means of fulfilling this mission was by establishing a worldwide
network of educational institutions. By the time of Loyola's death
in 1557, twenty-three years later, the seven students who met together in Paris had been joined by one thousand others, most of
them young men, who had established some one hundred educational mission centers around the world. By about 1600 there
were thirteen thousand of these young Christian visionaries and
more than two hundred colleges, many of which remain to the
present day.

Today, 184 Jesuit postsecondary institutions circle the globe
and enroll approximately 450,000 students: 36 are in the USA and
Canada, 24 in Latin America, 53 in Europe, 41 in India, 24 in East
Asia, 5 in Africa, and 1 in the Near East.[2] Together, they have been
and continue to be one of the more dynamic forces in the world
of higher education and, indeed, in the world at large.

Like the Pharisees of Jesus' day — and the fundamentalists of
our own — the Jesuits have tended to get a bad press that has, at
times, overshadowed the positive contributions of the movement.
Thus "Jesuitical" becomes a derogatory term like "fundamentalist"
— used to dismiss ideas and attitudes with which the speaker disagrees but does not wish to take time to refute! And, of course, there

2. James W. Sauve, "Jesuit Higher Education Worldwide," in *Jesuit Higher
Education,* ed. Rolando E. Bonachea (Pittsburgh: Duquesne University Press,
1989), p. 162.

is some reason for these negative feelings in the history of the Jesuit movement, as is the case with *any* religious or political movement that enjoys significant numerical growth and becomes something of a mass movement.

I am not an apologist for Jesuit theology (though I confess a profound attraction to Jesuit spirituality as encapsulated in the *Spiritual Exercises* and also to the educational and missionary vision outlined in the *Constitution of the Society of Jesus*) — nor am I blind to the weaknesses of the movement, past or present. But my purpose in this essay is to focus on the positive accomplishments of the Jesuits in higher education, and to see what we Protestants can learn from the Jesuit vision, strategy, and experience.

A Clear Mission

First, the Jesuits demonstrate the value and power of a clearly stated, continually repeated, and consistently reinforced mission. The Jesuit mission is not simply the mission of Christianity in general or of the Catholic Church in particular. Nor is it the same as that of the Franciscans or the Dominicans or any other religious order. The mission of the Society of Jesus is a unique mission encapsulated in particular documents: the spiritual vision of the *Exercises,* the strategic thinking of the *Constitutions,* and the educational program of the *Plan of Studies (Ratio Studiorum).*

With a clear mission, carefully stated in written form, the Jesuit movement did not die with its charismatic founder. Nor has there been a need constantly to reinvent the wheel, so to speak, with each change in leadership, or with extension into new areas. In spite of many ups and downs and even periods of interdiction, the educational and missionary enterprise of the Society of Jesus has remained amazingly true to its originally stated purpose.

A Global Perspective

Second, the Jesuits, much more than their Protestant counterparts, developed a global perspective. Despite their impressive theological insights, the Reformers developed neither a theology of, nor a strategy for, the Christian world mission. What could be clearer from a reading of Matthew or Luke-Acts or the Letters of Paul than that the Good News is to be shared with the whole world? But, as was the case with the majority of the leaders in the First Church of Jerusalem, the Reformers never really understood this fundamental aspect of the Christian faith. Instead, they focused on the renewal of the existing national churches of Europe.

But what a contrast with the Jesuits! From the beginning, they were themselves an international fellowship: Spanish, Savoyard, French, and Portuguese. Within a generation they were nearly as diverse as is the great multitude envisaged at the end of time in the Revelation of St. John. They quickly encircled the globe with the message of Jesus as they understood it, seeking to master the languages and cultures of the people to whom they came, thus providing models of cross-cultural missions that endure. Consider the examples of Francis Xavier and Matteo Ricci.

Francis Xavier (1506-1552), born into an aristocratic Spanish-Basque family, was the model multicultural missionary among the original group of Jesuits. Highly gifted as a linguist, he arrived in Goa, on the southwest coast of the Indian subcontinent, in 1542. There he ministered to the sick and taught the gospel (Jesuits tend to *teach* rather than *preach*) to people of every stratum of society and laid the foundations of the ongoing Jesuit mission there. During his brief three-year stint thousands were baptized.

From India, Francis moved on to Malacca, in what is today Malaysia. There he met Hachiro, who became the first Japanese Christian. With Hachiro and two others, Francis traveled to Japan in 1549, where he established a flourishing community of more than two thousand baptized believers but was driven out by the combined efforts of local warlords and jealous religious leaders. Undaunted, he moved on to establish friendships in China and then shortly thereafter returned to Goa. In 1552 he returned to China but was not allowed to enter the mainland and died the same year on the island of Sancian off the coast of China. At the time of his death at the age of 44 there were nearly three quarters of a million Asian Christians as a result of his brief but intense and highly effective ministry.

Matteo Ricci (1552-1610) took up the cause of reaching the Chinese where Francis Xavier left off. An even more brilliant linguist than was Francis, he reached Macao in 1582 and immediately set about mastering Mandarin Chinese. In 1583 he entered China proper at the invitation of the magistrate of Chao-ching, where he translated the Ten Commandments and initially was strongly opposed by the locals. But in due course his famous map of the world, his clocks, books, mathematical devices, mastery of the Chinese language and literature, superior intellect, and compelling apologetic approach won great respect at the highest levels of society.

Matteo Ricci attempted to build a bridge between the traditional wisdom of the Chinese sages and the wisdom of the biblical sages, culminating in the teachings of Jesus.[3] The emperor summoned him as a wise man to Beijing in 1601, where he lived until his death ten years later. At the time of his death there were thousands of Christians at the Imperial Court, some of them at the highest levels. Christianity flourished in China for a century, until his work was overturned as the result of (let me speak frankly) imperialistic and ignorant Roman bureaucrats who objected to the fact that the church in China had become too Chinese.

Francis Xavier and Matteo Ricci are merely representative of a great cloud of witnesses to the early Jesuit mission. The story could be told again and again. The Jesuit movement was forward-looking in nature, and it had a powerful, strategic plan for global impact. The lives of the Jesuits bear witness to the power of a combined commitment to rigorous intellectual activity and Christian mission. The Protestant world has never experienced the same combination on anything like the same scale. Is it any wonder that the Catholic "Counter Reformation" was so successful in reclaiming much of Europe from the Protestant Reformation and establishing Western Catholicism as the most ethnically diverse segment of Christendom?

3. See Jonathan Spence, *The Memory Palace of Matteo Ricci* (New York: Viking Penguin, 1985).

The Value of the Spiritual

A third lesson from the Jesuits concerns the importance of spiritual formation in the educational mission. At the heart of the Jesuit vision are the values and experiences of Ignatius' *Spiritual Exercises*. This is where we may see the greatest contrast between the Jesuit tradition and evangelical Protestant education today. The contrast between this vision and the outlook of contemporary secular education is, of course, even more striking.

I am a graduate of the college that is generally recognized as the premier college of the Coalition for Christian Colleges and Universities. When I was a student there some thirty-six years ago, chapel attendance was required and each class began with prayer. But this was the extent of the structured spiritual discipline required. It was easy to avoid becoming too deeply involved in spiritual formation. Certainly there were no formal structures to provide spiritual direction.

Most of the oldest colleges and universities in America, and generally those held in highest regard, were established as evangelical Christian institutions. Each one had an explicitly Christian mission statement and motto.[4] (Interestingly, only *Veritas* remains today of Harvard's original motto, *Veritas pro Christo et ecclesia*.) Each had an orthodox confession of faith as a part of its foundational documents; and some (e.g., Princeton University) required chapel attendance well into the twentieth century. Nevertheless, each of these institutions moved away from the views of its evangelical Christian founders. And the same story has been repeated hundreds of times among the less famous, originally evangelical, church-related colleges and universities of America. Why? And do we have any reason to believe that the situation will be different in regard to the current generation of evangelical Christian colleges?

I do not know. But I am not very optimistic. A required allegiance to carefully articulated Christian doctrines is rather hollow if it exists independent of any central commitment to spiritual formation, spiritual discipline, and worship. Most of the chapel services I

4. See George M. Marsden, *The Soul of the American University: From Protestant Establishment to Established Nonbelief* (Grand Rapids: Eerdmans, 1994).

have attended in my lifetime in a wide variety of Protestant institutions contain little, if any, worship. There is entertainment, the communication of information (some of which has spiritual implications), inspiring (and sometimes also boring) talks, a brief prayer or two, possibly a Scripture reading, gospel songs (in the days of my youth) or so-called "Scripture songs" (today), and very occasionally even a real hymn. But there is virtually no God-focused, Christ-centered worship in the classical Christian sense. In many Christian colleges today, the majority of the faculty prefer to spend the chapel hour in the faculty lounge drinking coffee or working in their offices rather than attend chapel. Some Christian college presidents rarely attend chapel. It is unlikely that spiritual development and worship will be important to students so long as faculty and administrators fail to consider it an essential part of their everyday lives.

A few years ago, when the newly appointed president of a Christian college in New England suggested that the college should (after years of nonenforcement) honor its officially stated policy of requiring all members of the faculty to be practicing Christians, a huge outcry was heard. Imagine what might happen if he had suggested that faculty not only should be members of Christian churches but also give as much attention to their growth in the grace and knowledge of Jesus Christ as they give to their advancement in the knowledge of their academic disciplines, or that they begin to take the commitment to the integration of faith, thought, and life seriously!

Contemporary Jesuit higher education has dropped its requirement that all faculty be Christians. Nevertheless, among the members of the Society of Jesus, who form the core faculty of all Jesuit universities, there is still a common commitment to the life of the *Spiritual Exercises* and to the values of the *Constitutions*. Every Jesuit professor begins with a journey through the *Spiritual Exercises,* the foundational document for their daily life and work.

At the heart of the *Spiritual Exercises* is conversion to Christ. This point of departure provides the Christian disciple with a worldview that includes "God, the universe and human beings with their place and function within it."[5] Ignatius sees all things as coming

5. George E. Ganss, Jr., "St. Ignatius and Jesuit Higher Education," in Bonachea, ed., *Jesuit Higher Education,* p. 156.

from God and then serving as stepping-stones by which people can achieve the chief purpose of their lives, which is the eternal happiness of loving, and being loved by, God. Thus, all of the world is worthy of study, because everything has inherent value as a gift of God and can become a stepping-stone into God's presence. This worldview is "focused squarely on the central marvel or 'mystery' in God's revelation: God's plan for the creation and redemption of humankind."[6] This worldview values everyone, everywhere, and embraces past, present, and future, this life and the next.

Holistic Education

The Jesuits were committed to the *integration* of the intellectual and spiritual, to a holistic education. The spiritual side of life, discussed in the previous section, was not to be left in some autonomous "God-compartment." Ignatius and the early Jesuits took the best of the older scholastic education that had originated in the thirteenth century, with its emphasis on contemplative theology and philosophy and knowledge for its own sake — and combined this with the best of the new humanism of the sixteenth century, which stressed education for character development and the application of knowledge in the service of the common good. Thus, the latest advances in the study of the humanities, the arts, and the sciences were celebrated along with theology, the queen of the sciences and the capstone of a Jesuit education.

Theology became the integrative factor for the Jesuits, but it was a robust theology that gave primacy to Scripture (in the original languages, studied by means of the new tools of Renaissance scholarship) and the study of the early Church Fathers, and a theology that was in constant dialogue with the arts and sciences (not an abstract theology).

Few members of college and university faculties today are able to integrate Christian and secular perspectives. Most of the academic movers and shakers on campus have received all of their advanced education in a totally secular context at a major state or private

6. Ganss, "St. Ignatius and Jesuit Higher Education," p. 155.

research university. In many cases, faculty members have never taken so much as one course in Bible or theology. Even those who attended religious colleges have taken only a few courses in biblical and theological studies — and then only at the most basic, unsophisticated level. Many who have received formal theological education all too often have not received academic training at the same level, or in the same disciplinary areas, as have their colleagues with doctorates from Harvard, Berkeley, and Chicago.

The situation is entirely different in the Jesuit tradition. Not only does every Jesuit professor have a solid and comprehensive academic education, each one is also a theological graduate. In fact, it is not unusual to find Jesuits who have two or more doctorates, in different fields. It is not hard to feel intimidated in the presence of such scholars.

A former colleague once made a rather untactful remark when speaking to an audience of Christian college presidents: "The trouble with Christian higher education," he said, "is that it is all too often *lower* education." Evangelical Protestant commitment to a high level of scholarship, in the twentieth century at least, only barely exists.[7] We are only now beginning to free ourselves from the anti-intellectualism of late nineteenth- and early twentieth-century revivalism and the secular pragmatism of John Dewey and his associates. However, few evangelical institutions have the resources to encourage significant scholarship among their faculty, and all too many faculty are enamored with the ideal of shared governance and seem to believe that by attendance at committee meetings they are somehow doing scholarship or otherwise increasing the quality of education being offered.

Progress has been made, however. Today thousands of men and women of faith are university and college professors with doctorates from the greatest universities, teaching in both secular and religious colleges. But the contemporary Christian college professor still has a very long way to go in terms of acquiring the solid theological foundation necessary for holistic, integrative academic work at a sophisticated level. What is needed is the expectation that

---

7. Cf. Mark A. Noll, *The Scandal of the Evangelical Mind* (Grand Rapids: Eerdmans, 1994).

Christian professors will acquire at least the equivalent of the training required of foreign missionaries (a minimum of one year of graduate theological studies). Ideally, following the Jesuit model, all should have an advanced theological degree. It is impossible for people with a doctoral-level education in an academic discipline, but only a "Sunday-school" education in theology and Scripture, to be able to integrate the two in a creative, convincing, illuminating, faithful manner.

Education as a High-Commitment Calling

The Jesuit educational movement demands a greater degree of commitment than do contemporary Christian colleges. There are no job advertisements in the *Chronicle of Higher Education* for Jesuits! Becoming a Jesuit demands a lifelong commitment (though there are, of course, those who drop out). The first commitment is to the mission of the community, as described in the *Spiritual Exercises,* the *Constitutions,* and the *Ratio Studiorum.* This is not entered into lightly. After making the decision to join, it takes years to become a permanent member.

The Christian college movement has no comparable literary legacies that shape the mission and commitment of Christian professors. The commitment asked of faculty is fairly minimal: sign a statement of faith and an annual contract, teach three or four courses each term, take a lower salary than you would get at a major secular institution, and do not fall prey to moral turpitude. If you get tenure (which nearly everybody does), you have a cushy job for life. You will not have to go overseas or even work particularly hard. And you probably will not have to think very hard either. Becoming (and remaining) a Christian college professor is about as demanding as joining an American Protestant church.

My point is not to run down professors at Christian colleges, but rather to indicate that the demands on them are not very rigorous. They are minimal in comparison to what is expected of a Jesuit. And there are probably at least twice as many Jesuit academics in the world as there are academics in CCCU-related institutions. Guess which group is making the greater impact upon world culture?

Administrative Genius

Ignatius Loyola was not merely a spiritual giant but an administrative genius. He was not merely an entrepreneur but a builder of both people and institutions. He knew that he had to have a group of associates to work with him if he was to realize his spiritual dreams, and that he had to create a structure that would endure as an instrument of service for future generations. And this he did in the Society of Jesus, in the documents that he produced to guide those who would join with him in the enterprise, and in the example of personal leadership that he left.

Ignatius's genius consisted, first of all, in his sincerity and integrity. Hypocrisy and dishonesty were not part of his character or behavior. All who encountered him bore witness to his transparent integrity. Second, Ignatius dearly loved people. He seemed to have an uncanny ability to reach out and touch almost anyone spiritually, which made him a tremendously successful recruiter, counselor, and motivator of people. He wrote tens of thousands of letters — and made thousands of appeals in person — calling on people to give financial support to the mission of the Society of Jesus. Influencing people to give was, to him, a deeply spiritual matter; giving was a means of grace not only to those who received but also to those who gave.

Ignatius hand-picked his key leaders and dispatched them to the tasks and places for which they seemed best suited. When he died, sixteen years after founding the movement, rather than languishing because of a change in leadership, the stage was set for even greater growth under the leadership of his successors: the ultimate testimony to the greatness of a leader.

Numerous observers have recently commented on the dominant influence of the large, twentieth-century parachurch organizations and mission agencies, many of which overshadow traditional church and institutional structures, and even many multinational business corporations. The majority of commentators on these new realities tend to decry these new structures and to see them as evils, or at least as potential dangers, rather than as positive evidence for what these groups are doing that is right (and perhaps also what traditional church institutional leaders are doing wrong). I tend to take the more positive view. Assuming that an organization is meeting a real need and that it does not demand resources that are totally inaccessible, the key to growth is the existence of appropriate and effective administrative structures and the gifted and trained personnel to fill them. This was true in the founding of the Jesuits, and it is also true in the case of key parachurch and new mission agencies in our time.

When we turn to the Christian college movement, only two or three schools have the resources (significant endowments, current assets, faculties, libraries, research facilities) to allow them to compete academically with the top schools in the nation. Their organizational structures seem ineffective and inefficient. Each school tends to operate in a vacuum — though the loose fellowship of the Coalition for Christian Colleges and Universities has been a significant boost in both group morale and professionalism. The development of a handful of professional associations and academic journals has also been a real help. But where is the Christian college that is making the impact on our society that the average Jesuit university is making (to say nothing of the impact of the top tier of secular colleges and universities)?

Moving Forward

Where are we then? The integration of faith and learning in North American higher education is an important and worthy goal. It is not only a theological mandate of the Christian faith to "love God with all our mind" and to "be transformed by the renewing of your mind"; it is a crucial contribution to our world. Our world of business, politics, education, and personal relationships cries out for moral and spiritual insight. And a global, culturally diverse marketplace makes it essential for Christians to understand *their* faith and its implications for life and work if they are to encounter constructively, in peace, those of other religious communities.

History provides us with many inspiring examples of individual colleges and universities, and still more examples of individual scholars and teachers, who have aimed, with various degrees of success, at a holistic education with God at the center.

Nevertheless, God, theology, and religious life have become marginal in today's higher education. As we have seen, even in the intentionally evangelical Christian colleges, the educational and intellectual life of the campus is secularized most of the time. Is it possible to change the situation? Can we perhaps learn from the Jesuit movement in higher education?

One possible response is to create a model Christ-centered research university. This would provide an alternative context in which to do serious academic research, in a manner that openly links the highest level of scholarship with the deepest commitment to Jesus Christ and theological truth.[8] It might be too expensive, and unnecessary, for such a university to replicate the science megaprojects of the large research universities; but by exploiting the new information technologies and by providing time and support for serious research, it would be possible to produce world-class scholarship in the humanities and social sciences (following the example of some of the smaller European universities).

Should this be an entirely new institution? I doubt it. The process of obtaining a new charter and also the foundational approval by the State Department of Education and accreditation by the appropriate regional accrediting body would be lengthy and very expensive. Unless there is a donor on the order of a Rockefeller or a Packard standing in the wings, waiting for an opportunity to invest a hundred million or so in the development of a Christian research university, it seems unlikely that the necessary money would be forthcoming.

Alternatively, an existing Christian college or university could take upon itself the mission of becoming a fully accredited Ph.D.-granting university. It would take a fresh infusion of significant capital and also a commitment to hiring research-oriented faculty and freeing them up from the responsibilities of heavy undergraduate teaching to do research and to supervise doctoral students. If only a carefully selected range of key disciplines were offered and the European emphasis on primary, largely independent research were followed, it would seem possible to launch a credible doctoral

8. But see Charles Habib Malik, *A Christian Critique of the University* (Downers Grove, Ill.: InterVarsity Press, 1983), pp. 106-8.

program. One can think of a dozen historic and highly regarded European universities, as well as some newer ones, which are much smaller and more people-centered than the large American research universities and which have produced outstanding scholars in the humanities and social sciences. But this cannot happen by simply building doctoral level studies into the responsibilities of existing faculty, as is often done in the development of masters-level programs.

Another alternative to starting a new Christian university from nothing would be to link together several existing institutions through the creation of a new, cooperative entity. This is the pattern of the Claremont Graduate School, of various ecumenical theological unions and institutes, as well as of universities like Cambridge, Oxford, and Toronto (consisting of clusters of independent, constituent colleges). A major problem is that few of the existing Christian colleges are located in close proximity to one another. This might be workable if the individual colleges choose to focus on only one or two areas at the doctoral level, building on the strengths they already have, and expanding them. It would take a very strong, well-financed parent body for such a university-of-colleges to be successful.

Launching a great Christian research university in one of the ways outlined above is not, however, the only way to promote holistic higher education. A range of other strategies is possible, depending on building networks and cooperation. Jesuit higher education has, from its inception, emphasized a constant interchange of ideas and experiences among scholars attached to different institutions and even from different national backgrounds. The *Ratio Studiorum,* which has been said to have "created the first real educational system that the world has ever known," was itself the product of a constant interchange designed to create a basic curriculum for the new schools established around the world.[9] What developed was a common vision that united the new schools through the shared perspective of its leading teacher-scholars. Although this continual exchange of ideas has not always come to pass to the degree desired, it is likely that it has been more of a

9. Suave, "Jesuit Higher Education Worldwide," p. 164.

reality among the Jesuit colleges and universities of the world than among most other institutions, due perhaps as much to the international nature of the Society as to anything else.

Outside of the academic area, say, in the areas of mission, evangelism, social ministries, church growth, and the like, evangelicals have, in recent years, been of all Christians the most cooperative. But cooperation and interchange has only barely begun among those Christians who teach and are engaged in scholarship. Within the CCCU family of institutions, there are, to be sure, programs drawing together administrators, workshops for new faculty, and think-tanks and special programs for intercollegiate intellectual exchanges. Academic and professional groups such as the Conference on Faith and History, Conference on Christianity and Literature, the American Scientific Affiliation, and the Institute for Biblical Research provide contexts for interchange among Christian faculty. The Pew Evangelical Scholarship Initiatives have also expanded the opportunities of scholarly partnerships and exchanges, along with the Templeton Science and Religion Course Program. All of this is certainly much more than would have been available two decades ago, but it is only a fraction of what needs to be done.

Here are a few possible ideas: (1) Establish a new series of seminars along the lines of the Staley Lectures but primarily aimed at faculty development. (2) Establish several research centers after the pattern of Tyndale House in Cambridge, England, adjacent to major university campuses in different parts of the continent (e.g., Berkeley, Princeton, Toronto, and New Orleans), where Christian faculty could come together in groups for sabbatical research and annual conferences, and where younger scholars who are just beginning doctoral research might find a community of like-minded individuals. (3) Establish an international exchange program for Christian scholars from other countries to spend a full academic year in North American Christian colleges, universities, and schools of theology. (4) Develop a graduate-level interdisciplinary theological degree designed to provide the foundation required for the integration of faith and learning by Christian scholars. (5) Publicize already existing opportunities for reasonably priced and academically rich centers for sabbatical research and interdisciplinary dialogue. (6) Establish a cooperative grants office to publicize appropriate grant opportunities for Christian professors and assist them in their writing of proposals. (7) Facilitate faculty exchanges among Christian colleges on a semester-by-semester or annual basis. And so the list could be extended.

Evangelical Protestants, I believe, have much to learn from the Jesuits.

If we learn from the Jesuits, we will not undervalue the importance of the integration of faith and learning.

And we will not fail to develop a clear mission and strategy for the accomplishment of this high goal.

The Evangelical Mind in America

Mark A. Noll

Several reactions can be imagined to an essay on "the evangelical mind in America."[1] The most uncharitable might suggest that this will have to be a very short paper. The most secular might look for a translation of religious mumbo-jumbo into privileged categories of reality as defined by Marx, Durkheim, Freud, or Foucault. The most sectarian might expect to hear nothing more than John Calvin, John Wesley, or perhaps the British founder of dispensational premillennialism, John Nelson Darby — with an American accent. The most precise might deny the possibility of the project altogether because of persistent ambiguity surrounding use of the term "evangelical" in American history and historiography.

Yet if we take care to establish coordinates, we can define a subject that exhibits reasonable integrity and considerable significance. It is also a subject of broader interest than might first appear. Evangelical impulses helped to shape America's first colleges. Evangelical concerns entered fully into mainstream American higher education through at least the 1880s or 1890s. In the twentieth century, evangelical colleges and (since the 1960s) universities have

---

1. For bibliographical coverage of the subject treated in this chapter, see Edith Blumhofer and Joel Carpenter, eds., *Twentieth-Century Evangelicalism: A Guide to the Sources* (New York: Garland, forthcoming), especially section II, "History and Character," and section III, "Life of the Mind." I have expanded on the arguments of this chapter in *The Scandal of the Evangelical Mind* (Grand Rapids: Eerdmans, 1994).

constituted one of the most important alternatives to the burgeoning sweep of state-sponsored higher education. Alongside a larger network of Roman Catholic colleges and universities and somewhat smaller sets of Mormon and Adventist institutions, evangelical higher education has been both a participant in, and a critic of, main patterns in modern higher education. Thus, to examine the evangelical life of the mind more generally is to discover something about a distinct tradition, but also a great deal about American intellectual life more generally.

A word of definition is in order at the outset. While not denying other legitimate uses of the term, the "evangelicalism" of this chapter refers to a tradition of mostly white, Protestant heirs of the English Reformation who share not only a relatively common history but also a relatively constant set of religious convictions. These convictions are succinctly summarized in an admirable recent history of British evangelicalism by D. W. Bebbington: "conversionism, the belief that lives need to be changed; activism, the expression of the gospel in effort; biblicism, a particular regard for the Bible; and what may be called crucicentrism, a stress on the sacrifice of Christ on the cross."[2]

Foundations

"The evangelical mind in America" took shape within a cultural context established by revivalism and the disestablishment of religion. The "awakenings" of the colonial period, occasioned especially by the itinerancy of George Whitefield and interpreted by the lucid commentary of Jonathan Edwards, provided the driving force for the American evangelical tradition. The social-political context in which that force took shape was provided by the First Amendment to the Constitution of the United States.

The effect of revivalism on the life of the mind lay precisely in its antitraditionalism. The form of revivalism that eventually came to prevail among evangelicals was activistic, immediatistic,

---

2. D. W. Bebbington, *Evangelicalism in Modern Britain: A History from the 1730s to the 1980s* (London: Unwin Hyman, 1989), pp. 2-3.

and individualistic.[3] As such, it was able to mobilize great numbers for the cause of Christ. But also as such — with its scorn for tradition, its concentration on individual competence, its distrust of mediated knowledge — American revivalism did much to turn evangelical thinking from doctrine to practice, from the consideration of first principles to the search for useful wisdom.

The decision by the founders, enshrined in the Constitution's First Amendment, to leave questions of politics and religion to the states led to what sociologist Roger Finke has recently called "religious deregulation." The national government refused to support any particular denomination. The consequences for the churches were immense. They were now compelled to *compete* for adherents, rather than being assigned responsibility for parishioners as had been the almost universal European pattern. The denominations now had to convince individuals, first, that they should pay attention to God and, second, that they should do so in *their* churches and not elsewhere. The primary way that the churches accomplished this task was through the techniques of revival — direct, fervent address aimed at convincing, convicting, and enlisting the individual. As Finke describes it, this process led to "a religious market that caters to the individual and makes religion an individual decision. Though religion is still a group phenomenon, which relies on the support, control and rewards of the local church, the open market stresses *personal* conversion and faith."[4]

One cannot exaggerate the importance of the effects of this combination of revivalism and disestablishment. Analyzed positively, the combination gave the American churches a new dynamism, a new effectiveness in evangelization, and a new vitality in shaping the life of the people by norms of Christian civilization. Analyzed negatively, the combination of revivalism and disestablishment meant that pragmatic concerns prevailed over principle. What the churches required were results — new adherents — or they would simply go out of business. As historian Sidney Mead once noted, the combina-

---

3. See esp. Nathan O. Hatch, *The Democratization of American Christianity* (New Haven: Yale University Press, 1989).

4. Roger Finke, "Religious Deregulation: Origins and Consequences," *Journal of Church and State* 32 (Summer 1990): 609-26 (quotation at p. 625).

tion of revivalism and disestablishment also predisposed believers to utilitarian apologetics and to a functional form of theology dominated by practical questions about how churches could expand and increase their influence in society.[5]

This was the situation in which the American evangelical mind took shape. American evangelicals never doubted that Christianity was the truth. They never doubted that Christian principles should illuminate every part of life. Yet in the years between the Revolution and the Civil War they transferred many questions of truth into questions of utility. What message would be most effective? What do people most want to hear? What can we say that will both convert the people and draw them to our particular church? The heavy pressure for results meant that very little energy was left for formal thought about God and nature, God and society, God and beauty, or God and the shape of the human mind. In the context of early America, facing the pragmatic challenge of subduing the wilderness and civilizing a barbarian society, these issues, which had regularly been a concern of some thinkers in previous generations, became largely irrelevant.

In this environment the *content* of evangelical thought came to be decisively influenced by events and ideas in the new American nation. The process by which evangelicals linked themselves so successfully with American ideals was an involved one, but for the sake of simplicity we can speak of four dimensions: evangelicals embraced republican theories of politics, they took as their own democratic theories of society, they accepted liberal views of political economy, and they domesticated the Enlightenment for Christian purposes. In each of these areas a common procedure was at work. Evangelicals adopted concepts from American culture at large in order to evangelize or reform that culture more effectively. In each case the process of adoption was successful insofar as believers, speaking the language of their culture, were able to present the gospel in such a way as to see individuals converted and to reform society. But in each case the influence also weakened the evangelical mind. Evangelical thinking, adapted so thoroughly to the norms of antebellum America, inevitably began to take on the shape of those norms.

5. Sidney E. Mead, "Denominationalism: The Shape of Protestantism in America," in *The Lively Experiment* (New York: Harper & Row, 1963).

It is difficult to find the proper metaphor to describe the content of evangelical thought that emerged in the course of religious development after the American Revolution. From one angle, it was an ideal adaptation that both preserved essentials of historic Christian faith and gave them great effect in the new world. From another angle, it was a ticking time bomb ready to explode when altered circumstances after the Civil War made for a new cultural climate. Within a generation after that conflict, America's hereditary Protestant churches lost control of the mushrooming cities; immigration brought vast numbers of new Americans and great problems of social cohesion; mammoth factories bestowed unrivaled influence upon their owners; freed slaves were forced back into inhumane conditions in the South and allowed a mere subsistence in the North; the Bible came increasingly under attack as a largely irrelevant mythological book; and new views in biology challenged both divine creation and the uniqueness of the human species. Against these challenges, the evangelical mind that was shaped in the crucible of antebellum events would flounder, but in its heyday it had been a mighty engine of Christianization and civilization.

Traumas of a New Era

The changing circumstances of postbellum America begin to explain why the evangelical mind suffered its severest strains in the transition from the nineteenth to the twentieth century. The particular developments of this period also bring into perspective differences between American evangelical thought and characteristic intellectual habits of evangelicals in other North Atlantic regions. No other body of evangelicals experienced such a complete alienation from mainstream academic life. In no other region would a fundamentalist-modernist controversy so decisively shape the perceptions of succeeding generations and the categories of historians.[6] These events also explain why in America the institutional divisions be-

6. See Bebbington, *Evangelicalism in Modern Britain,* and George M. Marsden, "Fundamentalism as an American Phenomenon: A Comparison with English Evangelicalism," *Church History* 47 (1977): 215-32.

tween self-defined evangelicals and other Christians are often sharper than are theological differences. Beliefs similar to those held by evangelicals continued to be found among a wide spectrum of Protestants. But Protestant institutions have been much more sharply divided between what was originally a protesting evangelical insurgency and a triumphant mainline establishment, which has more recently become a rising evangelical tide over against a defensive mainline decline.

Few historical events have been more important for the evangelical mind than the reorganization of American colleges at the end of the nineteenth century.[7] The years from 1865 to 1918 constituted a distinct era of transition for American higher education. When Charles Eliot became president of Harvard in 1869, he set that influential institution on a course of innovation and expansion. The Johns Hopkins University, founded in 1876, exercised leadership in the establishment of graduate education. Other major changes were also under way: new universities such as Cornell, Chicago, and Stanford were founded; older private colleges such as Yale, Princeton, and Columbia were transformed into universities with the addition of graduate and professional schools; major state universities such as Michigan and Wisconsin grew up almost overnight in the midwest and west. With this reorganization came also a steady influx of new students. Less than 1 percent of college-age people pursued higher education in 1860; by 1930 the proportion had risen to 12.4 percent.[8]

It is of the greatest significance that the money for this academic explosion did not come from the evangelical communities that had hitherto been the financial mainstay of American higher education.[9] Rather it was first the wealthy new entre-

---

7. See George M. Marsden, *The Soul of the American University* (New York: Oxford University Press, 1994); Alexandra Oleson and John Voss, eds., *The Organization of Knowledge in Modern America, 1860-1920* (Baltimore: Johns Hopkins University Press, 1979); and Laurence R. Veysey, *The Emergence of the American University* (Chicago: University of Chicago Press, 1965).

8. *Historical Statistics of the United States: Colonial Times to 1957* (Washington, D.C.: Bureau of the Census, 1960), pp. 210-11.

9. On larger economic-educational connections, see Burton J. Bledstein, *The Culture of Professionalism: The Middle Class and the Development of Higher*

preneurs and then the state governments that provided the funds for this expansion. Funding networks connected with churches and evangelical voluntary societies became less important with each passing year.

Almost unnoticed in the great influx of dollars and students was the decline of the evangelical habits that had marked most of American higher education in its earlier history. Neither the new donors nor the new breed of administrators were overly concerned about the orthodoxy of their faculties. Visible signs of this change abounded. At Harvard compulsory chapel ceased in 1886. The opening ceremonies at Johns Hopkins in 1876 contained no prayer, but did feature an address by "Darwin's Bulldog," the British evolutionary theorist Thomas Huxley. Businessmen replaced clergymen as trustees, and laymen replaced ministers as college presidents. In its curriculum, the new university incorporated a new German emphasis on research at the expense of an older British concern for character. New ideals of science, modeled especially after the striking proposals of Charles Darwin's *Origin of Species*, took on an unprecedented importance.

In almost every way imaginable, the new university posed difficulties for received habits of evangelical thinking. The reconciliation between Christian faith and the world of learning that had been a staple of American higher education before the Civil War became a thing of the past. Excess capital generated by industrialists after the Civil War arose from a widespread exploitation of new scientific technology. This excess wealth was generated, furthermore, by individuals who had largely laid aside the constraints of Christian altruism that the antebellum evangelical-American synthesis had tried to inculcate. American industrialists, to one degree or another, seemed to favor the kind of social Darwinism popularized by Herbert Spencer. One of the reasons that this new class of wealthy Americans funded education was to encourage more of the practical science and managerial theory coming from the new universities and less of the moralism coming from the old colleges.

Education in America (New York: W. W. Norton, 1976), and David F. Noble, *America by Design: Science, Technology, and the Rise of Corporate Capitalism* (New York: Oxford University Press, 1977).

The new breed of presidents focused much more attention on scholarship than on orthodoxy. Furthermore, the new scholarship that these presidents encouraged had been "liberated" from the pious certainties that once dominated American colleges. The new work tended toward naturalism in science and pragmatism in philosophy. In turn, and bringing the circle full, the new naturalistic science and the new pragmatic philosophy encouraged industrial giantism by providing training and technique to the capitalists while at the same time offering few criticisms of the new industrial wealth.

Against this combination of new money, social Darwinism, and naturalistic science, the old synthesis of evangelical convictions and American ideals stood almost no chance. The collapse of that synthesis signaled a momentous defeat for the evangelical mind in America. The effort to integrate religious faith with learning was abandoned under the assumption that the pursuit of science carried with it no antecedent commitments to a worldview.

The general sense of intellectual weakness that evangelicals communicated during the transformation of the American university was heightened by the events of the fundamentalist-modernist period.[10] Again it is possible to draw different conclusions about this episode. From one angle, fundamentalists can look like stalwart defenders (however selective) of time-tested Christian verities — the supernatural character of religion, the objectivity of Christian morality, and the timeless validity of Scripture. From another, they appear more as self-deluded defenders of dated intellectual conventions of the early nineteenth century. From both angles, however, it is clear that fundamentalism deeply influenced the intellectual habits of many evangelicals.

The most obvious fundamentalist concern for the mind came in response to the drift of American academic life. With naturalistic or secular ideas established in the leading universities, some fundamentalists attacked learning itself as a preserve of evil. For the most part, however, evangelicals did not abandon intellectual

---

10. The magisterial interpretation is by George M. Marsden, *Fundamentalism and American Culture: The Shaping of Twentieth-Century Evangelicalism, 1870-1925* (New York: Oxford University Press, 1980).

life so much as cling to earlier forms of reasoning.[11] Thus, works like the Scofield Reference Bible and the twelve-booklet series of *The Fundamentals* marked a flowering of realistic, commonsensical, and democratic thinking. But this very flowering drove a wedge even deeper between the received habits of evangelical thought and the standards becoming widely accepted in the academic world.

The fundamentalist era also strengthened evangelical individualism. Theological conservatives who left the major denominations were thrown on their own resources for maintaining the beliefs, practices, and institutions to which they were committed. Theological conservatives who stayed in the denominations were forced to develop strategies of survival that also emphasized resourcefulness and strength of individual effort. The result in both cases was to further underscore a conviction of the nineteenth-century heritage: to advance the kingdom of God it was necessary to rely primarily upon the ingenuity and resourcefulness of individual action.[12] The end result for intellectual life was to underscore the earlier suspicion of tradition, to restrict the possibility of learning from others, and so to hamper intellectual development.

Whatever else we may say of it, the populist character of fundamentalism had a negative effect on the life of the mind. In what had now become traditional American fashion, fundamentalism encouraged the translation of intellectual issues into political struggles. It encouraged evangelical leaders to solve problems by enlisting larger and larger numbers of followers rather than by carefully analyzing Scripture or the world. Historian Nathan Hatch has described the net result in these words: "Let me suggest somewhat whimsically that the heritage of fundamentalism was to Christian learning for evangelicals like Chairman Mao's 'Cultural Revolution' for the Chinese. Both divorced a generation from mainline

---

11. George M. Marsden, "The Collapse of the Evangelical Mind," in *Faith and Rationality: Reason and Belief in God,* eds. Alvin Plantinga and Nicholas Wolterstorff (Notre Dame: University of Notre Dame Press, 1983).

12. Joel A. Carpenter, "Fundamentalist Institutions and the Rise of Evangelical Protestantism, 1929-1942," *Church History* 49 (March 1980): 62-75.

academia, thus making reintegration [into larger worlds of learning] a difficult, if not bewildering task."[13]

From the perspective of 1930, the evangelical mind in America looked moribund, as many articulate commentators, including H. Richard Niebuhr, thought it was.[14] Not only were the nation's universities alien territory for evangelicals, but fundamentalists, the most visible evangelicals, had made a virtue of their alienation from the world of learned culture. Appearances, however, proved deceptive. At the apparent nadir of evangelical thought new signs of life were stirring that have contributed to at least a partial renovation of evangelical academic life in the decades since World War II.

A Measure of Intellectual Recovery

Four parallel developments in the 1930s and 1940s prepared the way for the more aggressive evangelical stance that has been visible in the academy over the last thirty years. The first and most dramatic was the emergence within American fundamentalism of younger leaders seeking an intellectually responsible expression of the Christian faith. Reverses for fundamentalists in the 1920s seemed to signal the end of intellectual vitality. Before too long, however, ambitious young fundamentalists were finding sectarianism and separation distasteful.[15] Harold John Ockenga (1905-1985), at various times the president of Fuller and Gordon-Conwell seminaries, called for a "new evangelicalism" that could value scholarship and take an active interest in society while maintaining traditional

---

13. Nathan O. Hatch, "Evangelical Colleges and the Challenge of Christian Thinking," *Reformed Journal* (Sept. 1985): 12.

14. H. Richard Niebuhr, *The Social Sources of Denominationalism* (Cleveland: World, 1957 [orig. 1929]), pp. 184-87; and "Fundamentalism," *Encyclopedia of Social Sciences*, vol. 6 (1937).

15. Key works on these developments are Joel A. Carpenter, *Revive Us Again: The Recovery of American Fundamentalism, 1930-1950* (forthcoming); George M. Marsden, *Reforming Fundamentalism: Fuller Seminary and the New Evangelicalism* (Grand Rapids: Eerdmans, 1987); and Rudolph Nelson, *The Making and Unmaking of an Evangelical Mind: The Case of Edward Carnell* (New York: Cambridge University Press, 1987).

Protestant convictions. Edward John Carnell (1919-1967), after completing doctorates at both Harvard and Boston University, championed at the new Fuller Theological Seminary in California an "orthodoxy" shorn of fundamentalist excesses. Carl F. H. Henry (b. 1913), also a professor at Fuller and then the founding editor of *Christianity Today* (1956), called fundamentalists to a new engagement with American society and a new concern for theological reflection. Together these and like-minded leaders soon spoke for a significant number of theological conservatives who sought an intellectually responsible expression of the faith.

The second development concerns theological conservatives who never became fundamentalists. The major American denominations always contained individuals who valued the traditional confessions and who sought to check the theological liberalism that found a home in these denominations. For such individuals the significant development was finding "fundamentalists" who, like themselves, possessed confidence in a traditional understanding of Scripture, but who also valued well-considered theological argumentation. As tumult from the fundamentalist-modernist wars receded into the historical background, it became easier for these theological conservatives to reestablish lines of contact with evangelicals outside of their denominations.[16]

The third development was one of assimilation. By the early twentieth century, German and Scandinavian Lutherans and the Dutch Reformed had established significant communities in America. In spite of efforts by leaders like Carl Henry, connections between America's "new evangelicals" and the Lutherans have always remained somewhat tenuous. The situation was different for the Dutch.[17] During the 1930s and 1940s, members of the Christian Reformed Church, representing the most recent immigration from Holland, continued a process of Americanization that had started in earnest during World War I. Evangelicals offered these Dutch Reformed an important refer-

16. For examples of such figures, see Mark A. Noll, *Between Faith and Criticism: Evangelicals, Scholarship, and the Bible in America* (San Francisco: Harper & Row, 1986), pp. 109-12.

17. See esp. James D. Bratt, *Dutch Calvinists in Modern America: A History of a Conservative Subculture* (Grand Rapids: Eerdmans, 1984).

ence point as they moved closer to American ways. As they grew closer to evangelical networks, the Dutch Reformed offered their American counterparts a heritage of serious academic work and experienced philosophical reasoning. In their native Holland, they had founded a major center of higher education, the Free University of Amsterdam; they had made significant contributions to political theory and practice (their leader, Abraham Kuyper, was prime minister of the Netherlands from 1900 to 1905); and they took for granted a full Christian participation in artistic and cultural life.

The most obvious link between these Dutch Reformed and the American evangelicals was in publishing. By the late 1940s, several firms in Grand Rapids, Michigan, a center of Dutch immigration, were bringing out the books of Carl Henry, E. J. Carnell, and other American evangelicals. In particular, the William B. Eerdmans Publishing Company was aggressively seeking new authors and markets from the world of American evangelicals.

Eerdmans also played an important part in drawing a fourth strand of intellectual renewal into the American picture.[18] Beginning in the 1930s, a number of British evangelicals inside and out of the Church of England united in efforts to expand the evangelical presence in the universities. The cradle for this effort was the British Inter-Varsity Fellowship (IVF); its nursemaids were graduate students and young professors convinced of the intellectual integrity of evangelical faith. Led by such preachers as Martyn Lloyd-Jones, scholars such as F. F. Bruce and David Wenham, and organizers such as Douglas Johnson, these British evangelicals made significant progress in a relatively short time. Forceful, yet dignified preaching missions to Oxford, Cambridge, and other universities led to the conversion of undergraduates. By the end of the 1940s, the Theological Students Fellowship of IVF established Tyndale House in Cambridge to encourage evangelical study of the Scriptures, and soon thereafter evangelicals began to gain research positions in major British universities. The British Inter-Varsity Press published many products of this renewed evangelicalism, often with Eerdmans as a co-sponsor or the American distributor. The printed word thus served as a medium

18. See Bebbington, *Evangelicals in Modern Britain*, pp. 259-61, and Noll, *Between Faith and Criticism*, pp. 62-90.

linking British evangelicals to American postfundamentalists, mainline conservatives, and Americanizing confessionalists. In addition, by the 1950s, American evangelicals were regularly crossing the Atlantic to pursue graduate work at the British universities with scholars either holding a similar faith or open to its emphases.

The glue uniting the different strands of evangelical intellectual renewal came in several forms. The American evangelist, Billy Graham, was a contact point of nearly universal recognition. What he did on a large scale through popular evangelism to establish networks of evangelical interest, British "missioners" to the universities — such as Martin Lloyd-Jones and John Stott — accomplished among more strictly academic groups. Cooperative publishing ventures such as the *New Bible Commentary* (1953) and the *New Bible Dictionary* (1962) from British Inter-Varsity, Carl Henry's work at *Christianity Today*, and several different projects at Eerdmans drew evangelical scholars from both sides of the Atlantic into common labor. Eventually, other institutions, such as the American InterVarsity Christian Fellowship and the Lausanne Committee for World Evangelism, also strengthened cross-cultural evangelical ties.

The result has been the establishment of an evangelical intellectual network with certain well-fixed reference points in the United States, Great Britain, Canada, and other parts of the world. The extended connections of British Inter-Varsity, the insights of Dutch Reformed confessionalists, the common valuing of the classical Protestant heritage, and an ingrained respect for an even broader range of historic Christian expressions have shaped the parts of this coalition. If the scholarly reinvigoration that resulted was most visible for its work in biblical studies, these evangelicals testified to a much more serious engagement of the mind through their thorough academic preparation and dedicated approach to learning. After World War II evangelicals also formed a series of academic associations, some focusing on biblical and theological subjects, but others aimed at the increasing numbers in philosophy, history, literature, sociology, economics, and other academic disciplines.[19]

19. Examples include the Evangelical Theological Society, the Society of Christian Philosophers, the Conference on Christianity and Literature, and the Conference on Faith and History.

In sum, since the era of the fundamentalist-modernist controversy the situation for evangelical scholarship has been considerably improved. At the same time, this contemporary renovation must be kept in perspective. Recent gains have been modest. The general impact of evangelical thinkers on even the *evangelicals* of the country, much less on the general culture, is slight. The best-known evangelical spokespersons — Jerry Falwell, Billy Graham, Kenneth Hagin, Tim LaHaye, Oral Roberts, Pat Robertson, Jimmy Swaggert, Chuck Swindoll — owe their influence to practical media skills rather than to theoretical ability in theology or the application of Christian insight to complicated modern problems. Often these most visible evangelicals still defend polemical stances defined in the fundamentalist era. At least when venturing beyond narrowly religious subjects (and sometimes even then), they are still more likely to express their thought in idioms from the antebellum period than in language familiar to modern intellectuals, evangelical, generally Christian, or secular.

Efforts by evangelical colleges have also yielded positive results in recent decades, but again success at reestablishing a vigorous academic presence has been limited. A recent essay by Princeton sociologist Robert Wuthnow spotlighted some of the problems of these institutions. Wuthnow pointed out that the deep structures of modern intellectual life are shaped largely by the works of non- or anti-Christians. Theorists like Marx, Weber, Durkheim, and Freud established the modern intellectual conventions of the academy. Their legacy, for good and for ill, provides the framework in which most believers of whatever sort pursue advanced studies. But more than just the framework of modern intellectual life affects the evangelical life of the mind. The widely varying distribution of academic resources is also a factor. A handful of national research universities act as gate-keepers, intellectual and physical, for most of the learned professions. If evangelicals are to be academically certified, they must pass through those gates. But then, if they would seek changes in the academic landscape, they must do so with resources that cannot begin to compare with those enjoyed by the major research universities. As Wuthnow put it, "those who would wish to see a distinctively evangelical scholarly orientation advanced are at a tremendous competitive disadvantage. To pit even the strong intellectual aspirations of a Wheaton College or a Calvin College, or the massive fund-raising network of a Liberty University, against the multibillion dollar endowments of a Princeton or a Harvard reveals the vast extent of this deficit in resources."[20] Charles Malik, a Lebanese Orthodox Christian, once put the case even more starkly in an address to an evangelical audience: "Who among the evangelicals can stand up to the great secular or naturalistic or atheistic scholars on their own terms of scholarship and research? Who among the Evangelical scholars is quoted as a normative source by the greatest secular authorities on history or philosophy or psychology or sociology or politics?"[21] In point of fact, a few academics who might be classed as evangelicals in a general sense now speak with such authority in their fields. But such academics, like historian George Marsden or the philosophers Alvin Plantinga, Nicholas Wolterstorff, and Robert Adams, remain quite rare.

On balance, the postwar resurgence of evangelical intellectual life has made a difference. But it has neither regained the hegemony for evangelical discourse that characterized American public life before the Civil War nor attained the sophistication that has marked university scholarship in the twentieth century. Despite the aspirations of a growing but still tiny number of evangelical academics, the evangelical mind in America remains the possession of media populists. It remains more in tune with the intellectual commonplaces of the nineteenth century than of the twentieth. And as illustrated by the rise of the New Christian Right, it remains more obviously dependent upon a hereditary symbiosis of American and Christian values than upon new applications of evangelical religious principles to the contemporary world.[22]

20. Robert Wuthnow, *The Struggle for America's Soul: Evangelicals, Liberals, and Secularism* (Grand Rapids: Eerdmans, 1989), p. 164.

21. Charles Malik, *The Two Tasks* (Westchester, Ill.: Cornerstone, 1980), pp. 33-34.

22. For an excellent overview, see Steve Bruce, *The Rise and Fall of the New Christian Right: Conservative Politics in America, 1978-1988* (Oxford: Clarendon, 1988).

Conclusion

From a standpoint within that mind, the fact that a common set of religious convictions — Bebbington's conversionism, activism, biblicism, and crucicentrism — has defined a relatively numerous and relatively distinct movement for now well over two hundred years is significant for the Christian religion itself. To the extent that these evangelical beliefs approximate, or grow out of, central teachings in the more general history of Christianity, study of "the evangelical mind in America" becomes one part of a more general study of "Christian thinking," a subject of infinite complexity but also, from a Christian perspective, of infinite importance. More specifically, when we study the relation between particulars of "the evangelical mind in America" and the panoply of Christian belief through the centuries, we are in a position to make a distinct American contribution to a task of universal Christian significance. That is the task of correlating the dazzling profusion of ways that this religion of the Incarnation has been incarnated — always pied, dappled, brindled, stippled, freckled, to be sure — in the dazzling profusions of human cultures around the globe. The history of "the American evangelical mind" does not provide a norm for these other incarnations, but it does offer an illuminating instance of faith enfleshed in the dwellings of a particular setting, an instance that has grown to global significance because of American leadership over the last century in missionary service around the world.

Second, and on a more pedestrian plane, a study of this subject makes possible a fruitful distinction between alternative forms of knowledge. From even this rapid survey, it is apparent that "the evangelical mind in America" has been rich in practical intelligence but relatively poor in theoretical intelligence. The evangelical Jonathan Edwards is one of America's greatest theoretical intellects. But for every Edwards in the history of American evangelicalism there has been a more widely visible Whitefield; for every example of theological creativity like the nineteenth-century theologians J. W. Nevin or H. B. Smith there has been a more charismatically persuasive spellbinder like Charles Grandison Finney; for every patient scholastic like Princeton Seminary's B. B. Warfield there has been a more compelling purveyor of celestial common sense like

D. L. Moody. In the course of American history it has been the canny shrewdness of the latter types much more than the creative brilliance of the former that has made the difference for the evangelical mind.

This circumstance is perhaps best explained by the conditions in which the evangelical mind was forged. In the dawning of the new American civilization there were no institutional supports for sustained thought, but everywhere a demand for applied intelligence. It is no accident that the highpoint of evangelical influence in the United States was reached in the decades between the Revolution and the Civil War, when the virtues of practicality were most in demand and the need for social mobilization was greater than it would ever be in the nation's history. The immense contributions of pious evangelical character to antebellum American civilization rested on a foundation of practical evangelical intelligence.

But, last, and perhaps most obviously, to speak of the practical cast of the evangelical mind in America draws attention to its profoundly paradoxical character, a paradox with much to ponder for those concerned about the course of American higher education, the integrity of faith, or both. As it has been evangelical, this mind has deeply influenced America. As it has been a mind, this evangelicalism has been deeply influenced by America. Both the capacity to influence and the capacity to be influenced arise from being so securely an evangelical mind *in America*. Over its history, this evangelical mind has excelled at translating the Word into the evolving languages of American popular culture. The thoroughness of that translation explains both the greatest strengths and the greatest weaknesses of the evangelical mind in America. It illuminates also a more common set of intellectual problems. For all who are concerned about domains of thought today, the evangelical story is an encouragement (about the ability of disciplined dedication to make a difference), but also a warning (about the intellectual danger of living in two conceptual worlds at once).

The Brethren and Higher Education: Tension and Tradition

Donald F. Durnbaugh

Historian Jacques Barzun began a wise and witty book — *Teacher in America* — with the observation that "education is indeed the dullest of subjects and I intend to say as little about it as I can." When we recall the endless streams of articles on education, full of jargon but slight of content, we are tempted to agree with the professor emeritus from Columbia University. Many will concur with his proposal that much of the endless debate about education misses the point. This is, he contends, because worthwhile education is the "lifelong discipline of the individual by himself" or herself, which can never be provided by another but can, at best, be encouraged and aided.[1]

Yet wordy debate and discussion of education continues with relentless intensity. That is because people rightly perceive that appropriate teaching and learning do offer possibilities for improvement in individual lives and in society. Politicians portray themselves as devoted to educational reform, study commissions pour out reams of reports, and hopeful prospects are painted, but actual progress seems limited.

Still, reformers of all ages have looked to the schools as the hope for the future. It is not alone the obvious fact that younger generations will, of necessity, have to be socialized and instructed

---

1. Jacques Barzun, *Teacher in America* (Garden City, N.Y.: Doubleday Anchor, 1955 [orig. Boston, 1944]), pp. 9, 12.

if the fabric of society is to be preserved. It is also that educational institutions are seen as strategic places for changing people's attitudes and concepts. Thus it is quite natural that religious bodies have always been concerned about the nurture of the younger generations. Many a struggle in ecclesiastical history has, therefore, centered on academic institutions. The Protestant Reformation of the sixteenth century grew, we recall, from the lectures of a professor named Martin Luther at a school in Wittenberg.

The Roman Catholic contribution to American higher education is well known. The contribution of mainline Protestantism is less visible today because of the secularization of Harvard, Princeton, Yale, and other great colleges and universities that began as Christian experiments in higher education. A third religious force that has played a part in American higher education is that of the "free," "sectarian," or "radical Protestant" churches. This part of the story includes the efforts of Mennonites, Quakers, Swedish Mission Covenanters, and many other groups who founded colleges. In this chapter I will examine one of those radical groups, the German Baptist Brethren, often known colloquially as the "Dunkers," as represented today by the Church of the Brethren. Those who sought reform in the nineteenth-century Brethren movement were in the forefront of establishing institutions of higher learning. Founded in 1876, Juniata College in Huntingdon, Pennsylvania, was the first of such schools to be able to maintain its existence (though not the first attempted).[2]

Early Attitudes of the Brethren on Higher Education

It is necessary to begin this historical sketch with some demythologizing. Many accounts of the first leaders of the Brethren movement (beginning in 1708) write of them as "university-trained" and as "ripe scholars." Typical portrayals of Brethren history see the eighteenth century in Europe and America as a kind of "golden age"; then, according to a common interpretation, that era was followed

2. Earl C. Kaylor, Jr., *Truth Sets Free: A Centennial History of Juniata College, 1876-1976* (Cranbury, N.J.: A. S. Barnes, 1977).

by the "dark ages" of withdrawal and ignorance, which was then supplanted by a "renaissance" with the return of schooling and publication. Such a recent work as the dissertation by Auburn Boyers on Brethren education (1969) accepts (with some qualification) this scheme. It is seen in full-blown form in Albert T. Ronk's history of the Brethren Church.[3]

Representative of the claims made for the Brethren of eighteenth-century Europe and colonial America is the following statement from John S. Flory, an educator from Virginia:

> Our educational history as a church abounds in paradoxes. At the beginning of our history we were among the most ardent advocates of higher learning, and possessed a liberal share of it in our own membership. We promoted educational institutions with an ardor that would do credit to any people. . . . From the first the church was characterized by a depth of conviction and solidity of character that it has never lost. Its leaders were sturdy and substantial, sound in faith and conviction. . . . Among them were men of university training, and others who had acquired liberal culture largely through their own efforts. Under the guidance of these men the church was prosperous. . . . It pursued an aggressive policy. It organized the first Sunday-school in America. . . . The church was among the most aggressive, most spiritual, and most liberal in the colonies.[4]

Martin G. Brumbaugh, esteemed president of Juniata College, stated in 1908:

---

3. Auburn Boyers, "Changing Conceptions of Education in the Church of the Brethren," Ed.D. dissertation, University of Pittsburgh, 1969; Albert T. Ronk, *History of the Brethren Church* (Ashland, Ohio: Brethren Publishing Company, 1968). This style of interpretation is discussed in D. F. Durnbaugh, "A Study of Brethren Historiography," *Ashland Theological Bulletin* 8 (Spring 1975): 3-18, and Carl F. Bowman, *Brethren Society: The Cultural Transformation of a "Peculiar People"* (Baltimore: Johns Hopkins University Press, 1995), pp. 251-55.

4. John S. Flory, "A History of Education in the Church of the Brethren," in *Educational Bluebook and Directory of the Church of the Brethren, 1708-1923*, ed. W. Arthur Cable and Homer F. Sanger (Elgin, Ill.: General Educational Board, Church of the Brethren, [1923]), pp. 23-24.

From the outset, the church was in the forefront of all religious progress. Its members, more than others, taught religion to the German pioneers of Colonial America. . . . [T]he church enjoyed the unique distinction of contributing more leadership to religious progress than any other equal group before the Revolutionary War. . . . [T]he fathers of the church were all trained and well-educated men — able to give answer for the faith that was within them, and the church today is weak or strong just in proportion as its individual members are trained and skillful defenders of a faith once delivered to these saintly spirits. . . . In proportion to their number, I challenge any historian to name a group who exercised a wider or better influence upon the development of American religious thought.

Brumbaugh challenged the Brethren during the bicentennial of the church's founding with this statement: "We began as an educated and powerful church. Let us try with all our energies to restore the church to its early and splendid history."[5]

A stalwart of early Brethren efforts at higher education, involved in many school foundings, and the early historian of Brethren higher education, Solomon Z. Sharp contended that the reason for the early success of Brethren evangelists was the training that they received from European scholars: "It is a matter of supreme satisfaction to know that the men who wielded so great an influence over the minds of our early church members were not ignorant enthusiasts like [Jakob] Boehme and [George] Fox, but men of education, who had their minds trained in some of the best universities in Europe, and some of them were themselves instructors in universities." These mentors, Sharp contended, included men such as Johann Arndt, Phillip Jakob Spener, Gottfried Arnold, and E. C. Hochmann von Hochenau. (Only Hochmann had direct connection with the Brethren.) Sharp claimed that the "first school of formal teaching established by the Brethren" was the gathering of the first

---

5. Martin G. Brumbaugh, "Introduction" and "The Church in the Fatherland: The Conditions in Germany about 1708," in *Two Centuries of the Church of the Brethren: Or the Beginnings of the Brotherhood,* ed. D. L. Miller (Elgin, Ill.: Brethren Publishing House, 1908), pp. 10-11, 25.

eight members at Schwarzenau, "where the Bible was the textbook and the Holy Spirit gave instruction."[6]

Of the early standard descriptions of Brethren history, only one writer, John Gillin, sounded a different note. In 1906 he concluded that "for many years after their arrival in this country, the Dunkers cared little for education. The Germantown congregation were in a degree an exception. . . . It is true that Mack and Beissel were interested in literary work of the religious sort, but they were self-taught and only by accommodation of language could they be called educated men. . . . The emphasis of general opinion among the Dunkers was all on the foolishness of human learning." Unlike the rhapsodies of Flory and Brumbaugh, Gillin's assessment was bleak: "Of the whole Dunker movement, truth compels one to say that it has brought forth no great literary men, and no statesman. No great poet, or philosopher, or educator was born or bred among the Brethren during the first one hundred and fifty years of their history. But the Dunkers have produced a great mediocre class of substantial, worldly-wise, industrious, economical, peaceful, moral, and religious citizens, possessed of more than the common virtue and with few vices."[7]

Should we side with the sober analysis of Gillin or with the enthusiasm of Flory and Brumbaugh? There is no doubt that Gillin has the better case. The exaggerated claims of the Brethren historians can best be explained by remembering their situation. They were themselves deeply involved in starting and directing Brethren schools. In doing so, they were continually beset with criticism from conservatives that they were innovators and radicals, departing from long-standing Brethren traditions and imitating the ways of the world. What better reply to this criticism than to demonstrate that they were merely restoring what the early church once had but then lost? To the cry of *innovation* they responded with the slogan of *restoration*. They were using history as an effective answer to the charges of novelty.

6. Solomon Z. Sharp, "Early Educational Activities," in *Two Centuries*, pp. 307-8, 310; see also his *Educational History of the Church of the Brethren* (Elgin, Ill.: Brethren Publishing House, 1923), pp. 19-32.

7. John L. Gillin, *The Dunkers: A Sociological Interpretation* (New York: author, 1906), p. 209.

One can also suspect that these Brethren educators also wanted to make an impact on their colleagues from other religious traditions. As the first Brethren to take graduate degrees they found that Brethren were either unknown to scholars or were looked upon patronizingly as part of the uneducated Pennsylvania-German element, as part of the "dumb Dutch." It was gratifying for Brethren, as they understood their history, to demonstrate that they were inheritors of a proud heritage with its own heroes and champions. They had no need to take back seats as country cousins.

This can be seen, for example, in a novel by J. Maurice Henry, pastor, professor, and college president in Virginia and Maryland; its title was *Heart of the Crimson Rose* (1929). The protagonist is an unlettered but brilliant farm boy from the hills who enrolls at the prestigious University of Virginia (Henry's alma mater). Despite supercilious treatment and underhanded attacks from wealthy fraternity types, the hero earns the admiration of all for his superb athletic and academic achievements. He eventually wins the hand of the beautiful daughter of a rich business tycoon, but only after superhuman — and noncombatant — exploits as a Red Cross staffer on the French battlefields of World War I. The once-scornful father finally sees the light; he apologizes for the mistake he made in overlooking the essential quality of the hero hidden in rustic garb.[8]

In comparable ways the pioneer Brethren educators and historians seem to have been seeking some recognition, some place in the sun within the broader American society of the late nineteenth and early twentieth centuries. They were not content, as were their ancestors, to be considered a "peculiar people." The tone of injured pride is sensed in the preface that Martin G. Brumbaugh gave to his pathbreaking *History of the German Baptist Brethren* (1899), written while concurrently president of Juniata College and professor of pedagogy at the University of Pennsylvania. Brumbaugh contended:

> Perhaps no religious sect is so little understood and so persistently misrepresented as the German Baptist Brethren. . . . It is of course not necessary to notice [but he obviously did!] the malicious

8. J. Maurice Henry, *The Heart of the Crimson Rose* (Boston: Stratford, 1929).

misstatements of prejudiced and bigoted zealots. . . . It is to be hoped that this volume will dispel all such errors and show the Brethren in their true light. . . . The aim has been not merely to give a relatively complete record of the early church, but to use this record as a defense of primitive Christianity as believed, interpreted and practiced by the church of the German Baptist Brethren. Without in any way perverting history the writer has aimed at making history defend doctrine and indicate future activities of the church.

Thus the Pennsylvania schoolman, who rose to the highest elective position of any member of the church (i.e., governor of Pennsylvania), laid out some of the motivations of his book. In doing so, he was in no way different in orientation from many of his contemporaries. Like him, they were concerned for the direction of their church and for its standing among the broader religious public.[9]

Anabaptist and Pietist Influences

What really was the Brethren attitude toward higher education? We must first look at the formative impulses that Brethren received from the religious influences that shaped them. By general agreement, these must be sought among the Anabaptist and Pietist movements. In so concentrating, we may be doing less than justice to the matrix of mainline Protestant traditions of German Lutheranism and German Calvinism (Reformed), which formed those who became Brethren and from which they departed.[10]

9. Martin G. Brumbaugh, *A History of the German Baptist Brethren in Europe and America* (Elgin, Ill.: Brethren Publishing House, 1899), pp. xii-xviii. See also Earl C. Kaylor, Jr., *Martin Grove Brumbaugh: A Pennsylvanian's Odyssey from Sainted Schoolman to Bedeviled World War I Governor, 1862-1930* (Madison, N.J.: Associated University Press, 1996 [1995]), pp. 116-17.

10. A general overview of these developments is in D. F. Durnbaugh, *Brethren Beginnings: The Origin of the Church of the Brethren in Early Eighteenth-Century Europe* (Philadelphia: Brethren Encyclopedia, Inc., 1992); for a more extensive discussion, see Dale R. Stoffer, *Background and Development of Brethren Doctrines, 1650-1987* (Philadelphia: Brethren Encyclopedia, Inc., 1989).

Representative of the consolidated position of the sixteenth-century Anabaptists or Radical Reformers are the writings of Menno Simons. Although Menno lamented that his learning, especially in biblical languages, was not more advanced, he clearly stated that heavenly wisdom was far more important. "Now this wisdom which affects such power and yields such fruits I consider to be the very finest that can be named, even if it is taught and recovered by an ignorant teamster or hod carrier. . . . You see, dear reader, for the sake of the sweetness of this philosophy, its nobility, its virtue, its delightfulness, and its beauty, which I have not learned from any famous doctors nor in any institution of higher learning, . . . I have preferred to be the fool of the world's learned ones, in order that I might be found of God to be wise." Again, he wrote: "I honor learnedness whenever it is properly and reverently employed. But above all things do I praise the simple and virtuous wisdom that is from above; for it will never perish but abide in glorious honor with all the pious in eternal life."[11]

Elsewhere, Menno addressed sharp words of reproof to the "learned ones" who as scribes and Pharisees sought only their personal gain and good fortune, not God's interest. He admitted that as a former priest, he had desired "only an empty, lazy soft life, praise and favor of men, yes, simply flesh and belly." But, contended the harried Anabaptist leader, "nothing avails in heaven nor on earth unto salvation, . . . neither eloquence nor erudition, neither councils nor usages . . . if we are not born of God."[12]

Comparable tones can be heard from the ranks of Pietist leaders. In the famous autobiographical confession of August Hermann Francke, describing his conversion, are these words: "Whereas earlier I had made an idol of learning, I now saw that faith as a mustard seed counts for more than a hundred sacks full of learning and that all the knowledge learned at the feet of Gamaliel is to be considered dirt beside the superabundant knowledge of Jesus Christ our Lord." Scholars of Pietism emphasize that its hallmark is Christian experience. Experiential religion, by definition, is open to all,

11. J. C. Wenger, ed., *The Complete Writings of Menno Simons, c. 1496-1561* (Scottdale, Pa.: Herald Press, 1956), pp. 791-92.
12. Simons, in *Complete Writings*, pp. 207-8.

and this emphasis undercuts academic attainment. Francke maintained as well that he valued a "drop of true love more than a sea of knowledge. . . . Our aim must be not to build up *scientia* [knowledge] but rather *conscientia* [conscience]." The foundational and searching criticism of Pietists against the dead hand of scholastic Protestant theology is well known.[13]

On the other hand, Francke himself created several outstanding educational institutions and remained personally a professor at Halle University as well as a parish pastor. This fact loses some weight when we recall that the form of Pietism that directly influenced the Brethren-to-be was Radical Pietism. This was known for its separatist tendencies in breaking from societal institutions, including the established church and official university. E. C. Hochmann von Hochenau, the spiritual mentor of many early Brethren, modeled this attitude by dropping out of a promising academic career to become an itinerant preacher. Likewise, Gottfried Arnold, an outstanding Radical Pietist leader, resigned his brief tenure as professor at the University of Giessen in 1698 because he could not stand the worldliness and clamor of academic life. From his secluded post as a tutor to a noble family he continued to write his massive compilations of church history. These were used by the Brethren as sources for their patterns of church life, as they sought to build their emerging movement along the lines of the early church, or as it was often phrased, of primitive Christianity.[14]

This Radical Pietist posture toward education is well caught in the autobiographical portrait of Johannes Lobach, one of the

13. August Hermann Francke, "From the Autobiography," in *Pietists: Selected Writings,* ed. Peter C. Erb (New York: Paulist, 1983), p. 106; Erich Beyreuther, *August Hermann Francke: Zeuge des lebendigen Gottes* (Marburg/Lahn: Francke-Buchhandlung, 1956); Gary Sattler, *God's Glory, Neighbor's Good* (Chicago: Covenant, 1982).

14. The best recent studies of Radical Pietism are by Hans Schneider, "Der radikale Pietismus in der neueren Forschung," *Pietismus und Neuzeit* 8 (1982): 15-42; 9 (1983): 117-51; "Der radikale Pietismus im 17. Jahrhundert," in *Geschichte des Pietismus,* ed. Martin Brecht (Göttingen: Vandenhoeck & Ruprecht, 1993), pp. 391-437; "Der radikale Pietismus im 18. Jahrhundert," in *Geschichte des Pietismus,* pp. 94-179. The most complete study in English is C. David Ensign, "Radical German Pietism, c. 1675–c. 1760," Ph.D. dissertation, Boston University, 1955.

Brethren from Solingen imprisoned because of their faith. This is his description of the German schools: "Although one can learn something from Latin, Greek, and Hebrew (which are in themselves very good), the fear of God is little considered in the learning of these languages, and is even forgotten. On the contrary, one learns pride most of all. . . . For my part, I admit that when I think of the tricks and sins which I committed at school with my fellow students I have to marvel at the great patience and forbearance of God that He does not cause the schools to sink into the depths." Lobach, however, continued his involvement with the education of small children, until the government shut down his private school in Krefeld.[15]

Although Christopher Sauer I was never a member of the Brethren (despite the claims of M. G. Brumbaugh and other historians), he was close to them in his views. His attitude toward higher education is clearly revealed in this statement: "Many are offered a whole manure wagon full of arts and sciences, for which many a rich father pays a lot of money, not a small amount of which goes to prevent him [the student] from receiving the proper discipline, to the detriment of his soul, [i.e.], the true understanding of Christ is eternal life. This knowledge is lacking in the schools and cannot be found there." Sauer played a leading role in blocking the ambitious Charity School scheme pushed by William Smith, Benjamin Franklin, and others in colonial Pennsylvania. He saw it as a device to Anglicize the German-speaking settlers and, at the same time, to further the ambitions of high churchmen and a certain political cabal. Modern scholars who have studied the event tend to agree with Sauer's interpretation.[16]

Against this negative view can be cited the active participation in the furtherance of education of Christopher Sauer II, who was a leader among the Brethren as an elder at Germantown. Sauer was

15. Quoted in English translation in D. F. Durnbaugh, ed., *European Origins of the Brethren* (Elgin, Ill.: Brethren Press, 1958), p. 191.

16. Quoted from Robert V. Hanle, "A History of Higher Education among the German Baptist Brethren, 1708-1908," Ph.D. dissertation, University of Pennsylvania, 1974, p. 50. A recent article on the Sauers is D. F. Durnbaugh, "The Sauer Family: An American Printing Dynasty," *Yearbook of German-American Studies* 23 (1988): 31-40.

influential in founding the Germantown Academy, still an active and respected institution. He was for many years one of the Academy's officers and raised large sums of money for its operation. The Germantown Brethren also supported a "select" (private) school run by a Sister Douglas. There seems to be good evidence for believing that the colonial Brethren favored elementary schools that could provide basic skills in reading, writing, and doing sums. The studies by Auburn Boyers and Robert Hanle demonstrate that over the years Brethren generally considered primary education in a positive light. When the first Brethren academies were proposed in the nineteenth century, critics of this development did not include the lower schools in their indictments, reserving their fire for education of advanced nature.[17]

There were, however, Dunkers who had no use for schooling at any level. Abraham Harley Cassel — the great antiquarian — was outstanding among nineteenth-century Brethren for collecting books and encouraging the preservation and writing of history. In fact, he may rightly be called the patron saint of Brethren historiography. (An important part of his library makes up the heart of the Juniata College rare book collection.) When he was a child, his father absolutely forbade Abraham to pursue his passion for learning in the then-available limited public schools. The father believed that he should bring up his children in what he called "pious ignorance." His position was: "If you give a child learning then you fit or prepare him for Forging, Counterfeiting, or any other badness that he may choose to do, which an unlearned or ignorant one would not be capable of doing." Also he noted that young Cassel was exceptionally bright and concluded that the lad could pick up needful information on his own. Cassel, however, persisted and was aided in slaking his thirst for education by sympathetic neighbors. In exasperation, the father finally gave in, saying: "I tried to bring you up according to my conscientious conviction, but I see I can't,

17. See esp. Auburn Boyers, "The Brethren, Annual Conference, and Education," *Brethren Life and Thought* 16 (Winter 1971): 15-47; James H. Lehman, *Beyond Anything Foreseen: A Study of the History of Higher Education in the Church of the Brethren* (Elgin, Ill.: Conference on Higher Education, 1976), pp. 4-6.

as you *will* learn in spite of all my opposition. Therefore learn, and if it leads you to evil, the fault is not mine." This opened the way for the six weeks (some say six months) of formal schooling that was all that Abraham Harley Cassel ever enjoyed.[18]

It should thus be clear, given these attitudes, that the early proponents of higher education among the Brethren would have no easy path. It is instructive to note the careful way in which Henry Kurtz and his collaborator James Quinter (later to become the first president of Juniata) went about dispelling antagonism toward schooling in the mid-1800s. They had as platform their periodical, *The Monthly Gospel Visitor*. One of their most persuasive arguments was to point to the drive for learning found in many young Dunkers, as illustrated in the life of young Cassel. Kurtz and others argued that the young people were demanding education. If the church did not provide it they would go elsewhere for it and thus be lost to the church. The remedy was for the church itself to provide "safe education" for their youth.[19]

This approach was never put more clearly than in the articles of association for the short-lived but ambitious Salem College of Indiana in 1870. One extremely long sentence read: "It has been the intention of the Brethren organizing and conducting Salem College to build an institution under the control and patronage of the church that shall be a school where the Brethren can safely place their children with the assurance that they will receive that training and admonition that shall endear the Church of the Brethren to their young hearts and cause their further lives to be spent in the service of the Lord, as believed and practiced by the Brethren in all its purity and simplicity, and as taught by the Scriptures, with nothing of the follies of pride or the frivolities of the world encouraged or tolerated in the school."[20]

18. D. F. Durnbaugh, "Abraham Harley Cassel and His Collection," *Pennsylvania History* 26 (Oct. 1959): 332-47.

19. Lehman discusses this point concisely in *Beyond Anything Foreseen*, pp. 7-17.

20. Quoted in Sharp, *Educational History*, p. 64; see also Steve Bowers, *Planting the Faith in a New Land: The History of the Church of the Brethren in Indiana* (Nappanee, Ind.: Indiana History Editorial Board, 1992), pp. 132-35.

In the same year Elder Peter R. Wrightsman published an article in which he claimed that

> hundreds of our Brethren's children [are] now away from home, receiving their education in the high schools of other denominations; some of the teachers of which are Universalists, Infidels, Deists, and to say the least, may do their best to explain away the simple commandments of Christ's Church. How shall we, who profess to be the true followers of Christ, lie still and suffer these sectarians thus to poison the mind of our dear children? God forbid it, Brethren, forbid it! . . . The time has come when the young people *will* have an education. If parents will not send them where they will have the advantage of a high school or college, many will go to other denominational schools and there be taught the peculiar view of those sects. How much better to have such a school among the Brethren and teach them the true Christian doctrine.[21]

Ironically, exactly the same kind of complaint — teachers misleading the young — was later to become a staple of criticism by conservatives against the Brethren-sponsored schools.

Two recurring complaints were raised against all proposals to sponsor church schools. One was that it would make for vanity and pride. The first question to the Brethren Yearly Meeting asking guidance on the subject of college attendance received this answer: "Considered [such attendance] not advisable, inasmuch as experience has taught that such very seldom will come back afterward to the humble ways of the Lord." When the conference was asked about a member teaching at a college, it concluded that "colleges [were] a very unsafe place for a simple follower of Christ, inasmuch as they are calculated to lead us astray from the faith and obedience to the gospel." Thus it was not surprising when the Yearly Meeting advised against a proposed school: "It is conforming to the world. The Apostle Paul says: 'Knowledge puffeth up, but charity edifieth.'" One response to the fledgling Juniata College came from an elder in Franklin County who claimed that such exposure to learning

---

21. Quoted in Sharp, *Educational History,* p. 65.

would cause students to "come home from college dressed in fine broadcloth, wearing a high bee gum hat, swinging a little cane, and acting like dudes."[22]

The other standing complaint was that the introduction of higher schools would inevitably open the church to professional clergy. First would come Bible departments, then schools of theology, and finally the practice of salaried clergy, referred to disparagingly as a "hireling ministry." As one critic phrased it: "Some say it is just to make preachers and they will want salary for preaching." The Brethren had long memories of oppression suffered by their ancestors at the hands of the clergy of the established churches. They wished no possible openings for the entry of such a development in their beloved Brotherhood. In 1873 an editorial in *The Pilgrim*, a publication issued by the Brumbaugh brothers in Huntingdon, Pennsylvania, attempted to scotch such fears: "There is an idea extant among part of the Brotherhood, at least, that were we to establish schools the design would be to prepare our brethren for the ministry, and that our ministers would finally drift into the same channel with other Churches. . . . We can assure you, brethren, that were this so, we would be among the number that oppose schools."[23]

This fear explains the otherwise curious feature of the earliest Brethren-sponsored schools that they omitted by design departments for the study of the Bible. They wished to assure the church that religious instruction would remain squarely in the hands of the family and local congregation.

Establishment of Brethren Schools

It is not necessary to trace here in detail the actual history of the birth of the first Brethren schools of higher learning. Veteran schoolman Solomon Z. Sharp did this as early as 1923. Later studies, such

22. General Mission Board, *Minutes of the Annual Meetings of the Church of the Brethren* (Elgin, Ill.: Brethren Publishing House, 1909), pp. 54, 138-39, 165; Kaylor, *Truth Sets Free*, p. 30.

23. Kaylor, *Truth Sets Free*, p. 30.

as that of Robert Hanle (1974), have analyzed and described the development. In *Beyond Anything Foreseen* (1976), James H. Lehman has provided a convenient and perceptive brief overview. Nevertheless, some further observations are appropriate.[24]

One of the problems of denominational history as usually written is that it stands in a vacuum. Little effort is made to relate the internal happenings of the church to the broader society in which it has its being. Not enough attention has been given to the correlation between the boom in the initiation of Brethren schools and the concurrent dynamic social and economic developments in late-nineteenth-century America. In many ways the pioneer Brethren educators were mirroring in smaller compass the age of industrial expansion of their day. The schools were established as private business enterprises and were reluctantly given church approval as such. They were typically organized as joint stock companies, raising money from shareholders. Although many of the early Brethren schoolmen indeed sacrificed their personal fortunes in their attempts to start schools, they originally hoped to make some money at it. Like other church leaders, before and since, they meant to do good but also hoped to do well for themselves if possible.

Similarly, a study of the early years of these schools reveals a remarkable amount of local boosterism. Towns competed to have educational institutions located within their boundaries, just as they schemed to induce railroad companies to run their tracks through their borders. Brethren understood how to take advantage of these desires, by locating their schools where the town fathers were the most accommodating. Businessmen saw the potential profits of attracting new residents among faculty and students. This motivation was well described by a historian of Mount Morris College in Illinois:

24. Sharp, *Educational History;* Hanle, "A History of Higher Education"; Lehman, *Beyond Anything Foreseen.* Murray L. Wagner compiled a bibliography entitled "Church of the Brethren Colleges and Universities," in *Religious Colleges and Universities,* ed. Thomas C. Hunt and James C. Carper (New York: Garland Publishing, 1988), pp. 163-67.

Concerning Mount Morris College, the pride of the town and community, we cannot speak too highly. . . . Here a polished education can be obtained under the most favorable moral and religious influences. . . . A home college is a great thing for the people of the place where the college is located. Viewed from the financial angle Mount Morris College is very valuable to Mount Morris and vicinity. . . . It saves the expense of sending away to college the young people of our community. . . . All this expense is saved to the people of Mount Morris in the education of their children, and in its stead they receive as an income thousands of dollars by those who come here from a distance.[25]

It should be admitted that the conservative critics of the new school movement were better prophets, or at least were more frank, than were the promoters when it came to changes that education was to bring to the Church of the Brethren. Many of the critical forecasts came true, including alteration in lifestyles. Critics correctly predicted the influence of higher education on the demand for a trained, and eventually a salaried, ministry. The church could not stay the same after Brethren schools began and their graduates came to have a voice in church policies.

After many church members received advanced education they became dissatisfied with the ministerial leadership of self-taught farmer-preachers. Publisher Henry R. Holsinger was noted for the vehemence of his criticism of the old-style ministry: "I can even now close my eyes," he wrote, "and name a dozen churches with whose elders I was personally acquainted who could not read intelligently a chapter from the Bible or a hymn from the hymnbook, nor write an intelligent notice or announcement of a communion meeting for the paper."[26]

For these reasons, the advent of schools played a significant role in the three-way schism that ruptured the denomination in

25. Kable Brothers, *Mount Morris: Past and Present. An Illustrated History* (Mount Morris, Ill.: Mount Morris Index Press, 1900), p. 234; Sharp, *Educational History*, pp. 103-21.

26. Henry R. Holsinger, *Holsinger's History of the Dunkers and the Brethren Church* (Lathrop, Calif.: Author, 1901), pp. 473-74.

1881-1883. The so-called Miami [Ohio] Valley Elders who spear-headed the reactionary drive saw that they were losing their place of leadership in the church to those who were advocating changes in education, missions, publications, and style of ministry. When the Annual Meeting pronounced, in answer to their complaints about these innovations, that while it was conservative it was also progressive, these elders read the handwriting on the wall and departed to form the Old German Baptist Brethren. The Progressives, on the other hand, who restlessly urged a faster rate of change, had in the process become anathema to the leaders of the larger, middle group. They were expelled to form the Brethren Church, with Ashland College in Ohio as the center of the movement.[27]

Once the dam was broken, the onslaught of Brethren-sponsored schools was amazing. Forty were attempted before 1923. Even though only seven of this number survive to this day, that is still an unusually large number for a denomination the size of the Brethren — with its largest North American membership in 1960 just over 200,000. Both major comprehensive studies of the interrelation of the Brethren schools, that of Noffsinger in 1925 and Kelly in 1933, rightfully concluded that there were too many for the Brethren to support adequately. It was, however, one thing for consultants to look at the figures and announce that there were too many schools. It was quite another thing to get schools to disband or merge voluntarily. Those mergers that did take place, such as Daleville with Bridgewater, Blue Ridge with Bridgewater and Elizabethtown, and Mount Morris with McPherson and Manchester, were triggered by catastrophes and financial distress. Loyalties had developed to schools by alumni and other constituencies that were deemed more important than sober economic calculations.[28]

27. The most complete account is found in Holsinger, *History,* pp. 470-551, written from the point of view of the Progressives. A recent balanced account is found in Bowman, *Brethren Society,* pp. 126-31.

28. John S. Noffsinger, *A Program for Higher Education in the Church of the Brethren, with Special Reference to the Number and Distribution of Colleges* (New York: Teachers College, Columbia University, 1925); Robert L. Kelly, *A Survey of Brethren Colleges* (New York: Association of American Colleges, 1933).

Relations of the Colleges to the Church

The shifting pattern of relationships of the colleges to the church is fascinating to study but is too complicated to recount here in detail. Again, some generalizations are possible and helpful.

Early permission given by the church for Brethren-initiated schools, as has already been mentioned, was based on their status as private business ventures. Founders were admonished not to use the term "Brethren" in college names and announcements, as this could imply official church sponsorship and approval. (For a time the Brumbaughs defied this by calling their college at Huntingdon the Brethren's Normal School.) Nevertheless, because of their own loyalty to the church and also to attract students, early educators took pains to see that church practices and customs were faithfully observed. Thus, early photographs of faculty groups show all teachers wearing the plain dress of the Dunkers (even if they were not church members).

Some colleges went from private ownership to direct church ownership through the districts in which, or near which, they were located. For example, Manchester College, although begun on a private basis, became the property of its related districts in 1902. Another tack was to ensure Brethren dominance on the board of directors or trustees. In schools created later, this arrangement was ordinarily called for in the articles of incorporation. More recently, colleges have worked to annul these provisions as part of the process of distancing themselves from church control and in order to qualify for certain government aid measures.

In 1890 the Brethren began appointing committees of respected church leaders to act as overseers of all of the Brethren-related colleges by means of regular inspection visits. This was meant to insure that educational philosophies and school practices were in line with denominational convictions. The precedent here was the custom of sending Annual Conference committees to those congregations where irregularities had occurred. The degree of severity of the school inspections varied. Already in 1892 it was suggested that members of the committee should be men of "broad views, who are in sympathy with our educational interests."

In his book Lehman traces the shift from the early committees of inspection to the current practice. In its present incarnation the committee is made up of the presidents of the colleges and seminary, with liaison through a staff member of the church denominational offices in Elgin, Illinois. Lehman points out that although this looks like a case of setting the fox to guard the geese, the development actually came about as an expression of trust placed by the church in the leadership of these institutions. It seems also, to quote Lehman, to evidence a "dim perception that the colleges would necessarily have to begin going their own way and [that] the presidents could be trusted to guide the movement." In fact, that trust was forthcoming. In this period of change, college and seminary presidents dominated in the tenure of moderators of Annual Conference, the highest elective office in the church. During a stretch of thirty years in the early twentieth century, presidents held the office no fewer than twenty-four times.[29]

This trust notwithstanding, the course of the twentieth century saw the distance increasing between the church and the colleges. Two of the contributing factors are: first, the increasing need of the colleges to look beyond the church for adequate numbers of students and sufficient financial support; and second, the desire to gain accreditation. The former need drove hard-pressed school administrators to seek allies among local business interests, industries, foundations, and, eventually, the government. Thus, for example, those with substantial means became more attractive as potential members of boards of trustees than were impecunious — if pious — Brethren pastors.

To secure accreditation, colleges had to show not only solid financial bases but also well-trained and well-supported faculties. This being the case, attachment to Brethren values became increasingly less important for teachers than possession of advanced degrees. This had the effect of bringing greater diversity to the teaching cadres. Since more and more students were recruited who were not Brethren, the shift was also perceived as fair.

Another possible option to meet this demand for better-qualified faculty members was to find degreed Dunkers. Some administrators, such as Otho Winger of Manchester College, did yeoman

---

29. Lehman, *Beyond Anything Foreseen*, pp. 57-72.

work in making it possible for already employed instructors to secure advanced training. Other presidents encouraged promising Brethren alumni to take graduate work, holding out to them the possibility of future appointments. These strategies, however, did not take care of the total demand. The result was an increasing percentage of non-Brethren members on the college faculties. An analysis of the data, nonetheless, shows that there has persisted a somewhat higher percentage of Brethren among the faculty than of Brethren among the student body.[30]

Stage by stage, therefore, the relationship of the church to the colleges has become less close. One clue has been the use of the term "church-related." One reason that the term has been found useful is that it says little about the kind of relationship involved or its intensity. Such relationships may be distant or may be close, along the analogy of human relationships. They may be as intimate as lovers; they may be supportive and confrontive as within the family. They may be cordial or critical; they may also be distant and slight, as with seldom-seen relatives.

The reality is that for the colleges the church has become one constituency among many. A very important constituency it is, to be sure, but not the only one. This becomes clear in times of tension or controversy. A case in point is that of military recruiters on campus. A little-discussed amendment to the denominational statement of war was passed at the 1970 Annual Conference of the Church of the Brethren. It declared that the presence of such recruiters on the campuses of Brethren-related colleges was "inconsistent with the church's position." A poll in 1971 conducted by the denominational periodical, the *Messenger*, showed that the standard policy was to allow low-profile visits of military recruiters. It further made clear that the colleges felt little need to defer to the pronouncements of Annual Conference. President Blair Helman of Manchester College stated: "A good deal of sentiment exists among students and faculty that there are real issues of academic freedom involved in various constituencies related to the college attempting to determine policies in areas such as recruitment, speakers, courses

---

30. Vernon F. Schwalm, *Otho Winger, 1877-1946* (Elgin, Ill.: Brethren Publishing House, 1952), esp. pp. 62-70.

of study, and the type of faculty who shall teach in the colleges." Then-president Leland Newcomer of the University of La Verne announced: "It is not the role of the college to predetermine . . . decisions by withholding information of vital importance to the 80 percent of its male members who are not conscientious objectors."[31]

It appears that Elizabethtown College may have changed its open policy because of the conference decision, however. The Department of Defense listed that school in 1980 as one of the six in the country that did not permit the military to recruit on campus. It is mentioned along with three Quaker and two Mennonite colleges.

Future Relationships

What then of the future? Is there reason to believe that the course of development of the institutions historically related to the Church of the Brethren will be any different from that which has held true for most other religiously sponsored schools? While most private colleges in this country were founded by church leaders, the seemingly inexorable trend has been for greater and greater academic independence, lesser and lesser church contact. Typically, the original church tie becomes a matter of passing mention in the introductory historical sketch in the college catalog. There is lingering recollection in the stained glass windows in the chapel, now used not for religious services but for secular convocations. This being the case, the answer given by an enrolling student at one of these colleges was understandable. When asked for church preference on the application form, the student wrote simply "Gothic."

There are exceptions to this trend. Fundamentalist schools such as Jerry Falwell's Liberty Baptist, Bob Jones University (known rather proudly as the "buckle on the Bible Belt"), and the burgeoning Oral Roberts University thrive by making demands on students.

31. *Minutes of the 184th Recorded Annual Conference of the Church of the Brethren, Lincoln, Nebraska, June 23-28, 1970* (Elgin, Ill.: Brethren Press, 1970), p. 66; Ronald E. Keeney, "Campus Recruitment for War and Peace," *Messenger* (1 May 1971): 2-3.

Some of these are quite specific, and are not restricted to lifestyle and academic questions. Oral Roberts University requires obese students (and faculty) to lose weight or face expulsion or loss of employment. Although challenged by civil libertarians, the University at last report was holding the line.

There are some signs that colleges of church origin are not content to allow the drift of estrangement to continue without addressing the issue. As competition for student enrollment increases and financial concerns pinch, college leaders have pragmatic reasons for looking more intently to the church as a source of support. In the shakeout for survival which faces liberal arts colleges, there is value seen in distinctive offerings and perspectives, something to set apart their school from Tic Tac Tech. Church perspectives may perhaps be recycled and again made relevant.

However, it seems unlikely that many Brethren-related colleges are ready to adopt the counsel offered by the late Kermit Eby, professor at the University of Chicago and perennial gadfly. He urged what he called "education for sectarians." In 1955 he wrote that

> if I were a Brethren educator, I should be avowedly sectarian. Otherwise, why be a Brethren educator at all? I am convinced that deep in our heritage there are particularistic values which are of transcendent importance for our entire society. For example, our emphasis on a 'rediscovery' of Jesus' teachings; on the evil of war, and especially of a world war which offers us not only personal — but generic — death; our subtle understanding of the futility of the oath, in this day of the informer; our emphasis upon the integrity of life and contract; and finally, our conviction that it is more important to win the man than the case. . . . I am pleading for education which gives Brethren youth a pride in their heritage and a sense of historical continuity.[32]

A more likely attitude was the proposition endorsed by participants in a study conference held by the Church of the Brethren in

32. Kermit Eby, "Education for Sectarians," *Gospel Messenger* (23 April 1955): 6-9.

1976. This urged that colleges related to the church provide a "forum where Christian views are critically examined along with other faith-communal affirmations." This is perhaps an echo of a recommendation made by President Calvert N. Ellis in 1955 in which he said that "every student coming to a church-related college has a right to expect that he [or she] will be exposed to the Christian faith. This is the minimum that the institution owes to its inheritance." The words "forum" and "exposure" are much less directive than the forthright sectarian teaching favored by Kermit Eby.[33]

Perhaps typical of this approach was the attitude toward the faith revealed by the eloquent statement by President Mark Ebersole of Elizabethtown College on the value of liberal arts education, published in the *Chronicle of Higher Education* in 1979. Ebersole commented on the need for guidance in an increasingly high-tech society:

> Through the giants of creative thought we come to know ourselves and to suffer life with compassion and courage and freedom. Great thinkers and great writers and great artists — it is they who represent the "summits from which man speaks to all epochs," and who set our sights upon the summits to which we ought to rise. Dostoyevsky and Socrates and Augustine and Michelangelo and Camus and Rembrandt and Bach and Stendahl and Beethoven and Dickens and Shakespeare and Emerson and Moses and Jesus — these are the people, and a host of others, who . . . help release the power and shed the light that will set us on course in the endless search for our true destiny.[34]

When Augustine, Moses, and Jesus make President Ebersole's liberal arts canon, there is evidence that some faith perspectives will

33. Lehman, *Beyond Anything Foreseen*, pp. 103-5; Elaine Sollenberger, "Higher Education: A Conference Whose Time Had Come," *Messenger* (Sept. 1976): 25-27; "Recommendations of the Conference on Higher Education and the Church of the Brethren," Earlham College, Richmond, Ind., June 27, 1976; Steve Simmons, "How 'Brethren' are the 'Brethren' Colleges?" *Messenger* (Sept. 1979): 12-13.

34. Mark C. Ebersole, "Why the Liberal Arts Will Survive," *Chronicle of Higher Education* (21 May 1959): 48.

secure "exposure" and be included in the "forum" of higher education. It is also clear that this represents a substantial change from the faith understandings that prompted the original beginnings of the Brethren-related colleges. The early founders, as we saw, understood their task as enlarging the outreach of the church and providing a "safe" educational environment designed to preserve the young people for the church.

This is not to say that there has been no continuation of earlier values. One of the most striking values is the Brethren emphasis upon peace. It is no accident that two of the six Brethren-related colleges — Juniata and Manchester — have strong and nationally recognized peace studies and conflict resolution programs and that the other schools have emphases on peace in their curricula. Further, the close interaction of faculty and students found on these campuses may be claimed as a modern equivalent of earlier Brethren egalitarianism.

Yet, it is clear that along with persistence have come many changes. In one of the recent studies of the development of education among the Brethren, Allen C. Deeter traced how attitudes have shifted. He concludes: "Still, a significant Brethren presence and imprint is clear on each campus. College administrations and some faculty have sought to perpetuate Brethren values. . . . Yet these values are not identical with traditional 19th and early 20th century Brethrenism; rather, they tend to represent a set of concerns generated by modern Brethren and non-Brethren faculty and youth engaged in the major issues of today's world and in the subjects they are studying."

Deeter's judgment is that diversity is the most striking quality of the current campus scene: "Brethren campuses are alive with religious, political, and intellectual diversity. Thus, the greatest transformation in the Brethren colleges . . . is in the continuing growth of diversity, openness to the outside world and engagement in the same national and international issues and causes about which educated people are concerned everywhere." Certainly few would quarrel with this analysis.[35]

35. Allen C. Deeter, "Education," in *Church of the Brethren: Yesterday and Today,* ed. D. F. Durnbaugh (Elgin, Ill.: Brethren Press, 1986), pp. 110-11.

Thus, more than a century after the first schools of higher learning were introduced by the Brethren for Brethren, we find fully accredited and generally respected colleges, dedicated to the instruction of students from a wide variety of ethnic, cultural, and religious backgrounds. Administrations and faculties commit themselves to excellence in the pursuit of teaching and encouragement of learning. In their various ways they pursue the motto of Juniata College, taken from the Gospel of John, of truth making free. They have both perpetuated core values of the Brethren and diverted young members (increasingly small numbers of whom attend these colleges) from earlier faith commitments. This diversity is the reality facing both those in the churches and in the schools in the late twentieth century.

Postscript:
J. Omar Good: The Man and His Legacy

Earl C. Kaylor, Jr.

In the course of its 120-year history, Juniata College has announced the creation of eight named professorships. Of that number only one, the J. Omar Good Chair in evangelical Christianity, is fully endowed. How that chair originated makes an intriguing story, a story heretofore untold. Rich in human interest, it revolves around the synergetic interaction of three devout urban parishioners, an elderly man, and a middle-aged couple, brought together into an intimate relationship at a time of special need. Their singular bonding would, in time, bestow upon Juniata College a distinctive mission in the field of Christian academics.

The old gentleman in this story was Jay Omar Good, the chair's benefactor. Born in 1877, Omar — he went by his middle name — grew up in a village near Waynesboro, Franklin County, Pennsylvania, near the Mason-Dixon Line.[1] His folks belonged to the Church of the Brethren, whose followers were known since colonial days, like the Quakers and Mennonites, for their simple life and plain garb. The Brethren, once opposed to higher education, began a golden age of college-founding during Omar's boyhood, Juniata being the first one, in 1876. Curiously, the college, because of local interest, very nearly got its start in a vacant hotel in Waynesboro, instead of in two unused print-shop rooms in its present hometown of Huntingdon.

1. Juniata College, Alumni Records file for J. Omar Good.

Small wonder, then, that the sixteen-year-old Omar headed for Huntingdon in 1894, apparently to prepare to teach. As a student, according to the campus paper, he "enlivened" the Hilltop scene by his "jovial" disposition.[2] He joined the Wahneeta Literary Society and earned kudos for the "keenness of his originality" as a speaker and writer.[3] In 1896, he received the two-year Bachelor of English diploma but stayed on another year to take courses in the Bible and the classics.

Instead of becoming a teacher, however, the Juniata alumnus entered the world of business. He first took an office position with a Brethren-owned farm implement firm in Waynesboro.[4] Then, in 1899, he began his quarter-century-long career with the William Mann Company, stationers and printers of Philadelphia.[5] He started out as "private clerk" to the president. By the time he retired in 1924, at age 47, his title had been upgraded to "assistant to the president." Meanwhile, he had inherited a small fortune from his parents, mostly in the form of securities. No doubt the dividends they earned enabled him to take an early retirement.

Married in 1902, Omar and his wife, Mabel, moved into a row house in Germantown, then one of the Quaker City's most desirable residential districts. His bride was a descendant of the famous colonial printer, Germantown's Christopher Sauer, through her mother's line. The Goods' thirty-five-year marriage ended in late 1937, when Mabel died. Omar would survive her death by more than three decades. The Goods had no children.

The couple had attended Philadelphia's First Church of the Brethren, where Mabel, organist, choir member, and Sunday-school teacher over the years, first caught Omar's eye. Omar himself gave a half-century of his long life to the congregation, at different times serving as trustee, clerk, and missionary treasurer. The two of them regarded First Church as the epicenter of their social life. It was no less so for Omar during his lengthy widowerhood.

As he aged, the former business executive, often bedecked in

2. *Juniata Echo* (Feb. 1899): 25.
3. *Juniata Echo* (April 1897): 78.
4. *Juniata Echo* (Oct. 1898): 180.
5. *Juniata Echo* (April 1899): 56.

a bow tie when dressed up, never lost his sense of humor.[6] He could be quick with the *bon mot* or pun, giving a hint of his "jovial" disposition of old. Pictures show him pleasant of mien with deep-set, mirthful eyes. Yet, First Church oldsters best remember him as a gentle man, soft-spoken, and deferential. Denied a father's role, he enjoyed the company of children, and he could charm First Church youth with tales of his capers as a teenage collegian. The choir loved him. It was a ritual with him to go to the choir room after every Sunday morning service and express appreciation for the anthem of the day, no matter how well — or poorly — it had been rendered.

He was beloved for another Lord's Day custom: putting his vintage black Buick sedan to use as a taxi for First Church worshipers. Well into his late years, he could be seen driving a carload of them on a Sunday at a poky speed of 15 MPH. At every intersection he deemed dangerous, he dutifully beeped the horn. One passenger he regularly chauffeured on the Sabbath recalled: "I used to hold my breath when we left the church after worship. Out we would go onto the main avenue, neither stopping nor looking to the right or left. His trust in God's care was something to marvel at."[7]

Soon after World War II, the area around First Church, which was located a few blocks north of Temple University, experienced a major ethnic change. The congregation's stone structure was in the middle of a rapidly-expanding ghetto. The membership roster dwindled away; church attendance declined by half, or more. Congregational leaders agonized about what to do. Relocate? Take up an inner-city ministry? The civil rights movement of the 1960s, of course, had not yet begun its work of breaking down the social and legal walls of racial discrimination that tarnished America's past.

It was Omar, then a septuagenarian, who early on in the debate about First Church's future brought a biblical perspective to the dilemma. It is the practice of the Brethren, in reenacting the Lord's

6. My profile of Mr. Good draws heavily on a pamphlet written by W. Clemens Rosenberger, "Selfless Philanthropy: In Memory of J. Omar Good" (Juniata College, 1972).

7. Rosenberger, "Selfless Philanthropy."

Supper, to observe the foot-washing rite — men wash the feet of "brothers" and women wash the feet of "sisters." So one night Omar ventured his opinion to fellow trustees within this basin-and-towel context. He said he would go along with whatever decision was made. But as for himself, he allowed, "I would welcome black brothers and be happy to wash their feet." One trustee was moved to remark afterward that Omar's testimony "burned into my memory as an example of true Christian love."[8]

Omar's stewardship was legendary, but people, unaware of his affluence, puzzled over how he managed to be so open-handed. Everyone knew why the missionary fund, which he oversaw for years, never seemed depleted. It was common knowledge, too, that his annual pledge accounted for about half of the congregation's budget of $50,000 by the mid-1950s. And his $35,000 commitment to the building fund guaranteed a successful capital campaign later that decade. Public charities enjoyed his regular support, as did Juniata College over the years. Many people, some of them from First Church, benefited from his covert philanthropy in times of financial adversity.

Yet his frugal lifestyle gave no clue about the source of his ready generosity. He lived in what had now become an unpretentious row house, once well-kept, where the lead pipes were so corroded that no hot water could be drawn in the upstairs bathroom.[9] He wore the cheapest off-the-rack suits — until they were all but threadbare. The last car he owned dated to 1938!

Omar had enjoyed good health over the years, but in 1962 he came down with what later was diagnosed as pneumonia.[10] Without a family, or close relatives, he had nobody to take care of him. He was missed at church, of course — especially by Lester and Pauline Rosenberger, from nearby Narberth. So one Sunday afternoon they took it upon themselves to stop by Omar's place and check on him, now in his mid-80s. They did not expect the sight that greeted them: their host making his bed on the living-room sofa and running a high fever. The Rosenbergers wasted no time rushing him

8. Rosenberger, "Selfless Philanthropy."
9. Rosenberger, "Selfless Philanthropy."
10. Rosenberger, "Selfless Philanthropy."

to the hospital, where doctors gave the gravely ill patient little chance to recover. But he did. Soon after he left the hospital, the Rosenbergers had him placed in a nursing home. He lived another seven years.

During that terminal interim, Lester and Pauline, whose son and daughter were adults and on their own, had the freedom to take complete charge of Omar's personal affairs. This kind service upon their part ensured his peace of mind. They were, as he had once been, proverbial "pillars" of First Church. Thus the three of them had been well-acquainted but not close friends. Now, however, there developed a deeply caring relationship, evoking in Omar a sense of total trust.

An alumnus of the Philadelphia College of Textile and Science, Lester was president of a long-established family business that served the textile, painting, and rubber industries. In 1952 he had been elected a trustee of Juniata College. He put in a stint as vice-chairman and served on the board until 1979, when he took emeritus status. Pauline, a homemaker and Penn graduate, gave a lot of her nonchurch volunteer time to the University's alumni relations office and to other civic activities.

So trusting was Omar that he proposed bequeathing half of his estate to the Rosenbergers.[11] They refused, however, to take a single cent from the retirement home resident, before or after his death. They did acquiesce in his plea to assume power of attorney for him and to act as executors of his will. A reading of the will convinced the Rosenbergers that it was too much a hodgepodge, so they helped him draft codicils that gave it more focus. When Lester opened Omar's lock box at the bank he found it stuffed full with untallied stock certificates. He discovered that their owner had absolutely no idea what they were worth. Omar died in January 1969, at age 91; the Rosenbergers had him buried at Waynesboro, near his parents' grave sites.

The securities, when all were sold off, added up to $3,000,000. Omar's will bequeathed large sums to First Church and to numerous

---

11. Much of this part of the story is based on an undated interview with Lester N. Rosenberger, taped shortly before his death, by then-Director of Alumni Relations, Dorothy L. Hershberger.

charities, including the Waynesboro hospital. Juniata College, at the instigation of the Rosenbergers, received $1,000,000, the largest gift to the institution until the 1990s. The campus's main academic building promptly got a memorial name: "J. Omar Good Hall."[12] There were residual funds in Omar's estate, however, left un-bequeathed. A testamentary clause stipulated that such funds, their disbursal to be at the discretion of the Rosenbergers, go toward "the perpetuation of the Historical Triune Faith of Protestant Christianity."

The Rosenbergers pondered several options for carrying out this commission. Then one day, while driving through the New England countryside on a business trip, Lester got a compelling idea. As he told it, he pictured "recognized authorities in the field of evangelical theology" as residents of Juniata College, teaching, writing, and available for off-campus speaking engagements. There would be a regular turnover of scholars, preferably on an annual basis — or maybe longer, in some cases.

At the time he hit upon the visiting professor scenario, Rosenberger was a veteran college trustee. As such, he deplored what had been happening on hundreds of campuses since before Omar Good's death.[13] Student unrest seemed epidemic. Drugs and alcohol appeared to define the life of collegians. Bi-gender dormitories had become the vogue. *In loco parentis,* once taken for granted by every-one, underwent erosion, thanks to state laws making adults of eighteen-year-olds. Long-cherished traditions at many schools suffered eclipse.

Juniata did not escape the ferment of the times. Gone by the early 1970s, for example, were compulsory chapel and required religion courses. As perceived by the Rosenbergers and others of their generation, increasing student autonomy had bred a confusing array of conflicting beliefs. They feared that contemporary colle-gians faced a serious crisis of values. A serial professorship at Juniata, the Rosenbergers opined, ought to be set up expressly to address the problems of Christian identity in an age of cultural confusion and rampant secularism.

---

12. Earl C. Kaylor, Jr., *Truth Sets Free: A Centennial History of Juniata College, 1876-1976* (Cranbury, N.J.: A. S. Barnes, 1977), p. 366.
13. Conversation by the author with Lester Rosenberger.

Accordingly, they submitted such a plan — in very general outline — to college officials in the fall of 1972. A select committee gave months of effort to working out details from the faculty and administration sides. In October 1973, the board of trustees placed its imprimatur upon the committee's labors.[14] Meanwhile, the trustees and the Rosenbergers had drafted a nineteen-page legal agreement creating the "J. Omar Good Fund." The document cleared the court the next year, making way for the first "J. Omar Good Distinguished Visiting Professor" to be recruited for the fall of 1975.

So far as college endowments go, the Good Fund is something of an anomaly; it imposes some unusual conditions upon its management. First of all, the assets of the endowment, which now exceed $2,500,000, must be kept segregated and separately audited, although the college is authorized to handle the investment portfolio. Second, there is an independent, self-perpetuating set of trustees, three in number.[15] Third, the Good trustees closely monitor the fund's integrity and growth and play an involved — albeit advisory — role in the search and selection of candidates for the Good chair and in making up the fund's annual budget. Fourth, under certain stated conditions, the Good trustees are empowered to unilaterally terminate the endowment.

The Rosenberger–Juniata College pact of 1973 sets forth precisely the qualifications for appointment to the endowed visiting professorship. The phraseology used, dictated by the Rosenbergers, is unconditional, meant to reflect the thinking of J. Omar Good:

> The Chair shall be occupied by a recognized authority in the field of evangelical theology and its allied or related disciplines, who shall be a person of high scholastic attainment, preferably with an earned doctor's degree from an accredited institution or the equivalent thereof. He or she shall be recognized as a person

14. Minutes of the Juniata College Board of Trustees, October 19-20, 1973.

15. The original set of trustees were the Rosenbergers and their dear friend, the late Dr. Calvert N. Ellis, Juniata's president from 1943 to 1968. The current trustees are Dr. W. Clemens Rosenberger (a Brethren pastor and member of the college's general trustee board), Dr. Nancy Rosenberger Faus (a seminary professor), and Earl C. Kaylor, Jr. All three are Juniata alumni.

learned in the field of evangelical Christianity and an active believer in the historical triune faith of Protestant Christianity. He or she shall be able to present and interpret sympathetically the field of evangelical theology; and shall be grounded in Biblical theology, the heritage of the Protestant trinitarian position, the heritage of the Reformation including personal salvation and eschatological doctrine and be able to interpret New Testament thought.

While the criteria laid out here seem to overemphasize demonstrated scholarship and academic performance, the purpose of the chair is certainly not to install "theoretical" Christians. Candidates must give clear evidence of being moored in a church. As for a definition of the term "evangelical," none appears in the document of 1973.[16] But there has been consensus among Good trustees, past and present, on its meaning. To them, it has signified bringing the power of the gospel to bear on young people's search for meaning, purpose, and hope in their lives — in other words, to unapologetically present contemporary collegians with the alternative choice of a Christian worldview. In style, "evangelical" denotes lifting up basic spiritual values: personal salvation; social awareness; ethical responsibility; moral courage — all this through a winning ecumenical, creative, enthusiastic exposition of the biblical and theological teachings of Protestantism in its historical evolution. Doctrinally, Good professors are expected to subscribe to the Apostles' Creed.

In its two decades of life, the Good chair, as attested by the chapters appearing in this book, has attracted a succession of outstanding Christian scholars. They have represented a variety of academic disciplines and have hailed from a wide range of geographical areas of the United States and Canada. Collectively, they have contributed, each in his or her own personal way, to the spiritual seasoning of countless numbers of Juniatians. Spouses of Good Professors have also left their mark on Juniata College.

16. When queried about his definition of "evangelical" at a general board of trustees meeting, Lester replied that it referred to the "doctrines of the four Gospels." He also said the term was synonymous with the Apostles' Creed.

Twenty-years time has enabled the Good trustees to broaden the fund's campus outreach through strategies other than academics. But the chair will always remain the fund's crowning work on College Hill. Its designers, the Rosenbergers, are both gone now.[17] With their deaths, the visiting professorship stands today as much a memorial to the two of them, who envisioned it, as it does to J. Omar Good, whose legacy endowed it.

The J. Omar Good Distinguished Visiting Professors of Evangelical Christianity, Juniata College

1975-77	Carnegie Samuel Calian
1977-78	Chad Walsh
1978-79	E. Earle Ellis
1979-80	George M. Docherty
1980-81	Richard J. Mouw
1981-82	Merold Westphal
1982-83	Mark A. Noll
1983-84	Robert G. Clouse
1984-85	Corbin Scott Carnell
1985-86	Bruce R. Reichenbach
1986-87	John C. Trever
1987-88	W. Ward Gasque
1988-89	Donald F. Durnbaugh
1989-90	Robert C. Roberts
1990-91	Lauree Hersch Meyer
1991-92	Paul A. Marshall
1992-93	H. Newton Malony
1993-94	Corbin Scott Carnell
1994-95	David W. Gill
1995-96	Jill Peláez Baumgaertner
1996-98	Kent Gramm

17. Lester Rosenberger died in 1984, Pauline Rosenberger in 1993.